Strategic Marketing
Planning and Control

1

6

Chartered Institute of Marketing/Butterworth-Heinemann Marketing Series is the most prehensive, widely used and important collection of books in marketing and sales currently lable worldwide.

the CIM's official publisher, Butterworth-Heinemann develops, produces and publishes the mplete series in association with the CIM. We aim to provide definitive marketing books for dents and practitioners that promote excellence in marketing education and practice.

e series titles are written by CIM senior examiners and leading marketing educators for ofessionals, students and those studying the CIM's Certificate, Advanced Certificate and stgraduate Diploma courses. Now firmly established, these titles provide practical study pport to CIM and other marketing students and to practitioners at all levels.

The Chartered
Institute of Marketing

Formed in 1911, The Chartered Institute of Marketing is now the largest professional marketing management body in the world with over 60,000 members located worldwide. Its primary ectives are focused on the development of awareness and understanding of marketing roughout UK industry and commerce and in the raising of standards of professionalism in the ucation, training and practice of this key business discipline.

Books in the series

Below-the-line Promotion, John Wilmshurst

CIM Handbook of Export Marketing, Chris Noonan

CIM Handbook of Selling and Sales Strategy, David Jobber

CIM Handbook of Strategic Marketing, Colin Egan and Michael J. Thomas

CIM Marketing Dictionary, Norman A. Hart

Copywriting, Moi Ali

Creating Powerful Brands, Leslie de Chernatony and Malcolm McDonald

Creative Marketer, Simon Majaro

Customer Service Planner, Martin Christopher

Cybermarketing, Pauline Bickerton, Matthew Bickerton and Upkar Pardesi

Effective Advertiser, Tom Brannan

Integrated Marketing Communications, Ian Linton and Kevin Morley

Key Account Management, Malcolm McDonald and Beth Rogers

Market-led Strategic Change, Nigel Piercy

Marketing Book , Michael J. Baker

Marketing Logistics, Martin Christopher

Marketing Research for Managers, Sunny Crouch and Matthew Housden

Marketing Manual, Michael J. Baker

Marketing Planner, Malcolm McDonald

Marketing Planning for Services, Malcolm McDonald and Adrian Payne

Marketing Plans, Malcolm McDonald

Marketing Strategy, Paul Fifield

Practice of Advertising, Norman A. Hart

Practice of Public Relations, Sam Black

Profitable Product Management, Richard Collier

Relationship Marketing, Martin Christopher, Adrian Payne and David Ballantyne

Relationship Marketing for Competitive Advantage, Adrian Payne, Martin Christopher, Moira Clark and Helen Peck

Retail Marketing Plans, Malcolm McDonald and Christopher Tideman

Royal Mail Guide to Direct Mail for Small Businesses, Brian Thomas

Sales Management, Chris Noonan

Trade Marketing Strategies, Geoffrey Randall

Strategic Marketing

Planning and Control

Graeme Drummond
Napier University Business School

John Ensor
Napier University Business School

Published in association with The Chartered Institute of Marketing

BUTTERWORTH
HEINEMANN

OXFORD AUCKLAND BOSTON JOHANNESBURG MELBOURNE NEW DELHI

Dedication to
The memory of Neil Macpherson, colleague, friend and mentor.

And to
Diane, Geraldine, Hannah, Brendan and Owen for their support, encouragement and help

Butterworth-Heinemann
Linacre House, Jordan Hill, Oxford OX2 8DP
225 Wildwood Avenue, Woburn, MA 01801-2041
A division of Reed Educational and Professional Publishing Ltd

 A member of the Reed Elsevier plc group

First published 1999

British Library Cataloguing in Publication Data
Ensor, John
    Strategic marketing: planning and control – (CIM student)
    1. Marketing – Management
    I. Title   II. Drummond, Graeme   III. Chartered Institute of
    Marketing
    658.8'4

ISBN 0 7506 4482 6

Composition by Genesis Typesetting, Rochester, Kent
Printed and bound in Great Britain

Contents

Preface   *xi*

Acknowledgements   *xiv*

1 The strategic perspective   1
About this chapter   1
Introduction   1
What is strategy?   2
Towards strategic management   3
Change – shaping strategy   5
Balanced scorecard approach   5
The role of marketing within strategy   6
What is marketing strategy?   7
Summary   9
References   10

Part 1   Strategic analysis

2 External analysis   13
About this chapter   13
Introduction   13
Scanning   13
Macro-environmental analysis   15
Industry analysis   16
Competitor analysis   18
The market analysis   21
Summary   22
References   22
Further reading   22

3 **Segmentation**   23
   About this chapter   23
   Introduction   23
   Why segment?   23
   The segmentation process   24
   Consumer buyer behaviour   25
   Consumer segmentation criteria   28
   Profile variables   29
   Behavioural variables   36
   Psychographic variables   38
   Organizational/industrial segmentation techniques   40
   Organizational buyer behaviour   41
   The Webster–Wind framework   43
   The Sheth framework   44
   Approaches to organizational market segmentation   46
   Summary   48
   References   49
   Further reading   49

4 **Internal analysis**   50
   About this chapter   50
   Introduction   50
   Organizational capabilities   50
   Organizational assets   51
   Organizational competencies   53
   Initial corporate-wide internal audit   53
   The internal marketing audit   54
   The innovation audit   55
   Auditing tools   58
   Summary   63
   References   63
   Further reading   63

5 **Developing a future orientation**   64
   About this chapter   64
   Introduction   64
   Forecasting   65
   Trend extrapolation   66
   Modelling   66
   Individual forecasting   66
   Consensus forecasting   67
   Scenario planning   70
   Market sensing   72
   Strategic questions   72
   People involved   73
   Summary   74
   References   74
   Further reading   75

Part 2 Formulation of strategy

6 Strategic intent   **79**
  About this chapter   79
  Introduction   79
  Mission   79
  Statement of strategic intent   83
  Nature of support for the mission statement   83
  Goals and objectives   84
  Hierarchy of objectives   85
  Long-term versus short-term objectives   87
  The balanced scorecard   87
  Gap analysis   89
  Summary   89
  References   89
  Further reading   90

7 Strategy formulation   **91**
  About this chapter   91
  Strategy formulation – an overview   91
  Competitive advantage   92
  Identifying sources of competitive advantage   94
  Experience and value effects   95
  Industry position   97
  Product and market strategies   101
  Strategic wear-out   104
  Difficult market conditions   104
  Summary   105
  References   106
  Further reading   106

8 Targeting, positioning and brand strategy   **107**
  About this chapter   107
  Introduction   107
  Evaluating market segments   107
  Establishing organizational capability   110
  Strategic alignment of assets and competencies (targeting)   111
  The strategic nature of making target segment choices   114
  Positioning   114
  Perceptual mapping   115
  Positioning alternatives   116
  Creating brand equity   117
  Brand strategy   118
  Summary   119
  References   120
  Further reading   120

9 **Product development and innovation**   **121**
   About this chapter   121
   The strategic agenda   121
   The nature of products and product development   121
   Why do products fail?   126
   Managing innovation   126
   Risk and the innovation dilemma   128
   Summary   129
   References   130
   Further reading   130

10 **Alliances and relationships**   **131**
    About this chapter   131
    Introduction   131
    Alliances   131
    Relationship marketing   134
    Developing relationships   135
    Summary   136
    References   137
    Further reading   137

11 **The strategic marketing plan**   **138**
    About this chapter   138
    Corporate and marketing plans   138
    Corporate planning   138
    Marketing plans – strategy or tactics?   140
    Why does planning matter?   141
    Barriers to successful planning   141
    The structure of a strategic marketing plan   143
    Approaches to marketing planning   143
    Summary   144
    References   145
    Further reading   145

Part 3   Strategic implementation

12 **Strategic implementation**   **149**
    About this chapter   149
    Implementation – stressing the importance   149
    Success vs. failure   150
    Fundamental principles   150
    Assessing ease of implementation   153
    People, power and politics   154
    Internal marketing   155
    Applying project management techniques   156
    Summary   158
    References   158
    Further reading   158

13 Control   **159**
   About this chapter   159
   Introduction   159
   Control – the basic principles   159
   What makes an effective control system?   161
   Management control   162
   Financial control   162
   Performance appraisal   166
   Benchmarking   166
   Controlling marketing performance   167
   Summary   168
   References   169
   Further reading   169

Index   *171*

Preface

The aim of this text is to enable the reader to develop a sound theoretical and practical understanding of marketing planning and control. Although primarily written for those studying for the Chartered Institute of Marketing's postgraduate diploma examinations, this text is equally useful for industry practitioners. This is not an introductory text to the subject of marketing, but builds on the existing knowledge that students and practitioners already hold about the principles of the subject. The aim has been to provide a clear, concise guide to the tools, techniques and concepts necessary to undertake strategic marketing decisions.

The text also covers contemporary issues, by exploring current developments in marketing theory and practice, including:

- The concept of a market-led orientation
- A resource/asset-based approach to internal analysis and planning

Innovation is a theme throughout the text, reflecting the growing importance of this issue, both in terms of its academic profile and current business practice. There is also an emphasis on developing a view of the future through various forecasting techniques.

Information for students studying for the CIM diploma

The text covers the CIM's Planning and Control syllabus, which is divided into five major areas:

- Market-led approach to planning
- Analysis
- Techniques for analysis and strategy development
- Strategy formulation and selection
- Implementation and control

Links with other papers

The Planning and Control syllabus acts as the central base for the other subjects to build upon at diploma level. This text will provide students with an understanding of the nature of strategic marketing decisions and the strategic marketing decision process. This is a necessary foundation for students before they progress to the other diploma papers, International Marketing Strategy, Marketing Communications Strategy and Analysis and Decision. In particular, this text acts as the underpinning of the Analysis and Decision paper. When studying this subject students should ensure that they are aware of these linkages and understand the inherent integration between these subjects.

The examination paper

The examination paper will be in two parts. Part A is a mini case study with two questions worth 20 marks each. Part B of the paper is made up of six questions, of which candidates are required to answer three. Again, each question in part B is worth 20 marks.

Part A is normally a mini case study, although it may be the abstract of an article. In either case it will not normally be longer than a side of A4. Students will be asked to analyse the material, make comments upon it and propose further actions. Normally the answers will be required in report format.

Part B will contain six questions from across the syllabus. These will require candidates to understand marketing theories and concepts and show that they can apply them to a given situation. Students will also need to demonstrate that they have an ability to critically appraise these models and concepts.

In the examination the examiners are looking for candidates to demonstrate interpretative skills, insight and originality in answering the questions. At the same time, it is expected that candidates will show a critical awareness and understanding of the relevant theoretical framework surrounding the issues being discussed.

To perform well on this paper candidates have to illustrate the following characteristics:

- Candidates need to concentrate on the strategic aspects of marketing and not make the mistake of drifting into tactical answers.
- Candidates have to demonstrate that they have the knowledge and skills required to critically appraise and apply models and concepts, not merely describe them.
- Candidates have to illustrate their answers, wherever possible, with relevant examples and provide the examiner with evidence that they have undertaken wider reading about the subject.
- Candidates need to ensure that they concentrate on the specifics of the question set, rather than answering in a generalised way, and that they answer all elements of the question.
- Lastly, candidates should ensure that they answer the question in the format requested. If the question asks for report format they need to ensure that this is provided. Generally candidates should try to give well-presented answers. Where possible candidates should use diagrams as this helps them to use their time more efficiently.

In order for candidates to do well on this paper they need to be fully prepared. The best preparation would include:

- Practice on selected questions from past examination papers.
- Reading the examiners' reports and specimen answers that are available for each past paper.
- Reading as widely as possible, not only textbooks but also the marketing and business press on a regular basis. *Note*: suggestions for further reading will be found at the end of each chapter in this text.

Candidates should also ensure that:

- They focus upon the application of models in a variety of market and industry sectors, e.g. the service sector, small business sector, business to business sector.

- Wherever possible, they make use of their own business experience and other illustrative sources to provide relevant examples. Regular reading of the business press is useful in order to identify illustrative examples.

- They make themselves aware of the broader implications of marketing planning and control decisions. In particular, as well as understanding the benefits of planning and control techniques, they should be aware of the drawbacks, in terms of costs, and other resource implications.

Acknowledgements

The authors and publisher wish to thank the following for permission to use copyright material:

The Free Press, a division of Simon & Schuster, Inc for Figures 7.2 and 7.7 adapted from Michael E. Porter, *Competitive Advantage: Creating and Sustaining Superior Performance*, Figure 1.3, p. 12, Figure 2.2, p. 37. Copyright © 1985 by Michael E. Porter.

Harvard Business Review for Figure 12.1 adapted from Thomas V. Bonoma, 'Making Your Marketing Strategy Work', *Harvard Business Review*, **62**(2), March/April 1984, p. 72. Copyright © 1984 by the President and Fellows of Harvard College.

The Controller of Her Majesty's Stationery Office for Figure 3.9 data from 'New Earnings Survey', Office for National Statistics. Crown copyright © 1991.

Pearson Education for Figures 7.8 and 7.9 from Kotler, Armstrong, Saunders and Wong, *Principles of Marketing*, 2nd European edition, Prentice Hall (1999), Figure 12.6, p. 531 and Figure 12.5, p. 527; and for Figure 1.2 from Johnson and Scholes, *Exploring Corporate Strategy*, 3rd edition, Prentice Hall (1993) p. 23.

Penguin Books Ltd for adapted material from Hugh Davidson, *Even More Offensive Marketing*, Penguin Books (1997), Table 120, p. 285. Copyright © Hugh Davidson, 1997.

John Wiley & Sons Ltd for Figure 4.9 adapted from J. R. Montnari and J. S. Bracker, article in *Strategic Management Journal*, **7**(3), 1986. Copyright © 1986 John Wiley & Sons Ltd.

John Wiley, Inc for Figure 13.7 from Watson, *Strategic Benchmarking* (1993) p. 4.

Whilst every effort has been made to contact copyright holders, the publisher would like to hear from anyone whose copyright has unwittingly been infringed.

CHAPTER 1

The strategic perspective

About this chapter

Increasingly competitive market conditions require strategic responses. Strategic decisions define core competencies and integrate activities. Strategic management recognizes the importance of implementation and managing change. Essentially, strategic marketing management, and subsequent marketing strategies, contribute to overall business goals via a three-stage process: analysis, formulation and implementation.

Introduction

The concept of marketing is inherently simple – business success via a process of understanding and meeting customer needs. Few would argue with this basic principle, and even the most inexperienced of business managers would intuitively see its sense. Given this basic simplicity, why do we need something as complicated, and time consuming, as a marketing strategy?

While basic business principles may be simple common sense, achievement involves many complex, interdependent or even conflicting tasks. Increasingly, such tasks are undertaken against a backdrop of constant change, intense competition and limited

resources. To further enhance the challenge, managers are often at the mercy of incomplete data and unexpected events, often being left to 'second guess' customer and competitor reactions. It is to this end that marketing strategy has become a vital component of success. A well considered, effectively implemented, marketing strategy should go some way to alleviating these problems and reducing the complexity of business tasks. Strategy should restore simplicity to the art of management. In essence, it is a series of tools and techniques that guide (hopefully) the organization to the marketing panacea – success via a process of understanding and meeting customer needs.

The modern business world now recognizes the importance of strategic issues and the contribution of strategic management to business success. While this has many benefits it also brings many problems. It could be argued that 'strategy' (or 'strategic') is the most overused/misused phrase in business today. Everybody seems to have a 'strategy' for everything. By attaching the term 'strategy' to an activity, it somehow becomes more important – more grand – but in reality very little actually gets done! To illustrate this, the authors recall the recent experience of sitting through a seemingly endless meeting, listening to people talk on and on about their 'strategy' or the need for a strategic view. Finally, someone said something sensible: '. . .

there's too much strategy and not enough people doing things!' This blunt comment is memorable for two reasons. Firstly, it ended a tedious meeting. Secondly, and more importantly, it illustrated a key point: strategy must lead to action, not be a substitute for it. Ultimately, all organizations need 'people doing things'. The goal of strategy is to ensure they are doing the right things. These actions have to be co-ordinated, efficiently executed and focused on meeting customer needs.

Essentially, strategy is a three-stage process involving analysis, formulation and implementation. During the analysis phase, management needs to look both internally and externally. Understanding the wider business environment is fundamental. It is then necessary to formulate plans appropriate to current and future circumstances. Finally, implementation is needed to put our plans into practice. Managers must ensure that due care and attention are paid to each of these stages. In this way, strategy avoids being little more than rhetoric and starts to become a practical reality of business life.

What is strategy?

Over the years, many definitions of 'strategy' have been developed. Close examination of such definitions tends to converge on the following – strategy is concerned with making major decisions affecting the long-term direction of the business. Major business decisions are by their very nature strategic, and tend to focus on:

- *Business definition.* A strategic fundamental is defining the business we are in. Organizations need to anticipate and adapt to change by keeping in touch with the *external competitive environment.* Business leaders need to define the *scope* (or range) of the organization's activities and determine the markets in which the organization will compete. We are

defining the boundaries of activity and ensuring that management face up to the challenges of change.
- *Core competencies.* The organization must be competitive now and in the future. Therefore, strategic decisions need to define the basis of *sustainable competitive advantage(s).* What skills and resources are needed in order to prosper within our defined markets and how can they be used to optimum advantage? It is essential that this issue is considered over the long-term in order to *match* organizational capability with desired goals and the external environment. This process often has *major resource implications,* both in terms of investment and rationalization.
- *Integrative.* Strategy has a wide-ranging impact and therefore affects all functional areas within the organization. Effective strategy is able to *co-ordinate* the different functions/activities within the organization in order to achieve common goals. By taking a 'whole organization' view of the corporation, managers should be better able to target resources, eliminate waste and generate synergy. *Synergy* occurs when the combined effect of functions/activities is greater than their individual contribution. It is vital that business leaders articulate a common *vision* and sense of purpose, in order to achieve an integrative approach.
- *Consistency of approach.* Strategy should provide a consistency of approach, and offer a focus to the organization. Tactical activities may change and be adapted readily in response to market conditions, but strategic direction should remain constant. Additionally, strategic management can provide common tools and analytical techniques enabling the assessment and control of complex issues, situations and functional areas.

The process aims to specify corporate objectives and establish ways of achieving such objectives. The intent is to react to, and of course influence, the competitive environment to the advantage of the organization. Any such advantage must be sustained over the long-term, but be flexible enough to adapt and develop as required.

Note that strategy and a *corporate/strategic plan* are not one and the same. Strategy defines the general concepts of future competitive advantage and reflects intent, whereas a strategic plan specifies the selection, sequence, resources, timing and specific objectives required to achieve the strategy.

Figure 1.1 summarizes the above issues. Issues of strategy, tactics and corporate planning are further developed in Chapter 11.

Towards strategic management

Over a period of some thirty years, we have seen the concept of strategy evolve. Aaker (1995) provides a historical perspective showing how this evolution has progressed and acknowledges that strategic activity has been described over the years as:

*   *Budgeting.* Early strategic activity was concerned with budgetary and control mechanisms. Structured methods of allocating, monitoring and investigating variances from budget provided a means of managing complex processes. The process was often based on past trends and assumed incremental development.
*   *Long-range planning.* Here greater emphasis was placed on forecasting. Planning systems and processes tended to extrapolate current trends (with varying degrees of sophistication) and predict factors such as sales, profits and cost. Management could use such forecasts as a basis for decision making.
*   *Strategic planning.* The 1970s and 1980s were the era of strategic planning, with emphasis placed on: (i) specifying the overall direction; and (ii) centralized control of planning activities. While still based around forecasting and extrapolation of past trends, far greater attention was paid to understanding the business environment. Managers hoped to be

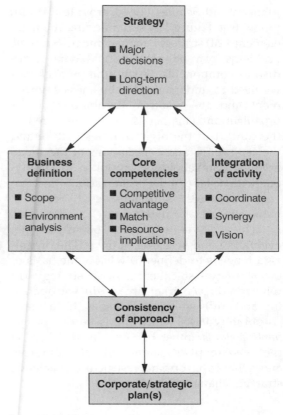

Figure 1.1 The basics of strategy

able to anticipate events via a detailed analysis of cause-and-effect relationships. Planning systems aimed to provide data and logic as a means of decision support. While promoting more awareness of strategic issues in terms of the external environment, the process still tended to focus on the preparation of corporate-wide plans. This was often achieved in a highly bureaucratic, centralized fashion.
*   *Strategic management.* We are currently in the age of strategic management. Strategic management concerns both the formulation of strategy and how such strategy is put into practice. While still undertaking analysis and forecasting, far greater prominence is placed on implementation. The concern is with managing change and transforming the organization within an increasingly turbulent business environment.

Johnson and Scholes (1999) provide a useful model (see Figure 1.2) summarizing the main elements of strategic management. Strategic problems can be viewed as having three distinct components. Firstly *strategic analysis* – we need to understand the business environment and the resource capabilities of the organization. This needs to be considered in the context of the organization's culture and the aspirations and expectations of the stakeholders. ('Stakeholders' are taken to be anyone with a stake in the organization – customers, employees, suppliers, etc.) Secondly, managers need to make *strategic choices*. This is achieved via a process of identifying, evaluating and selecting options. The organization needs to define: (i) what is the basis of our strategy – so-called 'generic' strategy; (ii) what product/market areas will we operate in; and (iii) specific strategies to achieve corporate goals. Finally, the issue of *strategic implementation* must be considered. There is the need to plan actions, allocate resources and, where appropriate, restructure to achieve strategic change.

It is important to remember that strategic management is not the orderly, logical sequence of events/activities that managers wish for. Practical reality means processes are interlinked and overlapping. For example, strategic analysis does not stop (or at least should not stop) when other stages take place. Analysis is an ongoing activity. Equally, creativity, vision and leadership are required to turn analysis into successful strategy. Given the volatility in today's business world, a contingency approach may be required. This provides flexibility by developing contingencies for a range of future scenarios.

Porter (1998) provides an interesting perspective and views strategy in terms of: (i) developing a unique position by choosing to perform differently from the opposition; (ii) making 'trade-offs' with other possible competitive positions, in order to protect your competitive advantage; (iii) combining activities to fit into, and reinforce, an overall competitive position; (iv) ensuring operational effectiveness when executing activities.

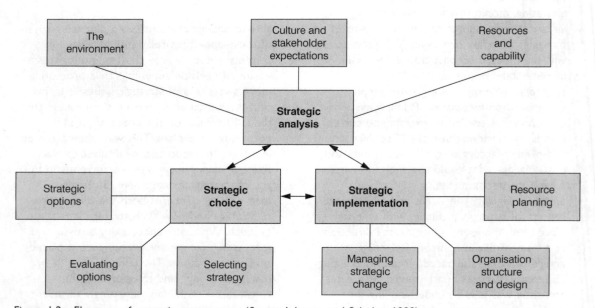

Figure 1.2 Elements of strategic management (*Source*: Johnson and Scholes, 1999)

Change – shaping strategy

Change is an accepted consequence of modern life. Indeed, the phrase *'change is the only certainty'* has become something of a business mantra. All organizations are subject to increasing levels of change. We can view change in terms of cyclical change and evolutionary change. Cyclical change involves variation that is repetitive and often predictable (e.g. seasonal variation in demand or fluctuation in economic circumstances). Evolutionary change involves a more fundamental shift. It may mean sudden innovation or a gradual 'creeping' process. Either way, the result can have drastic consequences for strategic development.

Given that strategic management is concerned with moving the organization to some future desired state, which has been defined in terms of a corporate vision and corporate-wide issues, it is important to see the concept of 'change' as an integral part of strategy. We can examine this in terms of the following questions: (i) What drives change? (ii) How does change impact on our markets/business environment? (iii) What is the result of change on the organization's strategy? Figure 1.3 summarizes these three questions.

- *Drivers of change*
  Consistently, current products and methods of operating are rapidly being displaced by a combination of competitors' actions and shifting customer needs. This discontinuity is being driven by factors which may be categorized as: **P**olitical, **E**conomic, **S**ocial (e.g. demographic) and **T**echnological. A so-called 'PEST' analysis (see Chapter 2) provides a useful analytical framework with which to study the business environment.
- *Impact of change*
  Quite simply, change means that we need to re-define our markets. While fast growth is still possible within certain 'sun-rise' industries, many industries have to accept that the days of incremental annual growth are over. Variation in consumer habits and demographic patterns means traditional markets are becoming more challenging. Change is accompanied by intense competition, which the phenomenon of business globalization can only intensify. Increasingly, we see shorter product life cycles and increasing difficulty in predicting the future.
- *Result of change*
  There are two main outcomes. Firstly, change creates opportunity. Organizations that are flexible and in touch with customer needs are likely not just to survive, but prosper. Secondly, past actions, strategies and methods offer no guarantee of future success. There is a need to guard against complacency and ensure that the strategic thrust of the organization does not drift from the true needs of the marketplace (beware strategic drift).

Balanced scorecard approach

As change pervades all aspects of business strategy, it is important to set appropriate measures of business success. Rather than

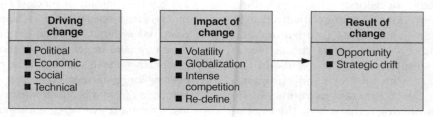

Figure 1.3   Strategy and change

relying on a few narrow financial measures, a system is needed which provides an overall view of business success. To this end, Kaplan and Norton (1992) advocate using a 'balanced scorecard' approach. This involves taking both financial/non-financial measures and examining the benefits delivered to all the organization's stakeholders. A balanced score-card approach involves four sets of measures:

- *Financial measures.* Here we examine how we are perceived by investors and shareholders.
- *Customers.* How do our customers view us?
- *Internal activities.* By examining the key areas of activity which deliver customer satisfaction, we can identify where the organization must outdo its competitors.
- *Innovation and learning.* To survive and prosper, all organizations need to improve and adapt. Any business activity can be viewed as a learning experience with the goal of continuously creating value.

Performance indicators are established within each of these areas. These become an objective basis with which to evaluate and formulate strategy. A winning strategy should address the above and offer a range of initiatives for the future.

The role of marketing within strategy

As noted earlier, all organizations need to make strategic decisions relating to their external environment. Strategy must address issues such as customers, competitors and market trends. It needs to be proactive as opposed to simply reacting to events. In this way, strategy can detect and influence changes in the business environment. By its nature, marketing defines how the organization interacts with its marketplace.

Consequently, all strategic planning, to a greater or lesser degree, requires an element of marketing. Only in this way can organizations become strategically responsive to customer need and commercial pressures. Indeed, it is possible to view marketing as more than a functional activity – it can be adopted as a business philosophy. Here the organization adopts a marketing orientation – *success by a process of understanding and meeting customer need.* Basically, the company's orientation defines its fundamental business philosophy, highlighting what is perceived as the primary route to success. Market orientations are now widely established within the business world (and often seen as the 'holy grail' of marketers) but other business orientations are equally common.

- *Production orientation.* Here business success is attributed to efficient production. The emphasis is on mass production, economy of scale and cost control. Management's key concern is with achieving volume and meeting production schedules. This philosophy has its place, but risks limiting operations to low added-value assembly work.
- *Product orientation.* The belief is that product innovation and design will have buyers beating a path to our door. Management's perception is that our products are so good they will, in effect, sell themselves. Little or no effort is put into establishing what the customer actually wants – a dangerous route! Naturally, product innovation is important, but it needs to appeal to the marketplace, otherwise it risks being innovation for the sake of innovation.
- *Sales orientation.* This views sales volume as the key determinant of success. The focus is on aggressive selling that persuades the customer to buy. Given that the process is driven by sales targets, a short-term perspective dominates, with little regard to building longer-term relationships. Often, this follows on from a production orientation, as management tries to create a demand for unwanted products.

- *Market orientation.* As previously stated, success is derived from understanding and meeting customer needs. This process starts with the customer and uses actual customer demand as a means to focus resources. In simple terms, we provide what the market wants. Additionally, the importance of building long-term relationships with customers is recognized. We seek to build loyalty and consistently offer superior value. An awareness of competitors' proficiency and strategy is required in order to optimize this process.

It is not our intention to decry production, product innovation or selling – indeed, they are vital. However, the truly 'world-class' organization understands how to marshal these factors into a coherent market-led orientation. Creating such focus will facilitate the sustainable competitive advantage required to prosper.

How do we go about achieving a market orientation? The answer to this question can be summarized as follows:

1 *Customer focused*
   Understand your customer base and be responsive to their needs. Treat loyal customers as assets and strive to build ongoing and long-term relationships. Regularly monitor levels of customer satisfaction and retention. To achieve this we must: (i) define our markets; (ii) effectively segment/target customers; and (iii) listen to customers.
2 *Competitor focused*
   In terms of competitors, be watchful and assess their objectives, strategies and capabilities. There is the need to 'benchmark' their products, processes and operations against our own.
3 *Integrate marketing into the business*
   Marketing should not be confined to the marketing department. Every function and person within the organization has a role to play in creating value and achieving the goal of being a market-led organization. This may require fundamental changes in culture and organization structure.

4 *Strategic vision*
   Develop a long-term, market-orientated strategic vision by viewing marketing as more than a series of promotional tools and techniques. It must be on the agenda of senior management, who should develop and implement market-led strategy and define the future in terms of creating long-term value for stakeholders.
5 *Realistic expectations*
   We cannot be all things to all people. Expectations have to be realistic and matched to capabilities, resources and external conditions. We may well need to make 'trade-offs' to ensure we focus on activities that add value.

What is marketing strategy?

In a strategic role, marketing aims to transform corporate objectives and business strategy into a competitive market position. Essentially, the concern is to differentiate our activities/products by meeting customer needs more effectively than competitors do. Marketing strategy can by characterized by: (a) analysing the business environment and defining specific customer needs; (b) matching activities/products to customer segments; and (c) implementing programmes that achieve a competitive position, superior to competitors. Therefore, marketing strategy addresses three elements – customers, competitors and internal corporate issues (see Figure 1.4).

Firstly, we consider customers. How is the market defined, what segments exist and who should we target? Secondly, how can we best establish a competitive position? A precursor to this is a detailed understanding of our competitors within targeted market segments. Finally, we need to match internal corporate capabilities with customer need. The successful achievement of these factors should enable

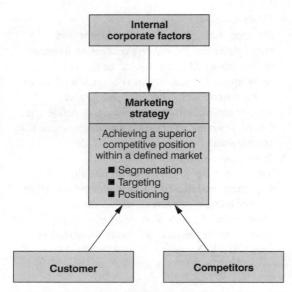

Figure 1.4   The basis of marketing strategy

the organization to develop, and maintain, a strong market position.

Essentially, a marketing strategy aims to deliver the following:

1 *Segmentation*
This process breaks the market down into groups displaying common characteristics, behaviours and attitudes. Fundamentally, this process aims to understand need and forecast reaction and/or demand.
2 *Targeting*
This involves evaluating and selecting market segments. We aim to look for opportunities which are sustainable, where we can build long-term relationships with customers.
3 *Positioning*
As previously stated, we establish a distinctive superior position, relative to competitors. The competitive position adopted should be based on matching product attributes to customer need.

It goes without saying that the three key constituents of marketing strategy – customers, competitors and internal corporate factors

– are dynamic and constantly changing. Therefore, organizations must develop and deploy processes, procedures and techniques that ensure market strategy is: (a) relative to the current/future business environment; (b) sustainable; (c) generating optimal benefits to both the organization and customers; and (d) correctly implemented. This is the process of *strategic marketing management*.

As a process, strategic marketing (and the subsequent structure of this book) has three distinct phases:

*   *Strategic analysis*
    To move forward, we must first answer the question: where are we? This stage entails a detailed examination of the business environment, customers and an internal review of the organization itself. Tools such as portfolio analysis and industry structure models help management to objectively assess the organization's current position. Equally, it is important to develop some view regarding future trends. This is achieved via forecasting and defining assumptions about the future market trends.
*   *Formulating strategy*
    Having analysed our situation, we then determine a way forward. Formulation involves defining strategic intent – what are our overall goals and objectives? Managers need to formulate a marketing strategy that generates competitive advantage and positions the organization's products effectively. To be successful, this must be based on core competencies. During this stage, product development and innovation are strategic activities, offering the potential to enhance competitive position and further development of products and brands. Additionally, formulation emphasizes the need to form relationships with customers and other businesses. Increasingly, we see organizations recognizing that they cannot do everything themselves and looking to form joint ventures and partnerships.
    The formulation stage culminates with the development of a strategic marketing plan.

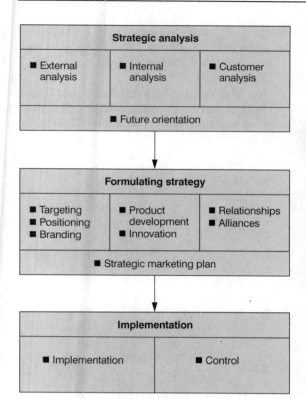

Figure 1.5 Strategic marketing

• *Implementation*

Consideration needs to be given to implementing the strategy. Marketing managers will undertake programmes and action that deliver strategic objectives. Such actions will often focus on individual elements of the marketing mix. Additionally, a process of monitoring and control needs to be put in place. This ensures compliance and aids decision making.

Figure 1.5 provides an overview of the process of strategic marketing management. Additionally, it provides a template to the structure of this text. The three components form a planning cycle (analysis, formulation and implementation) and are interactive in nature, with information being fed back to enable objectives and strategy to be reviewed and amended. Ultimately, the process will estab-lish the organization's marketing mix – products, price, promotion and place, which underpins and conveys our marketing strategy.

Summary

Today's business world recognizes the importance of strategy and strategic management. Normally, any strategic process has three distinct stages – analysis, formulation of plans and implementation. Increasingly, the importance of implementation is recognized as an integral part of the strategic framework. Strategy aims to define core competencies, understand the external environment and offer an integrative, consistent approach to decision making.

Any strategy is significantly influenced by environmental change. Political, economic, social and technological factors drive change and have an impact on the organization. This results in a volatile, intensely competitive marketplace. Organizations need to ensure they fully embrace the opportunities that change brings and guard against complacency and strategic drift. To this end, a 'balanced scorecard' approach is advocated, thus encouraging the organization to address wider strategic issues.

Marketing has a role to play within the strategic process. Namely, marketing can be adopted as a business philosophy. This sees commercial success as stemming from a process of understanding and meeting customer needs.

Marketing strategy involves achieving a superior competitive position within a defined market. Essentially, it involves segmentation, targeting and positioning. This must address customers, competitors and internal corporate factors. Strategic marketing management is the process of ensuring that our marketing strategy is relevant and sustainable.

References

Aaker, D., *Strategic Market Management*, 4th edition, Wiley, 1995

Johnson, G., and Scholes, K., *Exploring Corporate Strategy*, 5th edition, Prentice Hall, 1999

Kaplan, R., and Norton, D., 'The Balanced Scorecard: Measures that drive performance', *Harvard Business Review*, Vol. 70, No.1, 1992

Porter, M., 'What is Strategy?', cited in Segal-Horn, S. (ed), *The Strategy Reader*, Blackwell in association with The Open University, 1998

Part 1
Strategic Analysis

External Analysis
Segmentation
Internal Analysis
Developing a Future Orientation

Undertaking a strategic analysis is the foundation upon which strategic decisions are constructed. In this text strategic analysis is broken down into three constituent elements: external analysis, customer analysis and internal analysis. Undertaking the analysis is not, however, a linear process and there are areas of the analyses that overlap. The aim of the process is to develop a detailed and all-embracing view of the company and its external environment to permit the organization to formulate informed strategic decisions.

Chapter 2 explores the external analysis. This consists of an initial audit of the macro-environment. The organization's micro-environment is then considered and an initial analysis of the company's competitive position is undertaken.

Chapter 3 examines the customer. Consumer behaviour is explored to illustrate what the effect of changes in the external environment can have on customers. Market segmentation techniques are then discussed.

Chapter 4 describes the process of internal analysis. This looks at the ways of identifying the organization's assets and competencies.

These three chapters illustrate the groundwork that needs to be undertaken by an organization before it can begin to form a view of the future.

Chapter 5 discusses different approaches that organizations can take to develop a view of what developments may occur, and to carry out their activities, in the future. Part 1 also covers the process of matching the organization's resources and competencies to attractive market opportunities that is at the heart of strategic choice (the theme of Part 2 of this book).

CHAPTER 2

External analysis

About this chapter

The external analysis is the first stage of the auditing process. It creates the information and analysis necessary for an organization to begin to identify the key issues it will need to address in order to develop a successful strategy. The chapter explores the process of PEST analysis, industry analysis, competitor analysis and market analysis. The use of various approaches to facilitate this process, in particular the 'five forces' model and strategic groups, are covered.

Introduction

An analysis of the external environment is undertaken in order to discover the opportunities and threats that are evolving and that need to be addressed by the organization. A study by Diffenbach (1983) identified a number of positive consequences that stem from carrying out organized environmental analysis (see Figure 2.1).

An analysis of the external environment can be broken down into three key steps, becoming progressively more specific to the organization. The first step is an analysis of the macro-environmental influences that the organization faces. This is followed by an examination of the competitive (micro) environment the organization operates within. Finally a specific competitive analysis is undertaken.

Scanning

The environmental audit is reliant on the monitoring activity that is undertaken by the organization. The process is normally referred to as scanning.

There are four forms of scanning according to Aguilar (1967):

- *Undirected viewing.* This activity concerns the viewer exploring information in general without carrying a specific agenda. The viewer is exposed to a large amount of varied information but this is not an active search looking for particular issues, just a broad attempt to be aware of factors or areas that may have changed.
- *Conditional viewing.* Again this is not an organized search but the viewer is sensitive to information that identifies changes in specific areas of activity.
- *Informal search.* This is an organized but limited search for information to support a specific goal.

Awareness of environmental changes by management:	Industry and Market analysis:
■ Enhanced ability to anticipate problems arising in the longer term ■ Senior management awareness of a range of possible futures and their effect on the organization ■ Greater inclination to act in advance of changes	■ Quality of market and product forecasts improved ■ Identification of changes in buyer behaviour as a result of changes in social trends ■ Ability to identify future needs and anticipate new products
Strategic planning and decision making:	**Diversification and resource allocation:**
■ More flexibility and adaptability in plans as they reflect greater awareness of political events and economic cycles ■ Scope of perspectives broadened ■ Organization has greater ability to allocate resources to opportunities arising due to environmental change	■ Ability to focus resources in business areas that have long-term attractiveness ■ Guide the acquisitions process ■ Move away from products exposed to greater social and political pressure (environmental issues, etc.) towards other areas of the product portfolio
Relationship with government:	**Overseas busineses:**
■ Improved understanding and relationship with government ■ Ability to be proactive on government legislation	■ Improved ability to anticipate changes in overseas markets ■ Improved ability to anticipate how to undertake business in the overseas markets

Figure 2.1 A selection of benefits derived from organized environmental analysis (*Source*: Adapted from Diffenbach, 1983)

- *Formal search.* This type of search is actively pursued and specifically designed to seek particular information.

There is of course an unlimited amount of information that can be scanned. Any organization can only scan a certain amount of this information. A balance has to be struck between the resources allocated to this activity and the potential benefits. More information also does not lead to better decision making. Understanding the dynamics of the environment is the critical aspect to this activity, not the volume of information reviewed (see the section on Market Sensing in Chapter 5).

Managers search for information in five broad areas (Aguilar, 1967) (see Figure 2.2):

- Market intelligence
- Technical intelligence
- Acquisition intelligence
- Broad issues
- Other intelligence

(*Note*: Aguilar uses the word 'tidings' rather than intelligence.)

The study showed that 58 per cent of managers saw market intelligence as the most important area for obtaining external information, three times more important than the next most significant area, technical intelligence at 18 per cent. The importance placed on market intelligence was true across all functional areas. The most significant categories of information within this area was market potential, accounting for 30 per cent alone, and structural change, accounting for 10 per cent. The only other category that reached double figures was for the category of new products, process and technology under technical intelligence.

One crucial aspect of this activity, especially where it underpins futures forecasting, is to detect weak signals. That is, identifying fragments of information that indicate significant changes, but whose potential impact has generally not been perceived. This is

Area of external information	Category	General content
Market intelligence	■ Market potential	⇨ Capacity, consumption, imports, exports
	■ Structural change	⇨ Mergers, acquisitions, new entries
	■ Competitors and industry	⇨ Competitor information, industry policy
	■ Pricing	⇨ Effective and proposed prices
	■ Sales negotiations	⇨ Information on specific current or potential sales
	■ Customers	⇨ Current or potential customers, markets and problems
Technical intelligence	■ New product, processes and technology	⇨ Technical information relatively new or unknown to enterprise
	■ Product problems	⇨ Involving current products
	■ Costs	⇨ For processing, operations, etc. for suppliers, customers and competitors
	■ Licensing and patents	⇨ Products and processes
Acquisition intelligence	■ Leads for mergers, joint ventures or acquisitions	⇨ Information concerning possibilities for the organization
Intelligence on broad issues	■ General conditions	⇨ General information: political, demographic, etc.
	■ Government actions and policies	⇨ Decisions affecting the industry
Other intelligence	■ Suppliers and raw materials	⇨ Purchasing information
	■ Resources available	⇨ Availability of people, land, other resources
	■ Miscellaneous	⇨ Any other information

Figure 2.2 Critical areas of external information (*Source*: Adapted from Aguilar, 1967)

obviously difficult – especially as many organizations fail to recognize even major signals in the environment.

Macro-environmental analysis

The macro-environment audit examines the broad range of environmental issues that may affect the organization. This will include political/legal issues, economic factors, social/cultural issues and technological factors. This is normally referred to as a PEST (Political, Economic, Social and Technological) analysis, although some writers use the alternative acronym of STEP analysis (see Figure 2.3). The aim of this analysis is to identify the critical issues in the external environment that may affect the organization before moving on to judge the impact they may have.

- *Political/legal issues*
  There are a range of political organizations that have to be considered when looking at influences in this area of the audit. The structure of a political system defines the centres of political influence. A state with a federal political structure will differ from a unitary political system. In the UK there is a parliament for Scotland and an assembly for Wales. There are, however, a number of decision areas that are still the responsibility of the Westminster parliament. At the same time there is also an increasing range of decisions being taken both politically and legally within the framework of the European Union. Political pressure groups such as Greenpeace can also affect the political agenda. Therefore, when considering this area of the environment a much wider view has to be taken than just the domestic national government or the legal process.
- *Economic factors*
  Similarly, economic factors have to be viewed from a wider perspective than the

Political/legal issues	**Economic factors**
■ Taxation policy ■ Monopoly controls ■ Environmental protection measures ■ Employment law ■ Environmental legislation ■ Foreign trade agreements ■ Stability of the governmental system	■ Interest rates ■ Inflation rates ■ Money supply ■ Business cycles ■ Unemployment ■ GNP trends
Social/cultural issues	**Technological factors**
■ Age profiles ■ Social mobility ■ Changes in lifestyle ■ Family structures ■ Levels of education ■ Work behaviour ■ Leisure activities ■ Distribution of income ■ Patterns of ownership ■ Attitudes and values	■ Focus of government research ■ Rate of technology transfer ■ Materials ■ Developing technological processes

Figure 2.3   PEST analysis of influences in the external environment

organization's domestic economy. In the global economy, domestic economic conditions are heavily influenced by events in other areas of the world. Economics is concerned with the allocation of resources, therefore issues such as conservation of natural resources, costs of pollution, energy consumption and the whole area of the management of natural resources should be considered under this heading.

- *Social/cultural issues*
  Demographic changes are important and can be used as lead indicators in certain areas, such as healthcare and education. However, other critical areas such as social/cultural values and beliefs that are central to changes in consumer behaviour are harder to predict and can be subject to more dramatic shifts.

- *Technological factors*
  There is a great danger in using a particular technology to define an industry. In a situation where technological developments are fast-moving it is critical to understand

the fundamental consumer needs which the organization's technology is currently serving. Identifying new technologies that can service the consumer's needs more completely or economically is the critical part of this area of the analysis.

The central role of this PEST analysis is to identify the key factors that are likely to drive change in the environment. Then the aim is to establish how these key factors will affect the industry in general and the organization in particular.

Industry analysis

An organization has to understand the nature of the relationships within its industry in order to allow the enterprise to develop strategies to gain advantage of the current relationships.

A useful framework that can be utilized when undertaking this analysis is Porter's 'five forces' model of establishing industry attractiveness for a business (see Figure 2.4). This analysis should be conducted at the level of the individual strategic business unit (SBU) rather than at the level of the organization as a whole, otherwise the range of relationships facing a company with several divisions causes the analysis to lose focus. Porter identified five factors that affect the level of competition and therefore profitability within an industry:

- *Suppliers*
  The power of suppliers is liable to be strong where:
  - Control over supplies is concentrated into the hands of a few players.
  - Costs of switching to a new source of supply are high.
  - The supplier has a strong brand.
  - The supplier is in an industry with a large number of smaller disparate customers.

- *Buyers*
  The power of buyers is liable to be strong where:
  - A few buyers control a large percentage of a volume market. For example grocery and electrical goods retailers in the UK dominate the market and are in a very strong position versus their suppliers as a result.
  - There are a large number of small suppliers. In the meat industry in the UK there are a large number of small farmers supplying a retail sector dominated by a small number of large supermarkets.
  - The costs of switching to a new supplier are low.
  - The supplier's product is relatively undifferentiated, effectively lowering barriers to alternative sources of supply.
- *Potential entrants*
  The threat of potential entrants will be determined by a number of barriers to entry that may exist in any given industry:
  - The capital investment necessary to enter the industry can be very high in areas such as electrical power generation or chemical production.
  - A well-entrenched competitor who moved into the industry early may have established cost advantages irrespective of the size of their operation. They have had time to establish crucial aspects of their operation such as effective sources of supply, the best locations, and customer franchises.
  - Achieving economies of scale in production, distribution or marketing can be a necessity in certain industries.
  - Gaining access to appropriate distribution channels can be difficult. Peugeot/Citroën bought Chrysler's entire UK operations in order to gain an effective dealership network in Britain.
  - Government legislation and policies such as patent protection, trade relations with other states, and state-owned monopolies can all act to restrict the entry of competitors.
  - The prospect of a well-established company's hostile reactions to a new competitor's entry to the market may be enough to act as a deterrent.
- *Substitutes*
  Substitution can arise in a number of ways:
  - A new product or service may eradicate the need for a previous process. Insurance services delivered directly by producers over the phone or Internet are substitutes for the services of the independent insurance broker.
  - A new product replaces an existing product or service. Cassette tapes replaced vinyl records, only to be replaced by compact discs.
  - All products and services, to some extent, suffer from generic substitution. Consumers may choose to substitute buying a car in order to purchase an expensive holiday instead.
- *Competitive rivalry*
  The intensity of competition in the industry will be determined by a range of factors:
  - The stage of the industry life cycle will have an effect. Natural growth reaches a plateau once an industry reaches maturity – then the only way an organization can continue to grow in the industry is to take market share off its rivals.
  - The relative size of competitors is an important factor. In an industry where rivals are of similar size, competition is likely to be intense as they each strive for a dominant position. Industries that already have a clear dominant player tend to be less competitive.
  - In industries that suffer from high fixed costs, companies will try to gain as much volume throughput as possible. This may create competition based on price discounting.
  - There may be barriers that prevent companies withdrawing from an industry. This may be plant and machinery that is specialist in nature and therefore cannot be transferred to other uses. The workforce may have non-transferable specialist skills. If

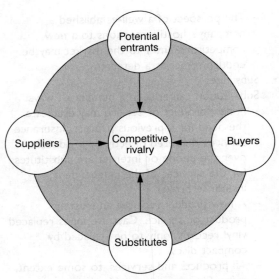

Figure 2.4   The five forces model (*Source*: Adapted from Porter, 1980)

the industry is in maturity, moving towards decline, and rivals cannot easily leave the industry then competition will inevitably increase.

The five forces model allows an organization to identify the major forces that are present in the industry sector. This can be related to the critical factors that were identified by the PEST analysis. Several issues then need to be considered:

- What is the likelihood that the nature of the relationships identified by the 'five forces' model will change given the trends in the external environment? Are there ways of benefiting from these potential changes?
- What actions can the organization undertake that will improve its position against the current forces in the industry? Can the company increase its power, relative to suppliers or buyers? Can actions be taken to reduce competitive rivalry, or are there ways of building barriers to dissuade companies from considering entering the industry? Are there ways of making substitute products less attractive?

- The organization will also need to consider their competitors. Given the forces in the industry, what is the relative position of the organization's rivals? Do conditions favour one particular operator? Could conditions change in favour of one particular competitor? Consideration of relative competitive position of rivals is an important aspect of an audit and needs now to be considered in more detail.

Competitor analysis

The 'five forces' analysis has examined the overall industry and is a starting point in assessing a company's competitive position. This is likely to be a rather broad definition of an industry and contains a number of companies that would not be direct competitors. Toyota is likely to have a number of natural direct competitors – TVR is not likely to be one of them, although both companies are in the car industry. Toyota's scale is global with car manufacture across the full range; TVR is a specialist, low volume prestige sports car manufacturer. Companies that are direct competitors in terms of products and customer profiles are seen as being in a strategic group. The car industry would be made up of a number of strategic groups.

Strategic groups

Strategic groups are made up of organizations within the same industry that are pursuing equivalent strategies targeting groups of customers that have similar profiles. TVR's strategic group is likely to contain Ferrari, Lotus, Lamborghini, Aston Martin, etc. All these companies are following similar strategies and facing similar strategic questions. They are also aiming at very similar market segments.

In the airline industry there are at least three strategic groups. One group consists of airlines with regional operations who offer

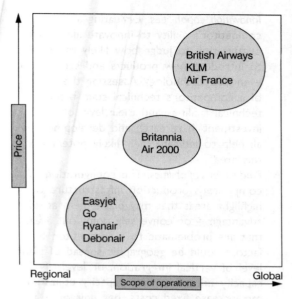

Figure 2.5   Strategic groups in the airline industry

scheduled flights and compete on cost. There is a group of major airlines who have global operations and offer scheduled flights with quality environments and service. The third group offer charter services to a range of holiday destinations (see Figure 2.5).

There is a range of attributes that can be used to identify strategic groups. Some examples are:

- Size of the company
- Assets and skills
- Scope of the operation
- Breadth of the product range
- Choice of distribution channel
- Relative product quality
- Brand image

For many companies, to analyse every competitor in its generic industry would be a difficult task in terms of management time and company resources. Defining an organization's strategic group allows a company to concentrate its analysis on its direct competitors and to examine them in more detail.

Tools which are used to analyse the internal environment, such as the value chain, can of course be used to analyse competitors (see Chapter 7). For each competitor in their strategic group an organization needs, as far as possible, to establish the information discussed in the following subsections.

Competitor's objectives

A competitor's objectives can be identified by analysing three important factors:

- Whether the competitor's current performance is likely to be fulfilling their objectives. If not, the competitor may initiate a change of strategy.
- How likely the competitor is to commit further investment to the business. Financial objectives may indicate this. Investment is more likely from companies that have objectives which are long-term in nature, such as market share and sales growth, rather than from those organizations under pressure to produce short-term profitability. This also reveals potential trade-offs the competitor may be willing to take. If short-term profitability is the key objective then the rival is likely to be willing to lose market share in the short term in order to achieve its profitability targets.
- The likely future direction of the competitor's strategy. The organization may have non-financial objectives, such as gaining technology leadership.

Competitor's current and past strategies

There are three areas that should be explored in order to establish a competitor's current activities:

- Identification of the current markets, or market segments, within which the competitor currently operates. This will indicate the scope of the business.

- Identification of the way the competitor has chosen to compete in those markets. Is it based on quality of service, brand image or on price? This may be an indication of whether a low cost or differentiation strategy is being pursued (see Chapter 7).
- Comparison between the current strategy and past strategies can be instructive. Firstly it can illustrate the direction the competitor is moving, in terms of product and market development, over time. It can also highlight strategies that the organization has tried in the past which have failed. The competitor is unlikely to attempt these approaches again without considerable reservations.

Competitor's capabilities

An analysis of a competitor's assets and competencies allows a judgement to be made about how well equipped they are to address the market, given the dynamics in the industry and the trends in the external environment. In order to evaluate a competitor's potential challenge to an organization a number of areas need to be examined (Lehman and Weiner, 1991):

- *Management capabilities.* The background and previous approaches of leading managers in a competitor company can give clues as to their likely future strategy. The level of centralization, or decentralization, of management decisions will also affect decision making. Recruitment and promotion policies, along with the remuneration and rewards scheme, all give an indication as to the culture and style of the management team.
- *Marketing capabilities.* An analysis of the competitor's actions, with the marketing mix, uncovers the areas where their marketing skills are high and also areas of vulnerability. There are a number of questions that can be asked: How good is the competitor's product line? Do they have a strong brand image? Is their advertising effective? How good are their distribution channels? How strong is their relationship with customers?

- *Innovation capabilities.* Evaluating a competitor's ability to innovate allows an organization to judge how likely the rival is to introduce new products and services, or even new technology. Assessing the quality of a competitor's technical staff, their technical facilities and their level of investment in research and development will all help to indicate their likely potential in this area.
- *Production capabilities.* The configuration of a competitor's production infrastructure can highlight areas that may place them at an advantage – or conversely point out areas that are problematic to a competitor. Such factors could be geographic spread of plant, level of vertical integration, or level of capacity utilization. Low capacity utilization can increase fixed costs, per unit of manufacture. On the other hand, it offers a competitor production capacity for new products. The flexibility of production staff is also an important issue to identify. In the service sector, capacity and staff flexibility are just as important. Factors such as the ability to pull in additional staff on a temporary basis gives a service company an important capability.
- *Financial capabilities.* The ability to finance developments is a critical area. Competitors that have strong cash flows, or are a division of a major group, may have the ability to finance investment not available to other competitors.

Competitor's future strategies and reactions

One of the aims of the competitor analysis so far has been to gather information on rivals to establish their likely future strategy. Equally important is to evaluate a competitor's likely reactions to any strategic moves the organization might instigate. The reactions of organizations can be categorized into four types of response (Kotler *et al.*, 1996):

- *Certain retaliation.* The competitor is guaranteed to react in an aggressive manner to any challenge. Market leaders, in particular, are likely to react in this manner against any threat to their dominant position. Companies that have an aggressive culture may also fall into this category.
- *Failure to react.* Competitors can be lulled into a false sense of security in an industry that, over a long period of time, has seen very little change. In this situation companies can be extremely slow to react to a competitive move. The classic example is British motorcycle companies failing to react to the entry of Japanese manufacturers into the lower end of the market.
- *Specific reactions.* Some competitors may react, but only to competitive moves in certain areas. For instance, they may always react to any price reductions, or sales promotions, as they believe these will have an important impact on their business. But they may fail to respond to a competitor's increase in advertising expenditure. The more visible the competitor's move the more likely a competitor is to respond. Actions that are less visible, such as provision of support material for the sales force or dealerships, are less likely to face a response.
- *Inconsistent reactions.* Some companies' reactions are simply not predictable. They react aggressively on occasion but at other times ignore similar competitive challenges.

Problems in identifying competitors

Analysing members of a strategic group provides crucial information on which to base strategic decisions. However, there are risks in the process of identifying an organization's competitors and a number of errors should be avoided:

- Overlooking smaller competitors by placing too much emphasis on large, visible competitors.

- Focusing on established competitors and ignoring potential new entrants.
- Concentrating on current domestic competitors and disregarding international competitors who could possibly enter the market.

The competitive analysis has allowed the organization to establish its relative position versus its competitors on a range of important criteria. However, the organization has to judge itself and its competitors against the market it is operating within. At this stage in the external analysis it is useful to establish a range of information about the market. The customer and market segmentation would also be considered in a market analysis – this will be explored in detail in Chapter 3.

The market analysis

A market analysis will be made up of a range of factors relevant to the particular situation under review, but would normally include the following areas:

- *Actual and potential market size.* Estimating the total sales in the market allows the organization to evaluate the realism of particular market share objectives. Identifying the key submarkets of this market, and potential areas of growth, is crucial to developing a marketing strategy, as is establishing if any areas are in decline.
- *Trends.* Analysing general trends in the market identifies the changes that have actually taken place. This can help to uncover the reasons for these changes and expose the critical drivers underlying a market.
- *Customers.* The analysis needs to identify who the customer is and what criteria they use to judge a product offering. Information on where, when and how customers purchase the product, or service, allows an organization to begin to understand the needs of the customer (Chapter 3 will look

at consumer behaviour in more detail).
Identifying changing trends in consumer
behaviour may begin to signal potential
market developments and opportunities (see
Chapter 5).

- *Customer segments*. Identifying current market
segments and establishing the benefits each
group requires allows an organization to
detect if it has the capability to serve
particular consumers' needs.
- *Distribution channels*. Identifying the changes of
importance between channels of distribution,
based on growth, cost or effectiveness,
permits a company to evaluate its current
arrangements. Establishing the key decision
makers in a channel of distribution also helps
to inform strategic decisions.

Summary

The external auditing process creates the
information and analysis necessary for an
organization to begin to identify the key
issues it will have to address in order to
develop a successful strategy. The PEST analysis uncovered the critical areas in the external
environment that the organization needed to
consider. The industry analysis revealed the
structure and strengths of players in the
industry that any strategy will be required to
address. The competitor analysis disclosed the
relative position of the direct competitors in
the strategic group. Finally the market analysis began to explore current trends and areas

of growth. More importantly, it began to build
a picture of the consumer.

The external analysis is the initial step in the
process of establishing the key issues facing
an organization. The next stage is to examine
the consumer, before establishing methods for
segmenting markets.

References

Aguilar, F.J., *Scanning the Business Environment*, Macmillan, 1967

Diffenbach, J., 'Corporate Environmental
Analysis in Large U.S. Corporations', *Long
Range Planning*, Vol. 16, No. 3, pp. 107–116,
1983

Kotler, P., Armstrong, G., Saunders, J. and
Wong, V., *Principles of Marketing: The European Edition*, Prentice Hall, 1996

Lehman, D.R. and Weiner, R.S., *Analysis for
Marketing Planning*, 2nd edition, Irwin,
1991

Porter, M.E., *Competitive Strategy*, Free Press,
1980

Further reading

Aaker, D., *Strategic Market Management*, 4th
edition, Chapters 4–7, Wiley, 1995

Davidson, H., *Even More Offensive Marketing*,
Chapter 5, Penguin Books, 1997

Mudie, P., *Marketing: An Analytical Perspective*,
Chapter 2, Prentice Hall, 1997

CHAPTER 3

Segmentation

About this chapter

The segmentation process is a crucial aspect of strategic marketing. This chapter explores both consumer and organizational segmentation. Initially both consumer and organizational behaviour is summarized to illustrate the areas from which segmentation criteria have developed. A full analysis of segmentation is then undertaken, to provide the foundation of the targeting and positioning activities that will be addressed in Chapter 8.

Introduction

At a fundamental level an organization's marketing objectives become a decision about which products or services they are going to deliver into which markets. It follows that decisions about the markets to be serviced are a critical step in strategy formulation. The segmentation process is therefore central to strategy and can be broken into three distinct elements: segmentation, targeting and positioning. This chapter examines the segmentation aspect of both consumer and organizational markets.

Successful segmentation relies on a clear understanding of the market. Knowledge of consumer behaviour is the crucial foundation on which that market understanding is built. This chapter will briefly summarize both consumer and organizational buyer behaviour as an introduction to market segmentation criteria.

Why segment?

There are a number of reasons why organizations undertake segmentation (Doyle, 1994):

- *To meet consumer needs more precisely.* In a generic market customers' demands will differ. By developing a distinct marketing mix for each consumer segment an organization can offer customers better solutions for their needs.
- *To increase profits.* Different consumer segments react in contrasting ways to prices, some being far less price sensitive than others. Segmentation allows an organization to gain the best price it can in every segment, effectively raising the average price and increasing profitability.
- *To gain segment leadership.* In any particular market the brands that have dominant shares of the market will be highly profitable. Their market leadership gives them economies of scale, while in marketing and production they will also have established access to distribution channels. Small companies or new

entrants in a market are unlikely to be able to gain leadership; they can, however, take a dominant share of a particular market segment. This focus can allow them to develop a specialist marketing mix to satisfy the needs of the consumers in that group while at the same time building a competitive cost position relative to other companies in that segment.

- *To retain customers*. Providing products or services aimed at different consumer segments allows an organization to retain that customer's loyalty as their needs change. For example, as an individual moves through life their needs in financial services will change. Young single individuals may need a minimum of credit and banking facilities and car insurance; younger families, however, will need in addition life insurance policies and mortgages; while in middle age these needs will turn to pension provision. If an organization can provide all these services they may retain a customer who otherwise would transfer to another brand.

  An organization may also be able to use segmentation as a way of moving a customer over time from entry level products or services to products at the premium end of the market.

- *To focus marketing communications*. Segmentation allows an organization to identify media channels that can specifically reach the target groups. For example, young women interested in fashion are likely to read certain fashion magazines. Rather than spending money on mass-market media that reach far wider than the target group, organizations can target their money and effort by using media focused directly on their potential consumer group.

The segmentation process

The segmentation process involves establishing criteria by which groups of consumers with similar needs can be identified. These criteria have to establish consumer groups that have the following characteristics:

- The consumers in the segment respond in the same way to a particular marketing mix.
- The consumers within the segment have to react in a clearly different way from other groups of consumers to the marketing mix on offer.
- The group has to be large enough to provide the return on investment necessary to the organization.
- The criteria used to identify the segment have to be operational. Recently a small company in the magazine market identified a group of customers that had clear needs. Overseas nationals living in the UK wished to buy magazines from their home country. The organization's proposed marketing offer was to import magazines from overseas and mail them out directly to the consumers' homes. This was a potential customer group that all responded in the same way to the proposed marketing mix. They clearly acted differently from other groups in the magazine market. This potential segment was large and potentially profitable; however, it was a difficult group to make operational. You cannot identify overseas nationals easily as no official organization or overseas institute will give you their names and addresses. The only way of pursuing this opportunity was to persuade overseas nationals to identify themselves. This could have been accomplished by attracting consumers to respond to a promotional campaign, allowing the organization to build a customer database. However, for a small organization this was likely to be a costly operation and the idea was dropped in favour of other options.

Given the fact that segments need to demonstrate these four characteristics, the next step is to examine the variables that can be used to usefully segment a market. Understanding of consumer buyer behaviour theory is central to the successful development and application of segmentation criteria.

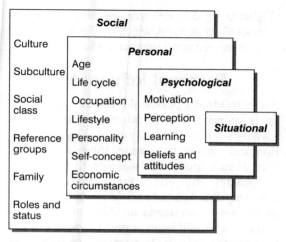

Figure 3.1   Influences on consumer behaviour

Consumer buyer behaviour

Consumer buyer behaviour relates to the end customer, the individuals who purchase products and services for personal consumption. This section summarizes the main sources of influence on consumer buyer behaviour (see Figure 3.1), in order to illustrate the influences that affect consumers' purchasing decisions. These influences can be broken down into four major categories; social, personal, psychological and the buying situation.

Social influences

There is a range of social influences on a consumer's purchasing behaviour, in particular culture and social class.

Culture

Behaviour is largely learned so the traditions, values and attitudes of the society an individual is brought up in will influence their behaviour. Cultural norms form the codes that direct behaviour. Therefore in an informal culture such as the USA or the UK the use of first names in a formal business meeting may be acceptable. In other cultures such as main-

land China more formal behaviour would be the norm. Within a larger culture there are obviously some subcultures, possibly based on religion, nationality, geographical areas or racial groups.

Social class

An individual's social class has been seen as an important influence on consumer behaviour, with individuals in lower social groups generally being seen to be more culture-bound. Social class groupings are heavily dependent upon a society's cultural background. Some societies are more hierarchical than others – many have a few people in the top and bottom classes with the majority in the middle. However, some societies, such as Scandinavia and Japan, have much flatter structures (see Figure 3.2). Some societies are more open than others, that is, individuals can move from one class to another; in a closed society this is not possible.

In western societies social classification has been criticized as a predictor of purchasing behaviour. In the UK a household in the higher AB category, after paying for a mortgage and private school tuition for their

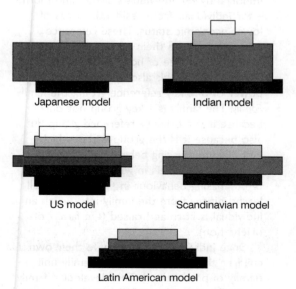

Figure 3.2   Examples of social class profiles in different cultures (*Source*: De Mooij and Keegan, 1991)

children, may have less disposable income than a lower category C2 or D household. There can also be wide discrepancies in purchasing patterns within social groups.

Individuals are also influenced by smaller social groups, such as friends, co-workers and family. These can be categorized into reference groups and family:

- *Reference groups.* Reference groups can be formal (members of a professional association or society) or informal groupings (social, friends, etc.). These reference groups influence an individual's attitude or behaviour. Individuals will tend to exhibit purchasing behaviour that is deemed to be acceptable by their reference group. Group norms and the role an individual plays within a group exert considerable influence on their behaviour. Recent research into the behaviour of first-time mothers illustrated the power of reference groups in shaping their expectations of the quality of service they would experience during their stay in the maternity ward. Doctors, midwives and information from antenatal classes were less influential than friends with young children – and more importantly the individual's sisters and mother – for individuals from residential areas of lower economic status. These reference groups influenced their subsequent behaviour in terms of choice of hospital and treatment (Tinson, 1998). This also underlines the power of one key reference group, the family.
- *Family.* The family is a key group not only because it is a primary reference group but also because it is the group within which individual purchasing behaviour is socialized. Attitudes and beliefs in general and patterns of purchasing behaviour in particular are all learnt initially from the family into which an individual is born and raised (the family of orientation).

  Once individuals start to have their own children they set up their own family unit (family of procreation). This developing family group also exerts an influence on the behaviour of individuals. There are, moreover, purchasing decisions that are taken by the household as a unit which reinforce the family as a key primary reference group.

Personal influences

An individual's personal attributes will have an influence on their purchasing behaviour. Factors such as the individual's age, occupation and financial situation, their personality, their family life cycle stage and their lifestyle in general will affect the pattern of their consumption decisions. These factors are commonly used as criteria to segment consumer markets and will be explored in greater detail in the section on consumer segmentation criteria.

Psychological influences

Four key psychological factors: motivation, perception, learning, and beliefs and attitudes are further influences on consumer behaviour.

Motivation

Individuals have a range of needs from basic biological needs, such as the need to satisfy hunger, thirst and physical distress, to psychological needs like the need for social recognition, esteem or belonging. These needs may lie dormant at any particular time but once aroused to a high enough level of intensity they become a motivational force. A motive is a need that has reached a level that drives an individual to search for ways to alleviate its demands. There is a whole body of theory in this area that cannot be explored in this text (see Further Reading at the end of this chapter); however, it is worthwhile summarizing two of the most influential theories to illustrate their influence on marketing practice:

- *Freud's theory of motivation.* Freud proposed that individuals are motivated by unconscious psychological factors. Moreover, as an individual grows up they conform to social norms which require them to repress a range of desires and passions (urges). This theory would suggest that an individual's consciously stated reason for buying a product may hide a more fundamental unconscious motive. An individual proposing to purchase an executive car may claim that this decision is based on the need for quality and reliability, whereas the unconscious desire may be for status.

- *Maslow's theory of motivation.* Maslow claimed that individuals have a hierarchy of needs. At the lowest level individuals are driven by basic physiological needs. When individuals are able to satisfy the needs at one level they will be motivated by the needs at the next level in the hierarchy (see Figure 3.3). The implication of the theory for marketers is that individuals will seek different products and services as they move up this hierarchy.

  This theory is not universal and is biased towards Anglo-Saxon cultural values, in particular individualism and need for self-development. These needs would not have the same prominence in Japan or Germany, for example, where the need for personal security and conformity take a higher priority.

Motivation theories relate to consumers' needs, and satisfying consumers' needs is a central tenet of marketing. These motivation

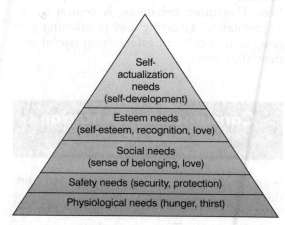

Figure 3.3 Maslow's hierarchy of needs (*Source:* Adapted from Maslow, 1970)

theories therefore have influenced approaches to market segmentation. It should be noted that although Freud's and Maslow's theories have been very influential in management and marketing theory and practice, they have been challenged on the grounds that the research evidence to support their utility as a psychological theory of motivation is weak (Steers *et al.* 1996). However, they are useful for marketers as they help to categorize consumers into groups based on needs.

Perception

The way an individual perceives an external stimulus will influence their reaction. Individuals can have different perceptions of the same stimulus due to the process of selective attention, selective distortion and selective retention:

- *Selective attention.* Individuals cannot observe all the potential stimuli in the external environment. Selective attention refers to the tendency of individuals to screen out the majority of stimuli to which they are exposed.
- *Selective distortion.* Individuals process information within the confines of their current set of attitudes and beliefs. The tendency to adjust perceptions to conform to their current mindset is called selective distortion.
- *Selective retention.* Individuals do not remember everything they perceive. Information that reinforces their attitudes and beliefs is more likely to be retained.

Perceptual behaviour is relevant to the segmentation process because of its links with learning, attitudes and beliefs.

Learning, attitudes and beliefs

Learning relates to any change in the content of an individual's long-term memory and is associated with how information is processed (covered above under Perception). There are various ways in which learning can take place, including conditioning, social learning and cognitive learning:

- *Conditioning.* This idea proposes that reinforcement is necessary for individuals to develop attitudes and beliefs. Therefore if an individual's experience of a particular product is positive this will reinforce their positive attitudes and beliefs about the brand. If the experience is negative it is unlikely the consumer will buy the product again. The negative attitude that has been formed to the product could also affect the individual's attitude to other products and services offered by the company or linked to the brand.
- *Social learning.* This suggests that learning can take place without direct personal reinforcement. Individuals may remember the slogan associated with a brand name and form an attitude about its attributes without any direct contact. An individual may also learn from observing the behaviour of others and the recognition or rewards they receive.
- *Cognitive learning.* In high involvement purchases an individual may use their own powers of cognitive reasoning to develop their attitudes and beliefs about a product.

Forming attitudes and beliefs about products effectively creates a position for the product or brand relative to other products and brands in the mind of the consumer. This lies at the heart of product positioning, which is central to the successful implementation of segmentation strategy (see Chapter 8).

The buying situation

The buying process (see Figure 3.4) an individual goes through when making purchasing decisions is affected by the particular situational factors surrounding the activity.

High involvement purchases refer to situations where both the information search and the use of referent group consultation and post-purchase evaluation is extensive. It occurs when the following factors are involved:

- *Self–image.* The purchase has a major effect on an individual's self-image, such as the purchase of a car.

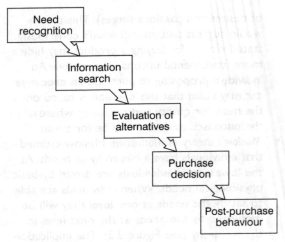

Figure 3.4   The buying process

- *Perceived risk.* The impact of a mistaken purchase would have a dramatic effect on the consumer. Expensive purchases would fall into this category, where any mistake could have a major effect on an individual's financial position.
- *Social factors.* An individual's level of social acceptance may depend on the right purchasing decision.
- *Hedonistic factors.* The purchase is concerned with products or services that are linked to providing personal pleasure.

Consumer behaviour theory is a complex area and only a brief overview has been provided here. Consumer behaviour is central to the segmentation, targeting and positioning process, in particular in establishing useful segmentation criteria.

Consumer segmentation criteria

Segmentation criteria can be divided into three main categories:

- *Profile variables.* These are used to characterize the consumer but in terms that are not expressly linked to, or predictive of, an individual's behaviour in the specific market.

- *Behavioural variables.* These relate to the behaviour of the consumer. Thus behavioural factors such as benefits sought, usage, and the purchase occasion all come under this category.
- *Psychographic variables.* These identify individual's attitudes, opinions and interests to build up a lifestyle profile that includes the consumer's consumption patterns. Thus these profiles are inextricably associated with specific purchasing behaviour.

Segmentation is a creative process and can be conducted using a range of different variables each bringing a particular perspective to the dynamics of the market. The air travel market could be segmented according to the benefits sought (value or status), or usage occasion (business or holiday), or stage in the family life cycle (young and single or middle-aged, married with children). On occasion it may be appropriate to use a single variable to segment a market, but more often than not they will be used in combination. For instance, a potential market segment in the air travel market could be middle-aged consumers with children who seek status benefits for business travel. Innovative combinations of variables from across the range can uncover new market segments, even in supposedly traditional markets.

There is no hierarchy to these variables. Marketers can use any variable as a starting point (first-order variables), and then add further variables (second-order variables) to give the grouping a clearer definition. Thus a segment of consumers seeking physical fitness may initially be determined using benefit segmentation. Profile variables may then be added such as age, gender, geodemographics, etc., to more clearly identify the consumer in order to allow the company to develop specific media communication and distribution plans.

There is a range of demographic, socio-economic and geographic segmentation variables in this category.

Demographic segmentation

The key demographic variables consist of age, gender and the family life cycle:

Age

Consumers' purchasing decisions will change with age. Older people are likely to be looking for different benefits from a holiday than younger people. However, age by itself may not be a sophisticated enough variable to help identify a consumer segment. Using the age range of 25 to 35-year-old individuals to identify a consumer group results in a rather unclear grouping. 25 to 35-year-old women will have different needs from 25 to 35-year-old men in certain markets. A 30-year-old woman who is single and has a professional job is likely to have different needs from a 30-year-old woman who is married with three children and has chosen not to work outside the home. Both will have different needs from a 30-year-old unemployed woman who is single with a child.

There is also the issue of psychological age to be considered when using this variable. That is, consumers may perceive themselves to be in a different age group to their true chronological age. Therefore a product or service aimed at 35-year-olds may attract older customers who still see themselves in this age range.

Age alone therefore has limitations as a method of breaking a market down into useful segments.

Gender

Sex, as a variable, has similar limitations to age. Clearly there are differences between consumer groups based on gender. However, this variable by itself only narrows the market down by around 50 per cent. There are still major differences within the gender category. Younger women may have different needs from older women. Cadbury's, when designing a box of chocolates called Inspirations, which was aimed at the female market, found that older women did not like the contemporary design used on a prototype while younger women liked the modern packaging (Ensor and Laing, 1993).

Obviously age and gender variables can be used together to help define a segment. Therefore we can define segments in terms of 25 to 35-year-old females, or 55 to 65-year-old males. However this still gives us quite broad customer groupings that do not take into consideration wider factors that may affect consumers in these particular age and sex groupings. One way of attempting to overcome these deficiencies is to look at consumer life cycles.

Family life cycle

The essence of the family life cycle is that consumers are likely to go through one of the alternative routes shown in Figure 3.5. The classic route would be for a consumer to move from being young and single, to young married without children, to young married with children, to middle-aged married with children, to middle-aged married without dependent children, to older married, ending up finally as older unmarried.

At each stage a consumer's needs and disposable income will change. Someone who is young and single has very few commitments so although their income in real terms may be low, they have high disposable income. Once an individual is married with children, commitments have increased. They are likely to have to move into the housing market, and in adddition they are now buying products for young babies and children. The couple may well start to take out savings and insurance policies to protect their children's future. In middle age they will begin to be more interested in pension arrangements. Quite obviously, as an individual moves

through these stages, their propensity to buy certain types of products will change. This approach is therefore useful in identifying these consumer groupings.

In western cultures there has been speculation that the family as a unit is of decreasing importance; however, there is contradictory evidence on this issue. In 1985 a Family Policy Studies Centre report looking at the UK claimed that:

- Nine out of ten people will marry at some time in their lives.
- Nine out of ten married couples will have children.
- Two in every three marriages are likely to be ended by death rather than divorce.
- Eight out of ten people live in households headed by a married couple.

There was one key change from earlier studies, however. This was a growing trend for individuals to go through the cycle belonging to more than one family group, with individuals divorcing and remarrying. Therefore parental figures in a family grouping may not both be blood relatives of the children. Also the siblings may not be blood relatives. From a marketer's point of view, however, the important fact is that family groupings are still a key feature in society. These family life cycle stages are therefore still relevant for segmentation purposes.

Another trend that Lawson (1988) identified after analysing demographic trends in the UK was that the stages have altered in both length and importance. Full-nest stages, when children live with their parents, are shorter due to the fact that couples are having fewer children and that these children are being born closer together. This means that individuals spend more time in the bachelor and empty-nest stages and there are more people in these groups.

As a result of this study, Lawson updated the family life cycle using the 1981 census, claiming this modernized version covers over 80 per cent of the population (see Figure 3.6).

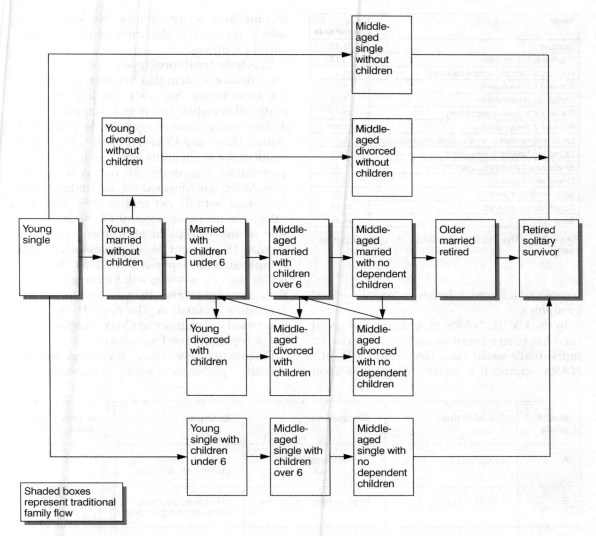

Figure 3.5   A contemporary family life cycle (*Source*: Adapted from Murphy and Staples 1979)

The 18.69 per cent of households excluded from this table are made up of young people living in joint households, households with residents other than family and households with more than one family.

Indeed, households can be a useful way of looking at social grouping. Individuals sharing a flat have to take part in group decision making for products such as furniture, electrical appliances, etc. Lawson claims, when discussing the 18.69 per cent of the population that do not fit into the family life cycle, that households are likely to be a better unit with which to analyse consumer behaviour than the family.

Socio-economic segmentation

In socio-economic segmentation, factors such as occupation, educational background, place of residence and income are used to classify

Stage	% of households
Bachelor	1.42
Newly married couples	3.11
Full nest 1 (with pre-school children)	11.91
Full nest 1 (lone parent)	1.26
Middle-aged no children	1.19
Full nest 2 (school-age children)	16.97
Full nest 2 (lone parent)	1.92
Launching families (with non-dependant children)	6.3
Launching families (lone parent)	1.45
Empty nest 1 (childless, aged 45–54)	9.45
Empty nest 2 (retired)	9.51
Solitary survivor under 65	2.66
Solitary survivor retired	14.17
Total	**81.31**

Figure 3.6   The modernized family life cycle (Lawson, 1988)

individuals into larger 'social class' groupings.

In the UK, JICNARS' classification of social class has been a common tool to categorize an individual's social class (see Figure 3.7). JICNARS' approach is heavily dependent upon income and occupation as the key factors which are used in determining its six major social groupings.

This is the traditional type of socio-economic classification system that has been used in the UK for censuses since 1911. The UK Office for National Statistics, however, is planning to use a new categorization system for the 2001 census (Rose and O'Reilly, 1999). This is as a result of the major shifts in make-up of the UK population. Currently 60 per cent of the population are deemed to be middle class compared with 51 per cent in 1984. The new categories also take account of the increased role in the workplace of women who now occupy 18 per cent of all professional posts compared with 4 per cent in 1984. Women, under the new system, will be categorized in their own right rather than according to their husband's occupation. The new classification was based on a survey of 65 000 people across 371 occupations (see Figure 3.8).

Despite this new classification there are still several problems with socio-economic

Social grade	Social status	Occupations	Examples	Approx % of households
A	Upper middle class	Higher managerial/ professional	Doctors, lawyers, professors, directors	3
B	Middle class	Intermediate managerial	Managers, teachers, computer programmers	10
C1	Lower middle class	Junior managerial, supervisory, clerical, administrative	Foremen, shop assistants, office workers	24
C2	Skilled working class	Skilled manual labour	Electricians, mechanics, plumbers and other crafts	30
D	Working class	Semi-skilled and unskilled manual labour	Machine operators, assembly workers	25
E	Subsistence	None	Pensioners, casual workers, unemployed, students	8

Figure 3.7   JICNARS' social grade definitions

New social class	Occupations	Examples
1	Higher managerial and professional occupations	
1.1	Employers and managers in larger organizations	Bank managers, company directors, financial managers, senior local government officers
1.2	Higher professional	Doctors, lawyers, dentists, higher civil servants, academics, engineers teachers, airline pilots, social workers, librarians, personnel officers, computer analysts
2	Lower managerial and professional occupations	Police officers, fire-fighters, prison officers, nurses, physiotherapists, journalists, actors and musicians
3	Intermediate occupations	Secretaries/PA's, airline flight attendants, driving instructors, computer operators, clerical workers, computer engineers, dental technicians, precision instrument makers
4	Small employers and own-account workers	
5	Lower supervisory, craft and related occupations	Electricians, TV engineers, car mechanics, train drivers, printers
6	Semi-routine occupations	Drivers, hairdressers, bricklayers, plasterers, welders, cooks, shop assistants, garage forecourt attendants, supermarket check-out operators
7	Routine occupations	Car park attendants, cleaners, road workers, refuse collectors, labourers, road sweepers

Figure 3.8   New social classes for the 2001 UK census (*Source*: Adapted from Rose and O'Reilly, 1999)

approaches to segmentation for marketing managers:

- Social class is not an accurate gauge of disposable income. An electrician or a plumber who would be classified as social class C2 may well have a higher disposable income than a junior manager who would be classified as social class C1.
- In western societies there has been a major trend toward women working. Social classification has used the head of household's occupation to define social class – however, if both adults are working then defining the head of household becomes more difficult.

Earlier in this chapter we have also seen that family structures themselves have become more complicated in the west. The new classification does attempt to address this issue but how does it help to predict family purchasing behaviour? Individuals from the same household may be in two completely different social classes.

- The variety and the changing nature of people's occupations make it increasingly difficult to apply social class categories consistently.

Most importantly in today's society, social class is a less important predictor of behaviour than other methods of segmentation. For instance, an individual whatever their social class who is interested in sport is more likely to buy products and services in the sporting area than an individual in the same social class who is not interested in sport. It may therefore be more important for marketers to identify individuals who share a common interest (e.g. sport) rather than identify social class groupings.

Geographic segmentation

Geographic and geodemographic variables come into this category.

Geographic

This variable was used more extensively in the past. There used to be clear consumer patterns in product areas such as food and alcohol across Europe, or even within a market such as the UK. Although some of these patterns still show through, mass communication and wider access to travel have tended to erode these regional differences. In the UK individuals are eating a much more cosmopolitan diet than thirty years ago. Pizzas and pasta dishes are common in many homes. Where geographic variables are used they tend to be used to reflect some wider cultural differences between markets. However, geographic variables can be useful if they are used in conjunction with other factors.

Geodemographics

Geodemographic segmentation combines information on household location with certain demographic and socio-economic data. This approach relies on information that is gathered in census returns. In the UK the census information on family size, household size, occupation and ethnic origin can be used to group residential housing into geographic areas that display similar profiles. There are several geodemographic forms of classification, one of the best known in the UK being

ACORN (A Classification Of Residential Neighbourhoods). The ACORN classification identifies six major categories (one group is unclassified) that can be further subdivided in seventeen groups (see Figure 3.9).

These seventeen groups can be further subdivided into fifty-four neighbourhood types. For instance, ACORN category C (Rising), group 7 (Prosperous Professionals, Metropolitan Areas) is made up of two neighbourhood types. One of these is neighbourhood type 19 that is categorized as 'Apartments, Young Professional Singles and Couples'. These types of neighbourhood areas are heavily concentrated in London. Outside London these neighbourhoods are found in such places as Edinburgh, St Albans and Cambridge.

These neighbourhood areas allow specific patterns of consumption to be identified. For instance, ACORN neighbourhood type 5 'Mature, Well-off Suburbs' is a subgroup of category A, group 1 'Wealthy Achievers, Suburban Areas'. This group is made up of mature suburbs found all over the UK, particularly in Surrey, Hertfordshire, South Glamorgan and Outer London. Individuals in this group buy above average levels of fresh and dried pasta, ground coffee, fresh fish and fruit. Ownership of most financial products in this group is above the national average except for personal pensions. This type of detailed profile allows for highly sophisticated targeting.

This segmentation approach can be used to aid decision making in a variety of areas:

- Identifying favourable retail locations for a specific retail format.
- The specific mix of products and services delivered in a particular retail location.
- Decisions on direct mail campaigns.
- The boundaries of specific sales territories.
- Location of poster sites.
- Selection of media.

There are criticisms of this approach. It is claimed that all these geodemographic systems contain inaccuracies because of the

Category	% Pop.	Groups	% Pop.
A – Thriving	19.8	1. Wealthy achievers, suburban areas	15.1
		2. Affluent greys, rural communities	2.3
		3. Prosperous pensioners, retirement areas	2.3
B – Expanding	11.6	4. Affluent executives, family areas	3.7
		5. Well-off workers, family areas	7.8
C – Rising	7.5	6. Affluent urbanites, town and city areas	2.2
		7. Prosperous professionals, metropolitan areas	2.1
		8. Better-off executives, inner-city areas	3.2
D – Settling	24.1	9. Comfortable middle-agers, mature home-owning areas	13.4
		10. Skilled workers, home-owning areas	10.7
E – Aspiring	13.7	11. New home-owners, mature communities	9.8
		12. White collar workers, better off multi-ethnic areas	4.0
F – Striving	22.8	13. Older people, less prosperous areas	3.6
		14. Council estate residents, better off homes	11.6
		15. Council estate residents, high unemployment	2.7
		16. Council estate residents, greatest hardship	2.8
		17. People in multi-ethnic, low income areas	2.1
Unclassified	0.5		0.5

Figure 3.9   The ACORN consumer targeting classification (CACI, 1993; ACORN is a registered trademark of CACI Ltd)

difficulties in lining up the census enumeration districts with postal codes. There are also problems in reflecting the changes in housing that take place between each census.

The geodemographic systems referred to so far are used at a relatively local level. There have been developments to try and use this approach at a much larger regional level. Geodemographic techniques have been used on a European scale to identify consumers who have common characteristics but may live in different countries. Using demographic (age), economic (income), cultural (language), and geographic (longitude and latitude) factors six Euro-consumer segments can be identified (see Figure 3.10).

This approach illustrates the point that consumers in different countries can share similar characteristics. For instance, the consumers in segment 4 show more similarities to

Segment	Geographical boundaries	Description	Pop.
1	UK and Ireland	Average age and income profile; English as a common language	60.3m
2	Central Germany, Central and Northern France, Southern Belgium and Luxembourg	High proportion of older people and low proportion of middle-aged; average income; German and French languages	54.5m
3	Portugal and Spain	Young population; below average income; Portuguese and Spanish languages	50.4m
4	South-eastern France, Southern Germany, Northern Italy	High proportion of middle-aged people; above average income; French, German and Italian languages	71.5m
5	Southern Italy and Greece	Young population; below average income; Italian and Greek languages	31.2m
6	Northern Germany, the Netherlands, Northern Belguim, Denmark, Sweden, Finland, Norway, Iceland and Switzerland	High proportion of middle-aged people; very high income; multilingual; German, French, Italian and Scandinavian languages	57.6m

Note: Norway, Iceland and Switzerland are not currently in the European Union

Figure 3.10   Euro-consumer segments using geodemographic segmentation (*Source:* Adapted from Vandermerwe and L'Huillier, 1989)

each other than to other consumers from their own country. This is the first step at European segmentation, and may well lead to the identification of subsegments within these larger groups and to the ability for marketers to target relatively large geodemographic segments that transcend national boundaries.

Behavioural variables

The segmentation approaches that have been discussed so far all use characteristics of the consumer as a way of identifying clear groupings. However, identifying consumer behaviour rather than their personal attributes can be a more effective way of identifying market segments.

The main behavioural variables in this category are benefits and usage segmentation, and purchase occasion.

Benefit segmentation

Benefit segmentation uses the underlying reasons why an individual purchases a particular product or service, rather than trying to identify an individual's particular personal attributes.

Benefit segmentation is based on the concept that the key reason a consumer buys the product or service is for the benefit that product or service gives them. Identifying groups of consumers that are seeking a common benefit in a particular market allows a producer to develop specific products or service offerings. An example of benefit segmentation would be in the management education market. A survey in the USA found that there were several benefit segments in the market for MBA qualifications (see Figure 3.11).

The advantage of benefit segmentation is that it is a market-orientated approach, which by seeking to identify consumers' needs

MBA Benefit Segments

Quality seekers wish to have the highest quality education available. They believe a top ranked education will benefit them during their entire business life, and will lead to job advancement or a career change.

Speciality seekers wish to have a specialized education and to become experts in their areas of particular interest. Concentrated courses tend to fit their needs, and they will search for institutions that offer them.

Career changers are seeking new jobs or employers and believe an MBA qualification will open up opportunities for career advancement and mobility. They have several years work experience and feel that they are in a career cul-de-sac.

Knowledge seekers wish to learn and feel that increased knowledge will lead to power. They believe an MBA will be an asset not only in their career but also in all aspects of their life.

Status seekers feel that an MBA will lead to increased income and prestige.

Degree seekers believe that a first degree is no longer sufficient and that an MBA is needed in order to be competitive in the contemporary job market. These individuals tend to be active, self-orientated and independent.

Professional advancers are striving to climb the corporate ladder. They are looking for professional advancement, higher salaries and job flexibility. They are upwardly mobile, serious, future orientated and wish to build a career within the current corporate structures.

Avoiders look for MBA programmes that require the least effort to complete. They believe that all Business Schools provide essentially the same education. Their motivation is 'other directed' and they will seek low cost, 'lower quality' programmes.

Convenience seekers will join MBA programmes that are located near their homes or place of work and which have simple entry procedures. They are interested in any Business School which provides these conveniences and are low cost.

Non-matriculators wish to undertake an MBA course without completing any formal application procedures. They are therefore attracted to a Business School that allows them to begin an MBA programme without any formal application.

Figure 3.11 MBA benefit segments (*Source*: Based on Miaoulis and Kalfus, 1983)

allows organizations to set about satisfying them.

Usage segmentation

The characteristics and patterns of consumer usage are the essence of this segmentation approach. Consumers will generally fall into categories of heavy users, medium users, occasional users and non-users of a particular product or service. Identifying heavy users can be useful as they are likely to consume a larger percentage of an organization's sales than other groups, as the Pareto effect would suggest (see Figure 3.12). This can lead to the identification of new segmentation opportunities for an organization.

For example, Mangers identified that the heavy users of their cleaning product Sugar Soap, which was a universal non-silica based household cleaner, were professional house-hold painters and decorators. In fact the reason this group were heavy users of the product was because it could be used to clean surfaces that needed to be painted, and because it was a non-silica based cleaner that allowed them to paint straight onto the surface after cleaning. Once managers had identified this group of heavy users they relaunched the product to the Do It Yourself market for individuals wishing to decorate their own houses.

Airlines use frequent flyers programmes to retain the heavy user of their services. Many other companies in other sectors use incentives to retain this important customer grouping.

Banks and building societies may wish to have charging scales on their accounts that give incentives for heavy users while at the same time increasing relative charges for light users as they are relatively more expensive to manage.

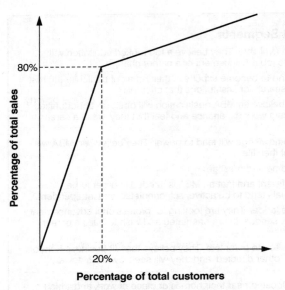

Figure 3.12   The Pareto Effect, also known as the 80/20 rule

Psychographic variables

The techniques that have been discussed so far have used either consumer characteristics or behavioural variables as the basis for identifying consumer groupings. Psychographics is a more recent approach that attempts to identify segments based on lifestyle characteristics, attitudes and personality. Rather than concentrating on single factors such as age, sex and marital status it attempts to build a broader picture of consumers' lifestyles based on their activities, interests and opinions. Asking a series of questions about consumers' activities, interests and opinions as well as questions about product and service usage identifies these lifestyles (see Figure 3.13).

Several models have been developed using this approach, all with broad similarities. Two of them will be discussed in more detail here: the VALs framework and the Monitor framework.

Purchase occasion

Consumer groups can be identified on the basis of the type of occasion for which they buy a particular product or service. Some products may be bought as gifts, or for specific formal social occasions such as weddings or New Year celebrations. The convenience store concept is an example of occasion segmentation, where individuals can make purchases at a time and place that are agreeable to them.

The VALs framework

This model was developed in the USA by asking 2713 individuals 800 questions. The VALs framework identified nine lifestyle groups in the American population. The model also identifies three developmental stages that individuals may pass through.

Activities	Interests	Opinions	Demographics
Work	Family	Themselves	Age
Hobbies	Home	Social issues	Education
Social events	Job	Politics	Income
Vacation	Community	Business	Occupation
Entertainment	Recreation	Economics	Family size
Club membership	Fashion	Education	Dwelling
Community	Food	Products	Geography
Shopping	Media	Future	City size
Sports	Achievements	Culture	Stage in life cycle

Figure 3.13   Questions posed in lifestyle studies (*Source*: Plummer, 1974)

Developmental stage	Grouping (% of US population)
Need-driven	**Survivors.** This is a disadvantaged group who are likely to be withdrawn, despairing and depressed (4%). **Sustainers** are another disadvantaged group, but they are working hard to escape poverty (7%).
Outer-directed	**Belongers** are characterized as being conventional, nostalgic, reluctant to try new ideas and generally conservative (33%). **Emulators** are upwardly mobile, ambitious and status conscious (10%). **Achievers.** This group enjoys life and makes things happen (23%).
Inner-directed	**'I-am-me'** tend to be young, self engrossed and act on whims (5%). **Experientials** wish to enjoy as wide a range of life experiences as possible (7%). **Societally conscious** have a clear sense of social responsibility and wish to improve society (9%).
Nirvana	**Integrateds** are completely mature psychologically and combine the positive elements of outer and inner directedness (2%).

Figure 3.14   The VALs framework developed by Arnold Mitchell at the Stanford Research Institute

Normally individuals would move from one of the need-driven stages to either an outer-directed or an inner-directed stage. This is a hierarchical model and relatively few would reach the integrated stage (see Figure 3.14).

The framework is divided into a series of segments:

- The needs-driven segment identified by this model have relatively little purchasing power and are therefore of marginal interest to profit-making organizations. This is a declining group in western societies.
- The outer-directed groups are more affluent and are interested in status products that other individuals will notice. They are therefore interested in brand names such as Rolex and Cartier.
- Inner-directed individuals in contrast are more concerned with their individual needs rather than external values. This is an important sector, as they tend to be trend-setters. This group is also the fastest growing group in western societies.

- Very few individuals reach the integrated stage.

The Monitor framework

This framework was developed by the Taylor Nelson research agency. The model similarly divides consumers into three main groups each with its own subgroups (see Figure 3.15).

The advantages of this lifestyle approach are:

- It takes into account factors other than status and class.
- Purchasing patterns are encompassed in the lifestyle profile.
- Well-defined communication channels may emerge as part of the lifestyle.
- Brand personalities can be built to appeal to specific lifestyles.

These models allow a more rounded view of consumer groups to emerge. Identifying the

Groups	Subgroups (% of UK population)
Sustenance-driven are concerned about material security	**Aimless.** Includes the young unemployed and elderly drifters (5%).
	Survivors are working-class people who retain traditional attitudes (16%).
	Belongers straddle the sustenance-driven and outer-directed groups. they are a conservative family-orientated group. (The subgroup is 18% of the UK population in total with 9% in the sustenance-driven group).
Outer-directed	**Belongers.** This half of the subgroup are still conservative and family orientated but are also status driven (9%).
	Conspicuous consumers are driven by a desire for status (19%).
Inner-directed	**Social resisters** are caring and tend to hold doctrinaire attitudes (11%).
	Experimentalists are individualistic and interested in the good life (14%).
	Self explorers hold less doctrinaire attitudes than the social resisters and are less materialistic than the experimentalist subgroup (17%).

Figure 3.15   The Monitor framework developed by the Taylor Nelson research agency

lifestyle of potential consumer segments allows the marketer to develop sophisticated marketing mixes that tie in with a particular lifestyle group. The lifestyle profile may highlight the type of retail outlets that the consumer group is attracted to, or the publications they are more likely to read. This allows managerial decisions to be made about the distribution and promotional aspects of the mix.

Weaknesses with psychographical models are that they currently tend to reflect a western social hierarchy and culture. As a result these frameworks are not always easily transferred to different social settings. Cultural values may mean that aspirations are different from those represented by western values of individualism, self-development and status. These models also do not easily represent the flatter social class structures that occur in certain cultures such as Scandinavia.

Some critics of the approach would also argue that these broad lifestyle profiles are not accurate predictors of consumers' purchasing behaviour in any particular market sector. An outer-directed individual who may in general buy status products may not buy branded goods in a market area where there is very little risk of damage to their self-image. The soap powder they buy is unlikely to be of major significance to the way they feel about themselves or about the way other people see them. However, the car they drive or the clothes they wear are likely to be a much more significant indicator of their status to both themselves and others.

Lifestyle segmentation has led to the proliferation of acronyms to describe consumer groupings (see Figure 3.16).

Organizational / industrial segmentation techniques

So far this chapter has concentrated on segmentation of consumer markets. Obviously many companies' main markets lie in the organizational or industrial sphere. In these markets companies have to sell products and services directly to organizational purchasers. There are differences between the type of

Yuppies	Young upwardly mobile professionals
Dinks	Dual income no kids
Bumps	Borrowed-to-the-hilt, upwardly mobile professional show-offs
Silks	Single income lots of kids
Glams	Greying leisured affluent middle-aged
Jollies	Jet-setting oldies with lots of loot

Figure 3.16   Acronyms developed from lifestyle groupings

segmentation variables used in an organizational market and the ones that have so far been outlined for consumer markets. The difference in approach lies in the nature of organizational buyer behaviour.

Organizational buyer behaviour

An organization's purchase decisions are likely to be more complex because of the number of individuals and groups involved in the purchase decision and the possibility of the actual product/service being more expensive and sophisticated. All the individuals that participate in the decision-making process will have interdependent goals and share common risks although they may face different systems of reward. What emerges is a decision-making unit (DMU) made up of all these individuals and groups. Individuals in the DMU will play one of six main roles:

- *Initiator.* Identifies a problem that can be overcome by the purchase of a product or service. An individual in a retail company may for instance identify a problem in the merchandising function of the company that could be resolved by a new piece of software. (The merchandise function develops the buying plan for a retail company, and monitors sales and product margins amongst other things.)
- *User.* Uses the product in the merchandising function of the company in this case. They may well be the initiator, although this role may be someone outside the user group.
- *Buyer.* Undertakes the negotiation with potential suppliers. The brief for the technical requirements of the software needed, however, is likely to come from one of the other areas of the DMU.
- *Influencer.* Does not directly make the product or supplier choice but has a major impact on the decisions made. In this case an individual from the computer services unit in the organization will lay down the technical requirements of the software based on the need for it to integrate with the current hardware system.
- *Decider.* This is the individual who actually makes the decision to purchase. This individual may not have direct line management control of the merchandise or IT areas of the business but occupies this role because of the power and influence they have over the area being investigated. This is a crucial position in the DMU and yet it can be the most difficult to identify because several individuals may potentially play this role. In this case it may be the merchandise director, the finance director (many finance directors are responsible for the IT function) or the managing director.
- *Gatekeeper.* Determines the flow of information within the DMU without being directly involved in the buying decision. They control whether a potential supplier gains access to other individuals in the DMU. The flow of promotional material and information about suppliers is also under their guidance. Secretaries are very obvious gatekeepers but any individual in the DMU can potentially play this role. A technical person may favour one particular supplier and will pass only their promotional material to other members of the DMU.

The size of the DMU will depend in part on the type of purchase decision being undertaken. Where a simple low-risk purchase is being made one or two individuals could undertake all the roles in the DMU. A high-risk expensive purchase may involve a large number of people from different functional areas in the company. Organizational purchases can be classified in terms of their level of risk as follows:

- *Routine order products*. These are used and ordered on a regular basis. The products or services are unlikely to pose any problems regarding their use or performance and are therefore low risk (e.g. office stationery).
- *Procedural problem products*. These products may involve some level of training in order for individuals to successfully adopt them. This will increase the risks associated with the successful introduction of the purchase to the company (e.g. personal computers or word processors).
- *Performance problem products*. The risks here lie with the question of whether the product can perform at the level required to meet the users' requirements. There may also be concerns about the product's ability to be compatible with the company's existing

resources and current equipment (e.g. introducing new technology).
- *Political problem products*. Political problems could arise where a purchase takes away resources from another area within the organization. A high investment in a product for one area of the business may mean that another area has to forgo investment. Political problems can also take place where it is planned that the same product will be used by several different units, each having their own requirements (e.g. a new information system).

Political pressures also build up in the DMU because individuals look for different attributes from a particular product. This is partly based on the operational needs of their department. Individuals also pursue their own self-interest and are motivated by the formal rewards available to them. Individuals in different areas of the company may be given incentives in different ways. Buyers may be evaluated and/or given incentives to save the organization money. Production managers may be given quality and output targets.

This can lead to strange effects. Bonoma (1982) talks of an organization that reduced its

PURCHASING OBJECTIVES

| of finance department | of production function | of accounting function | by others in the company | of legal function | of engineering function | of marketing function | of purchasing function |

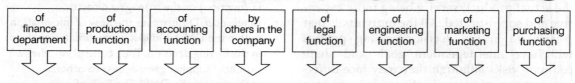

REWARD-BASED BEHAVIOUR WITHIN THE BUYING CENTRE

| by finance personnel | by production personnel | by accounting personnel | by others in the company | by legal personnel | by engineering personnel | by marketing personnel | by purchasing personnel |

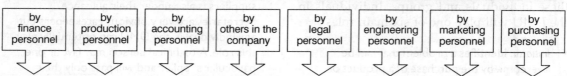

BUYING CENTRE DYNAMICS

Figure 3.17 Rewards/incentives as a source of conflict in organizational decision-making units (*Source*: Adapted from Morris, 1988)

list price to well under its competitors', but gave only small discounts off this list price. All the competitors charged higher prices but gave larger discounts. Even though the company had lower prices, organizations favoured the competitors. The main reason for this turned out to be that the buyers were evaluated and given incentives based on the price concessions they were able to obtain during negotiations rather than on the end price paid.

Figure 3.17 shows how each unit may have its own set of rewards. These disparate incentives can also lead to conflict within the DMU. Buyers may feel they cannot save money because the production engineers are setting technical specifications on a product that are too high. Alternatively production engineers may not be able to reach their output targets because the buyer has bought a cheaper product from a supplier who has less dependable delivery times.

This demonstrates that organizational buying decisions are more complex than general consumer buyer behaviour. Frameworks have been developed to give a more comprehensive view of the complex factors involved. These also act as a foundation for developing meaningful segmentation criteria in organizational markets. The Webster–Wind and the Sheth frameworks both try to develop logical models of this process.

The Webster–Wind framework

This framework identifies four categories of variables that have an influence on organizational buying decisions (see Figure 3.18).

* *Environmental.* Any aspect of the external environment that may affect the organization buying behaviour is embraced under this heading. This includes political, economic, cultural, legal, technological and physical environments. Competitors' marketing actions are also deemed to be in the external environment.

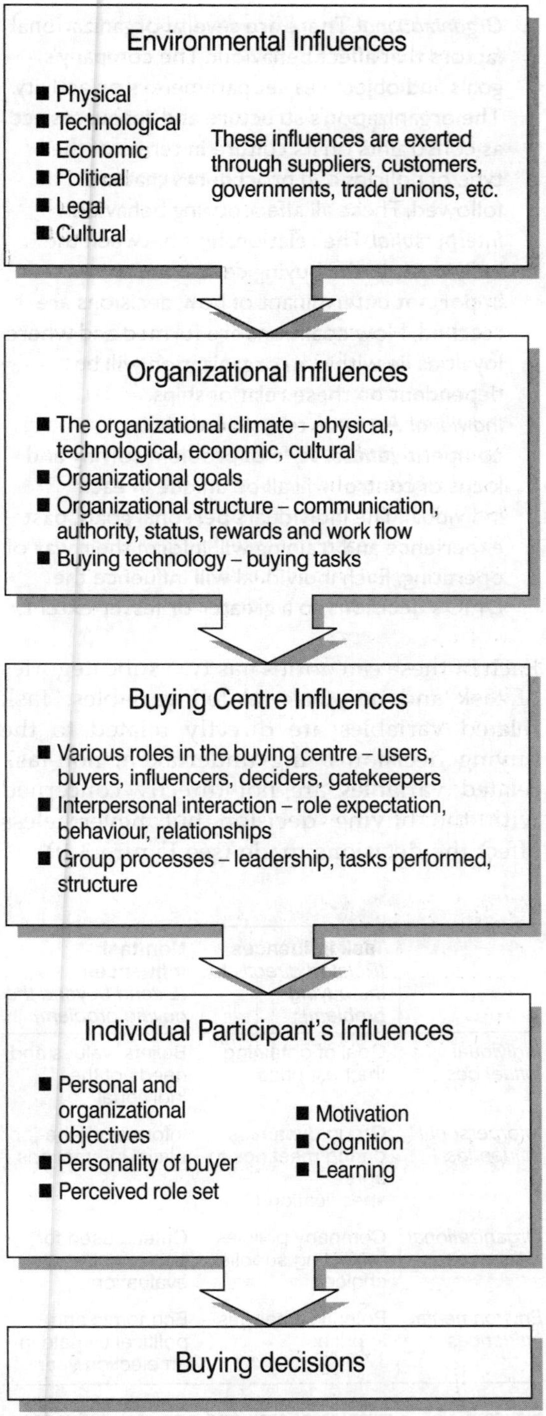

Figure 3.18 The Webster–Wind framework (*Source:* Adapted from Webster and Wind, 1972)

- *Organizational.* There are several organizational factors that affect behaviour. The company's goals and objectives set parameters on activity. The organization's structure and resources act as constraints on its culture in terms of the type of policies and procedures that are followed. These all affect buying behaviour.
- *Interpersonal.* The relationships between the individuals in the buying centre are an important determinant of how decisions are reached. How coalitions are formed and where loyalties lie within an organization will be dependent on these relationships.
- *Individual.* Attitude to risk, creativity, competitiveness, style of problem solving and locus of control will all be unique in each individual. The individual's personal goals, past experience and training will inform their way of operating. Each individual will influence the DMU's decisions to a greater or lesser extent.

Each of these categories has two subcategories of task and non-task related variables. Task related variables are directly related to the buying decision being undertaken; non-task related variables are not directly concerned with the buying decision but nevertheless affect the decisions made (see Figure 3.19).

	Task influences (Related directly to the buying problem)	Non-task influences (Extend beyond the buying problem)
Individual influences	Goal of obtaining the best price	Beliefs, values and needs of the individual
Interpersonal influences	Group dynamics during meetings to agree specifications	Informal off-the-job social interactions
Organizational influences	Company policies restricting supplier choice	Criteria used for personnel evaluation
Environmental influences	Potential changes in prices	Economic and political climate in an election year

Figure 3.19 Examples of task and non-task influences on organizational buying decisions (*Source:* Adapted from Webster and Wind, 1972)

The Sheth framework

The Webster–Wind framework identifies and helps to assess key variables that influence an organization's purchasing decisions, but does not concentrate on the process to any great degree. Sheth (1973) developed a model that has some elements in common with the Webster–Wind framework but has more of an emphasis on the psychology of the decision-making process.

He identified the importance of four main factors that influence organizational buyer behaviour:

- The expectations of the members of the DMU.
- The factors influencing the buying process.
- The character of the decision-making process.
- Situational factors.

The model is constructed so that the flow of the actual decision-making process can be illustrated (see Figure 3.20).

The expectations of the members of the DMU

Every individual in the DMU will have their own attitudes and particular background that shapes the way in which they judge a supplier. An engineer will use different criteria to an accountant. Individuals' expectations will be determined by their educational background, their job or task orientation and their lifestyle in general.

Individuals will also be influenced by information from a range of sources. When the purchase being considered contains a high level of risk to the organization it is likely that a rigorous process will be undertaken to identify as many sources of information as possible. This information search is likely to be undertaken by the professional

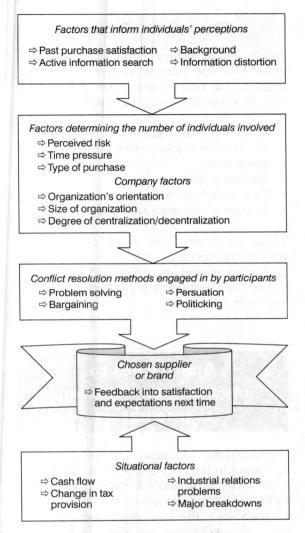

Figure 3.20 A model of organizational buyer behaviour (*Source*: Adapted from Sheth, 1973)

buyers and can lead them to play an important gatekeeping role by choosing what information is passed on to other members of the DMU.

The information provided, as with any communication, will be subject to perceptual distortion by the individuals in the DMU. Individuals' expectations will also be influenced by their previous experience of the product or service.

The factors influencing the buying process

The Sheth model outlines two sets of factors that will determine the particular buying process for a specific product or service. The first set of factors relate to the product itself:

- *Perceived risk.* If the purchase is high risk then a detailed search for information will take place, drawing more individuals into the DMU. This could occur if the purchase was a major capital expenditure.
- *Time pressure.* If a decision has to be made under time pressure a smaller number of individuals will be drawn into the DMU. The fewer people involved the quicker the decision.
- *Type of purchase.* A routine repurchase of a product is likely to be undertaken by an individual who has been delegated the responsibility.

The second set of factors that influence the buying process are related to the organization itself:

- *The organization's orientation.* An organization may be, for example, engineering orientated or marketing orientated. This orientation will, to an extent, reflect the balance of power within the DMU and have an important influence on its attitude to a purchase decision. An organization that has a dominant engineering orientation will perceive a purchase by using engineering values.
- *Size of the organization.* A small organization may have only one individual responsible for buying. This individual may undertake all the information searches themselves. Large organizations are likely to have more individuals involved in purchase decisions.
- *Degree of centralization/decentralization.* A central buying department would be common in a strongly centralized organization. A much greater spread of individuals would be involved in a decentralized company.

The character of the decision-making process

Sheth's model identifies two types of decisions:

1 Autonomous decisions are taken by an individual and are relatively straightforward.
2 Joint decisions are undertaken by more than one individual. As the model has already indicated, each individual has a unique set of factors influencing them and therefore some level of conflict is likely.

The manner in which these conflicts are resolved affects the final decision. The model outlines four approaches to making decisions:

- *Problem solving.* This involves gathering information and using a systematic approach to weighing up the alternative options. A disadvantage of this approach is that it inevitably takes time.
- *Persuasion.* Time is taken in order to get everybody to put the organizational needs and objectives above personal agendas. Again the disadvantage is that this can slow the decision process down.
- *Bargaining.* This is used in order to reach a compromise. Individuals in the buying centre trade concessions. This may result in a sub-optimal decision – individuals may be satisfied, but the decision may not be in the best interest of the organization as a whole.
- *Politicking.* Power and influence are used to coerce individuals into supporting majority positions within the DMU.

The model would suggest that problem solving and persuasion are the most rational approaches to decision making. Many practising managers will be well aware, however, that the bargaining and politicking options are common practice in many organizations.

Situational factors

Finally, the model highlights situational variables that are outside the control of the organization but influence the DMU. These variables would be such things as:

- A strike at a key supplier.
- A supplier is suddenly taken over by a competitor.
- Financial problems.
- Production breakdown.
- Changes in corporate taxation.

These two models illustrate the complexity of the buying process in organizations. They also give some insights into potential factors that can be used to identify organizational market segments.

Approaches to organizational market segmentation

Organizational markets can be segmented according to the characteristics of the organization. This is sometimes referred to as segmenting at the macro level. Factors that would be analysed at this level would be:

- *Industry sector.* Standard industry classification codes (SIC codes) will identify an organization's primary business activity. Different industry sectors may have unique needs from a product or service. In the computer hardware and software market, for example, the needs of retailers, financial services companies and local government will be different.
- *Size of the organization.* This can be judged using several variables such as the number of employees, volume of shipments and market share. This method of segmentation has to be used with caution – just because an

organization is large does not mean that it will be a large purchaser of your product. However, larger organizations will differ from smaller companies by having more formalized buying systems and increased specialization of functions.

- *Geographic location.* Traditional industries can tend to cluster geographically, an example being the car industry in Detroit, USA. However, even emerging technologies show a tendency to locate in the same geographical area. The UK computer industry has clusters in central Scotland (Silicon Glen) and along the M4 motorway in southern England. Internationally there may well be different regional variations in purchasing behaviour, for example between Western and Eastern Europe.
- *End-use application.* The way in which a product or service is used by a company has an important effect on the way the organization views its value. A truck that is used 12 hours a day by a quarrying company may represent great value. But for a construction company who only use the same piece of equipment for two hours a day it may represent a much lower value-for-money purchase. Establishing end-use application can help establish the perception of value that will be used in particular segments.

Organizational markets can also be segmented according to the characteristics of the decision-making unit. This is sometimes referred to as segmenting at the micro level. The factors used include:

- *The structure of the decision-making unit.* This is directly related to the models covered earlier in this chapter on organizational buyer behaviour. The type of individuals involved in the DMU of an organization will vary, as will its size and complexity.
- *The decision-making process.* This can be short and straightforward or complex and time-consuming. This will largely be dependent on the size and complexity of the DMU.
- *Structure of the buying function.* The buying function can be centralized or decentralized. Centralized buying allows an individual buyer to specialize in purchasing particular types of product categories. An individual is responsible for buying much larger volumes per purchase than under a decentralized structure. This allows them to negotiate larger discounts. In centralized structures the professional buyer has much greater influence within the DMU over technical advisers compared with buyers in decentralized systems.

- *Attitude towards innovation.* There may be specific characteristics that mark out innovative companies. Identifying companies that exhibit this profile will allow a segment to be established at which new products can be initially targeted. There are organizations that are followers and only try a product once innovators have already adopted it. Identifying these companies can also be useful to a marketer.
- *Key criteria used in reaching a decision on a purchase.* These can include product quality,

Variables	Examples
Macro segmentation	
■ Size of organization	Large, medium or small
■ Geographic location	Local, national, European Union, worldwide
■ Industrial sector	Retail, engineering, financial services
■ End market served	Defined by product or service
Micro segmentation	
■ Choice criteria	Quality, delivery, value in use, supplier reputation, price
■ Structure of decision-making unit	Complexity, hierarchical, effectiveness
■ Decision-making process	Long, short, low or high conflict
■ Buy class	New task, straight or modified re-buy
■ Importance of purchasing	High or low importance
■ Type of purchasing organization	Matrix, centralized, decentralized
■ Innovation level of organization	Innovative, follower, laggard
■ Purchasing strategy	Optimizer, satisfier
■ Personal attributes	Age, educational background, risk taker/adverse, confidence level

Figure 3.21   Organizational macro and micro segmentation

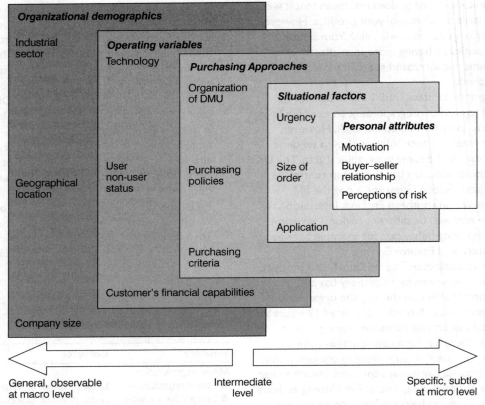

Figure 3.22   The major factors for segmenting organizational markets (a nested approach) (*Source*: Adapted from Bonoma and Shapiro, 1983)

price, technical support, supply continuity and reliability of prompt deliveries.

- *Personal characteristics of decision makers.*
  Factors such as age, educational background, attitude toward risk and style of decision making can potentially be used to segment the market.

Figure 3.21 summarizes macro and micro segmentation.

A more systematic method to organizational market segmentation has been developed, called the nested approach. This method moves through layers of segmentation variables starting with the demographics of the organization (the macro level) down through increasingly more sophisticated

levels reaching the complex areas of situational factors and personal characteristics. This approach effectively establishes a hierarchical structure in which to undertake the segmentation process (see Figure 3.22).

There is a balance to be struck with this approach between the macro level which is generally inadequate when used in isolation, and the micro level which may be too time-consuming and expensive to establish and operate in markets with limited potential.

Summary

This chapter has illustrated how an in-depth knowledge of both consumer and organizational buyer behaviour is needed to successfully identify useful segmentation criteria. This led to an exploration of a wide range of criteria that can be used to segment both consumer and organizational markets. This is the first step in the critical strategic process of establishing market segments that are available for a company to serve. Companies have to evaluate the potential of these segments and to make choices about which groups to serve (targeting) and on what competitive basis (positioning). The next steps to successful segmentation will be explored in detail in Chapter 8: Targeting, positioning and brand strategy.

References

Bonoma, T.V. and Shapiro, B.P., *Segmenting the Industrial Market*, Lexington Books, D.C. Heath and Company, 1983

Bonoma, T.V., 'Major Sales: Who Really Does the Buying?', *Harvard Business Review*, 60 May–June, pp. 111–119, 1982

CACI Limited (Data source BMRB and OPCS/GRO(s)), © Crown Copyright (1991), 1993

De Mooij, M.K. and Keegan, W., *Advertising Worldwide: Concepts, Theories and Practice of International, Multinational and Global Advertising*, Prentice Hall, 1991

Doyle, P., *Marketing Management and Strategy*, Prentice Hall, 1994

Ensor, J. and Laing, S., *Cadbury's Project Gift*, European Case Clearing House, 1993

Family Policy Studies Centre Report (1985). Cited in Rice, C., *Consumer Behaviour: Behavioural Aspects of Marketing*, Butterworth-Heinemann, 1993.

Lawson, R.W., 'The family life cycle: a demographic analysis', *Journal of Marketing Management*, Vol. 4, No. 1., C.I.M., 1988

Maslow, A.H., *Motivation and Personality*, 2nd edition, Harper and Row, 1970

Miaoulis, G. and Kalfus, D., '10 MBA benefit segments', *Marketing News*, 5 August, 1983

Morris, M.H., *Industrial and Organizational Marketing*, Merrill Publishing Company, 1988

Murphy, P.E. and Staples, W., 'A Modernised Family Life Cycle', *Journal of Consumer Research*, June, 1979

Plummer, J.T., 'The Concept and Application of Life Style Segmentation', *Journal of Marketing*, Vol. 38, January, 1974

Rose, D. and O'Reilly, K. (eds), *Constructing Classes: Towards a New Social Classification for the UK*, ESRC/ONS, 1999

Sheth, J.N., 'A Model of Industrial Buyer Behaviour', *Journal of Marketing*, Vol. 37, No. 4, pp. 50–56, 1973

Steers, R.M., Porter, L.W. and Bigley, G.A., *Motivation and Leadership at Work*, McGraw Hill, 1996

Tinson, J., *Customer Service Interface: Implications for Maternity Service Provision*, Conference Paper, Academy of Marketing, 1998

Vandermerwe, S. and L'Huillier, M., 'Euroconsumers in 1992', *Business Horizons*, Jan.–Feb., pp. 34–40, 1989

Webster, F.E. and Wind, Y., 'A General Model of Organizational Buying Behaviour', *Journal of Marketing*, 36, April, pp. 12–17, 1972. © American Marketing Association

Further reading

Hooley, G.H., Saunders, J.A. and Piercy, N.F., *Marketing Strategy and Competitive Positioning*, 2nd edition, Chapters 9 and 10, Prentice Hall, 1998

McDonald, M., *Marketing Plans. How to Prepare Them, How to Use Them*, 4th edition, Chapter 4, Butterworth-Heinemann, 1999

Rice, C., *Consumer Behaviour: Behavioural Aspects of Marketing*, Butterworth-Heinemann, 1993

CHAPTER 4

Internal analysis

About this chapter

The internal analysis of an organization's resources is the final stage of the auditing process. It creates the information and analysis necessary for an organization to identify the key assets and competencies upon which a strategic position can be built. This chapter explores the nature of organizational assets, competencies and capabilities. The auditing process used to identify these assets and competencies includes the elements of an innovation audit. The use of various auditing tools to facilitate this process, in particular the portfolio models and the SWOT analysis, are also covered.

Introduction

So far in Part 1 the external environment, the market and the customer have been analysed. However before an organization can begin to review its strategic options it has to evaluate the enterprise's relative ability to compete and satisfy customer needs in attractive market areas. The organization's current and potential capabilities have to be identified and this can be achieved by evaluating the assets and competencies that make up the company's resources. Once this has been undertaken an organization can begin to develop a com-

Figure 4.1   Matching organizational capabilities to market needs through competitive positioning

petitive position that matches organizational capabilities to the needs of consumers in market sectors identified as attractive (see Figure 4.1). This approach builds on two sources: a resource-based view of the firm and market orientation. A resource-based view of the firm emphasizes the need for an organization to exploit its distinctive capabilities whereas market orientation emphasizes the need to be responsive to market needs.

This chapter explores aspects of an organization's capabilities, before illustrating the component parts of an audit and the tools available to facilitate the audit process.

Organizational capabilities

In this chapter resources are defined as all the assets and competencies to which the organization has access. Assets are given a broad definition to include both the tangible and intangible capital of the organization. Competencies are the skills that are contained within the organization. The application of these skills to effectively deploy the available assets delivers the organization's strategic capabilities in the market. Corporate capabilities are therefore defined as the combination of assets and competencies that denote the organization's competitive capacity.

Establishing an organization's current and potential capabilities is therefore reliant upon an evaluation of two aspects of its resources: assets and competencies:

Organizational assets

Organizational assets are the accumulated capital, both financial and non-financial, that a company has at its disposal. These assets are both tangible and intangible (Hooley *et al.*, 1998) and include:

- *Financial assets* – such as working capital, or access/availability of investment finance, and credit worthiness.
- *Physical assets* – ownership or control of facilities and property. In the retail sector ownership of an outlet in a prime location could be a significant asset.
- *Operational assets* – production plant, machinery and process technologies.
- *People assets* – the quantity of human resources available to the organization and the quality of this resource in terms of their background and abilities.
- *Legally enforceable assets* – ownership of copyrights and patents, franchise and licensing agreements.
- *Systems* – management information systems and databases and the general infrastructure for supporting decision-making activities.
- *Marketing assets* – of particular concern in the development of marketing strategy are of course marketing assets.

These marketing assets fall into four main categories:

- *Customer-based assets*
  These are assets that the customer perceives as being important, such as:
  - *Image and reputation.* These relate to the company and the recognition of its corporate identity.
  - *Brand franchises.* These are important because of the time and investment required in building them. Once established, effective brands have high levels of customer loyalty. They create competitive positions that are defendable and obtain higher margins because customers feel a higher price is merited by the added value that the brand provides to them. Weak brands of course show the opposite characteristics.
  - *Market leadership.* A strong brand may not be the market leader but a brand leader enjoys distinct advantages such as excellent market coverage, widespread distribution and beneficial shelf positions in retail outlets.
  - *Country of origin.* Consumers associate particular attributes with different countries; these then become associated with an organization or a brand that derives from that particular state. So for instance Germany is associated with efficiency and quality. Products like Mercedes and BMW benefit from this perception of their country of origin and it reinforces their quality positioning in the market.
  - *Unique products and services.* These are key assets. Their distinctiveness in the market can be built on a number of attributes such as price, quality, design or level of innovation.

- *Distribution-based assets*
  Distributing a product or service successfully into the market is a critical marketing activity. Therefore a number of potential assets lie in this area, such as:

– *The size and quality of the distribution network*. The size of the distribution network should be seen in terms not only of geographic spread but also of the intensity of that coverage on the ground. An organization may only distribute over a specific geographic region of a national market, but have built up a strong presence in that area and be locally dominant. Quality should be seen in terms of fitness for purpose. There is a range of factors that could be used to judge quality, such as ability to guarantee supply, lead times, or ability to react quickly.

– *Level of control over distribution channels*. An organization that can exert control over the main channels of distribution in a market is at a huge advantage, making control a key marketing asset. For example, Irn-Bru is the market leader in the soft drinks market in Scotland. However, Coca-Cola successfully stopped Irn-Bru being distributed through McDonald's fast food restaurants in favour of Coca-Cola. Coca-Cola were able to apply control over that channel of distribution due to their global relationship with McDonald's.

• *Internally-based assets*
There are a number of internal organizational assets that lie outside the marketing function but can be deployed to give advantages to marketing activities. It is important to identify the underlying asset rather than just the activity. It is the asset that has the potential to be deployed in new ways to create additional advantages. There are a range of organizational assets that may give advantages to marketing activities:

– *Cost structure*. The organization may be able to achieve lower costs than competitors through higher capacity utilization, better economies of scale, or by applying newer or more innovatory technology. This could allow marketing to

set lower prices for their products and services than the competition. The asset is the manufacturing cost base, and can be deployed to give advantage to the marketing activity of pricing.

– *Information systems*. These can be applied to marketing research activities to collect and analyse customer, competitor and market information. These systems could also be used to create customer databases, a marketing asset that can be exploited.

There are also some organizational competencies that lie outside the marketing function that can be used to create advantages in marketing activities such as:

– *Innovatory culture*. The ability to be able to create and maintain a culture for innovation is an important competence. This competence facilitates activities such as new product development, customer service through empowering front line staff to develop creative solutions to customers' problems and advertising through a willingness to adopt creative ideas.

– *Production skills*. These may allow an organization's production to have more flexibility, higher quality or shorter lead times, all of which can be used to advantage by the marketing function.

• *Alliance-based assets*
There are a number of areas where the asset is linked to a formal, or informal, external relationship. These agreements with third parties can allow an organization to gain the following:

– *Access to markets*. Through local distributors that the organization could not cover with its existing resource base.

– *Management expertise*. From outside agencies not available within the company.

– *Access to technological developments or processes*. Through licensing or joint ventures.

– *Exclusive agreements*. With third parties, such as Coca-Cola and McDonald's already mentioned above, that effectively exclude competitors.

Organizational competencies

These are the abilities and skills available to the company to marshal the effective exploitation of the company's assets. The combination of assets and these skills allows an organization to undertake specific activities. Activities such as producing innovative products are a capability that arises out of the underlying assets and competencies of the organization. These competencies can lie at the three decision-making tiers – strategic, functional and operational; and at three levels in the organization's structure – corporate, team and individual (Hooley *et al.*, 1998):

- *Strategic competencies*. These relate to the management skills, the drive and the strategic direction of the organization. Skills should be assessed in a range of areas, including ability to create strategic vision, communicate, motivate, implement strategy, assess changing circumstances, learn and innovate.
- *Functional competencies*. These refer to the skills available to the organization to manage its activities in the various functional areas such as finance, operations and marketing. The marketing function should be assessed on its skills such as handling customer relationships, channel management, product management, product innovation and new product development.
- *Operational competencies*. These skills are necessary to run the day-to-day operations across the functional areas of the organization. As an example in the marketing function these would include skills of co-ordinating and implementing sales force activities, promotional campaigns, public relations activities, special offers and discounts, and the updating of product packaging and labelling. Where these activities are subcontracted to third parties such as PR agencies, the skills that need to be assessed are the abilities of co-ordinating and controlling these external relationships.
- *Individual competencies*. These are the abilities and skills that lie with individuals in the organization. These competencies are based not on individuals' skills in isolation, but on whether individuals have the required skills to execute the tasks they face in their area of responsibility, whether at strategic, functional or operational level.
- *Team competencies*. It is necessary for individuals in organizations to work together in teams. These may be teams formed on a formal or informal basis. Despite the specific skill base of the individuals involved, a group also requires the skills necessary to work together as a team. A key element of successful project management relies on these team competencies.
- *Corporate-level competencies*. These are the skills that apply to the organization, in its entirety, to execute tasks at strategic, functional and operational level. This could relate to the ability to foster innovation throughout the organization or the ability to exploit and continually update the organizational knowledge base, by effective communication of critical learning throughout the business.

Once the assets and competencies of an organization have been identified there are likely to be some assets that are more important than others. The relationship between these assets and competencies can be mapped to uncover the key relationships (see Figure 4.2).

Initial corporate-wide internal audit

As has already been stated, some assets and competencies that can be deployed to create advantage in marketing activities are found

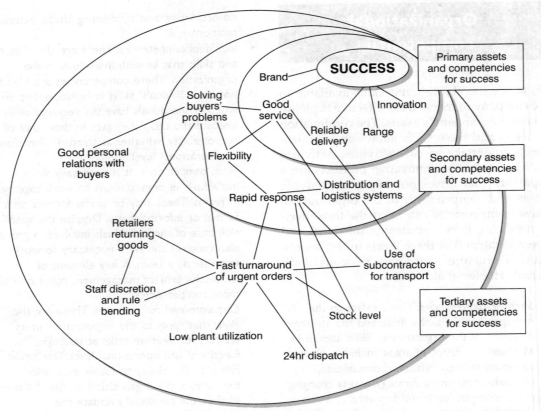

Figure 4.2 Hierarchy of assets and competencies for a consumer goods company supplying major retail outlets (*Source*: Adapted from Johnson and Scholes, 1999)

in functional areas other than marketing. Any audit will therefore need to carry out a thorough analysis of the company's resources to establish assets and competencies that either currently, or potentially, could assist the marketing function and support strategic marketing developments. Hooley *et al.* (1998) suggest that these wider non-marketing assets and competencies will fall into five categories: financial resources, managerial skills, technical resources, organization and information systems. Once this overview has taken place the specific marketing activities of the organization should be evaluated. This can be undertaken by an internal marketing audit.

The internal marketing audit

The internal marketing audit is specifically aimed at reviewing the marketing activities of the enterprise and is split into five distinct areas (Kotler *et al.* 1996):

• *Marketing strategy audit.* This analysis examines the organization's current corporate and marketing objectives to establish if they are relevant and explicit. The current strategy is evaluated in terms of its fit with the set objectives. This element of the audit also highlights whether adequate resources have been allocated for the successful implementation of the strategy.

- *Marketing structures audit.* This examines the structure of the marketing function and its relationship with other areas of the business. In particular the profile that the marketing function has, within the business, is reviewed. For instance, is the head of marketing a member of the board of directors? This is an indicator of how influential marketing considerations are in strategic decisions. Communication within the marketing function, and between marketing and other functions, should also be analysed to see how effective the function is at co-ordinating its activities. The internal structure should be examined to establish whether marketing activities are carried out efficiently.
- *Marketing systems audit.* This part of the audit inspects the planning systems, control measures and new product development processes in the organization, as well as examining the information systems that support these activities.
- *Productivity audit.* This element of the audit examines the organization's activities using financial criteria such as profitability and cost-effectiveness applied to assess the relative productivity of products, market sectors, distribution channels and geographic markets.
- *Marketing functions audit.* This element of the audit looks in detail at all aspects of the marketing mix: the products and services the organization produces, pricing policy, distribution arrangements, the organization of the sales team, advertising policy, public relations and other promotion activities.

The innovation audit

One other area that should be examined is the organization's innovation activities. The ability to carry out innovation activities may have been identified at the initial stage in the audit when wider organizational resources were reviewed. However, this area is of increasing importance to organizations and deserves further attention.

This part of the auditing process reviews how effectively the organization is able to deliver the level of innovation necessary to create new products, new services, and new ways of undertaking activities. Success in these activities is likely to depend on the company successfully harnessing the latent creativity in individuals at all levels in the organization. The innovation audit examines whether the necessary assets and competencies are present and examines four key areas:

- The current organizational climate with regard to innovation.
- Hard measures of the organization's current performance in innovation.
- Review of the organization's policies and practices that are currently used to support innovation.
- The balance of the cognitive styles of the senior management team.

Current organizational climate with regard to innovation

There are two components to the audit of the organization's climate, as discussed here.

1 Attitude survey of key areas of the organizational climate that affect creativity

The aim of this component of the audit is to discover the current feelings of staff about the organizational climate. There are eight influential factors that are crucial in supporting innovation and four areas that act as constraints (Burnside, 1990). Support for creativity and innovation include:

- *Teamwork* – the level of commitment to the current work, the level of trust between team

members and the willingness to help each other.
- *Resources* – the amount of access to appropriate resources in terms of facilities, staff, finance, and information.
- *Challenge* – the challenge involved in the work undertaken in terms of its importance and the very nature of the task. Is it intriguing in itself?
- *Freedom* – the amount of control individuals have over their work and ideas. How much freedom are they allowed to decide how a project or task will be undertaken?
- *Supervisor* – managerial support in terms of clear goals, good communication and building morale.
- *Creativity infrastructure* – level of senior management support and encouragement of creativity and the structures necessary for developing creative ideas.
- *Recognition* – the level of recognition and the type of rewards given for innovative ideas.
- *Unity and co-operation* – factors such as a collaborative and co-operative atmosphere and the amount of shared vision in the organization.

Factors that act as constraints on innovation in an organization include:

- *Insufficient time.* There is a lack of time in which to consider alternative approaches to undertake work.
- *Status quo.* A traditional approach. An unwillingness of managers and other staff to change the current way of doing things.
- *Political problems.* Battles over areas of responsibility and lack of co-operation between different areas of the organization.
- *Evaluation pressure.* The evaluation or feedback systems are perceived to be inappropriate. The environment is focused on criticism and external evaluation.

Two other areas should be included in the audit of the staff's perceptions on organizational climate:

- *Creativity.* How creative is the organization perceived to be overall?
- *Productivity.* How productive is the organization perceived to be?

2   Metaphors

This audit is about innovation and it should therefore use proven creativity tools as part of the process. The second part of the evaluation of the organizational climate uses the technique of metaphorical description (Morgan, 1993).

The power of the metaphor approach is that it can overcome the limitations of literal language and describe far more complex relationships and connections.

Individuals are asked to describe their organization in terms of a metaphor. For example: 'This organization is like a well-oiled machine. It runs well and doesn't make too much noise,' or 'This organization is like a supertanker – it takes a long time to change direction.' These metaphors can then be analysed. They are likely to be either positive or negative observations based around seven organizational practices:

- Managerial skills
- Organizational structure
- Operations
- Organizational life cycle
- Strategic orientation
- People orientation
- Power orientation

The use of metaphor allows a more rounded perspective of the organizational climate to emerge.

Hard measures of the organization's current performance in innovation

There is a range of hard measures that can be reviewed to establish the current organizational performance in the areas of creativity and innovation:

- The rate of new product development in the last three years. Davidson (1997) suggests that both total innovation development and percentage success rate are analysed (see Figure 4.4).
- Customer satisfaction ratings. These should be reviewed not just in terms of the actual core product but across all areas of customer service.
- Staff turnover.
- An innovation/value portfolio analysis (see Figure 4.3) should be undertaken on the organization's strategic business units or products to establish whether they are:
  - *Settlers*. Businesses or products that offer the normal (me-too) market value.
  - *Migrators*. Businesses or products that offer value improvements over competitors.
  - *Pioneers*. Businesses or products that represent value innovations such as the Dyson vacuum cleaner or the Sony Walkman.

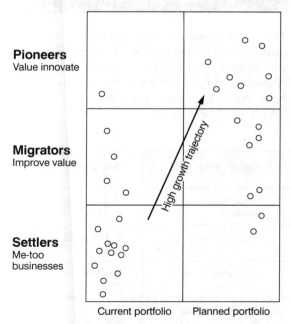

Pioneers
Value innovate

Migrators
Improve value

Settlers
Me-too
businesses

Current portfolio   Planned portfolio

Figure 4.3   The innovation/value matrix (*Source*: Kim and Mauborgne, 1998)

INNOVATION PERFORMANCE MEASURES

Innovation criteria	3 years ago	This year
Number of significant innovations in the past 5 years	11	6
Number successful	4	4
% Success rate	36%	66%
% Total sales in product/service launched in past 5 years	16%	28%
% Incremental sales	11%	14%
Average annual sales per new product/service (£m)	6	12.5
Incremental payback per new product/service (years)	3	4

Figure 4.4   Product and service innovation performance measures (*Source*: Adapted from Davidson, 1997)

These product and service innovation performance measures show the following:

- New product and service developments are lower in the last 5 years, but the rate of successful market launches has risen from 36 per cent of developments to 66 per cent.
- Sales per new development have risen from £6m to £12.5m.
- Although 28 per cent of sales in the last 12 months are from products launched in the last 5 years (up from 16 per cent three years ago) only half of these sales are new (incremental) sales. The remaining half are sales that have cannibalized current products. This is an indication of poor planning.
- The payback period for new developments is lengthening.

One action the organization could take is to have more effective segmentation and targeting processes, so that new product sales are developmental rather than cannibalizing existing sales. This type of analysis allows an organization to explore its current performance using hard output measures.

Research undertaken on a hundred new business launches (Kim and Mauborgne, 1998) discovered that 86 per cent of them were standard market value (me-too) launches, or only offered incremental improvements. These businesses only generated 62 per cent of launch revenues and 39 per cent of profits. The remaining 14 per cent of launches were businesses that created markets or re-created markets that were already in existence. These 'pioneering' businesses, although only 14 per cent of the sample, generated 38 per cent of revenues and a massive 61 per cent of profits. The clear implication of this study is that organizations that are driven by future profitability need to have a spread of business across the portfolio. Companies that find the majority of their businesses or products are in the settler area are paying insufficient attention to the innovation process.

Review of the organization's policies and practices that are currently used to support innovation

This consists of identifying current policies that may be in place to support innovation. It would also review whether any structures or procedures have already been developed to try and facilitate creativity and innovation.

Balance of the cognitive styles of the senior management team

The final part of the innovation audit is to evaluate the cognitive preference and behaviours of the management team. Although individuals have the capacity to make use of all their cognitive functions, one area tends to dominate. The four cognitive areas are shown in Figure 4.5.

It is important to have a mix of cognitive styles in the senior management team that will influence the business's orientation towards creativity and innovation. Researchers have hypothesized the likely influence of a range of senior management teams' potential cognitive profiles as illustrated in Figure 4.6.

The whole issue of the nature of groups and the need for balanced teams is considered further in Chapter 5.

Auditing tools

There is a range of tools that can be applied during the auditing process that are capable of providing useful insights into the company's situation. Three of these tools are discussed here: the value chain, portfolio analysis and SWOT analysis.

Cognitive area	Concerned with...	Handle these with...	Tends to be...
Intuition	Possibilities, patterns and ideas	Metaphors and symbols	Ingenious and integrative
Feeling	People and values	Force of personality	Enthusiastic and insightful
Thinking	Cause and effect	Regulations and language	Reliable and orderly
Sensation	Activities, events	Spontaneity and action	Adaptable and practical

Figure 4.5   Cognitive areas (*Source*: Adapted from Hurst *et al.*, 1989)

Cognitive composition	Time orientation	Strategy orientation
Mainly intuitives with some feelers	Future	Prospecting
Mainly thinkers with some sensors	Near term, future and past	Analytical
Mainly sensors	Current	Reflective
Mostly feelers with some Intuitives	Past	Preserving
Mix of intuitives, feelers thinkers and sensors	Future through to the past	Renewing

Figure 4.6   The senior management's cognitive composition and its likely relationship to business strategy (*Source:* Adapted from Hurst *et al.*, 1989)

Value chain

The value chain is an obvious analytical tool to use in the internal audit. This tool specifically looks at the primary and support activities of an organization and therefore directly relates to identifying organizational capabilities. See Chapter 7 for a full explanation of this tool.

Portfolio analysis

There are a number of portfolio models that are used to identify the current position of business units or products. This position will be the result of the organization's current resources and can be seen as a symptom of the competencies and assets of the organization. They reflect the organization's current performance and identify strengths on which the marketing strategy can be built, or weaknesses that the strategy is required to overcome.

The Boston Consultancy Group (BCG) growth share matrix

This is one of the most well known portfolio models. The growth share matrix is concerned about the generation and use of cash within a business and can be used to analyse either

SBUs or products. The two axes on the model represent relative market share and market growth (see Figure 4.7). Relative market share is seen as a predictor of the product's capacity to generate cash. The proposition is that products with a dominant position in the market will achieve high sales, but will need relatively less investment as they are already an established brand and should have lower costs through economies-of-scale advantages. Market growth, on the other hand, is seen as a predictor of the product's need for cash. Products in high growth sectors require

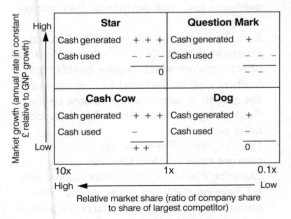

Figure 4.7   The Boston Consultancy Group's growth share matrix (BCG)

investment to keep up with the increased demand.

The model uses market share relative to competitors as an indication of the product's relative strength in the market. To do this the axis uses a log scale. At the mid-point of the axis, represented by 1.0 (or 1×) on the scale, the product's market share is equal to its largest competitor's market share. At the extreme left-hand side of the axis, represented by 10.0 (or 10×), a product has ten times the market share of the largest competitor. At the other extreme of 0.1 on the axis, the product would only have a tenth or 10 per cent of the largest competitor's market share.

Products or SBUs are represented on the model by circles and fall into one of the four cells into which the matrix is divided. The area of the circle represents the product's sales relative to the sales of the organization's other products. The four cells in the matrix represent:

- *Cash Cows*. These products have high profitability and require low investment, due to market leadership in a low-growth market. These products are generating a high level of cash. These products should be defended to maintain sales and market share. Surplus cash should be channelled into Stars and Question Marks in order to create the Cash Cows of the future. Current Cash Cows will inevitably over time lose their position as their market changes.
- *Stars*. These are market leaders and so are generating high levels of cash, but are in areas of rapid growth which require equally high levels of cash (investment) to keep up with the growth in sales. Cash generated by the Cash Cows should be channelled to support these products.
- *Question Marks*. These are also sometimes referred to as Problem Children or Wildcats. Question Marks are not market leaders and will have relatively high costs. At the same time these products require large amounts of cash as they are in high-growth areas. An organization has to judge whether to use cash

generated by the Cash Cow to try and develop this product into a Star by gaining market share in a high-growth market or to invest in other areas of the business.
- *Dogs*. These are products with low levels of market share in low-growth markets. Products that are in a secondary position to the market leader may still be able to produce cash (Cash Dogs). For others the organization's decision is likely to be a choice between moving the product into a defendable niche, harvesting it for cash in the short term, or divestment.

The overall aim of an organization should be to maintain a balanced portfolio. This means investments should flow from Cash Cows into Stars and Question Marks in an effort to make products move round the matrix from Question Marks into Stars and from Stars into Cash Cows. This movement of cash and products round the matrix thus ensures the future cash flows of the business.

There have been a number of revisions and adaptations to this basic model in order to accommodate different factors. Figure 4.8 highlights the fact that products in the research and development stage also need investment which cash generation provides, an issue the standard BCG model overlooks. Figure 4.9 applies the basic portfolio analysis technique but in the context of the public sector. On one axis of this matrix is the organization's ability to effectively deliver a service within the constraints of current resources, on the other is the level of the political requirement to offer the service. This allows a key consideration of the public sector bodies: the need to provide services to satisfy political objectives, to be accommodated within a portfolio analysis approach.

The BCG model is criticized for having a number of limitations. Amongst these are:

- Market growth is seen as an inadequate measure of a market or of an industry's overall attractiveness. This measure does not consider such issues as barriers to entry,

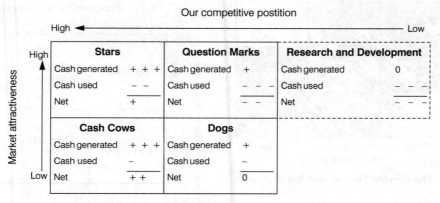

Figure 4.8 Matrix to accommodate research and development (*Source:* McDonald, 1985)

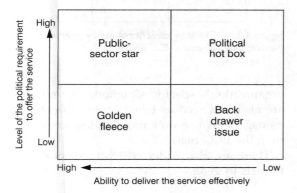

Figure 4.9 Public sector portfolio matrix (*Source:* Adapted from Montanari and Bracker, 1986)

strength of buyers or suppliers or investment levels.
• Market share is an inadequate measure of a product's relative ability to generate cash. Other factors such as product positioning, brand image and access to distribution channels may allow an organization to gain higher margin and strong cash flows as a result.
• The focus on market share and growth ignores fundamental issues such as developing sustainable competitive advantage.
• Not all products face the same life cycle. Therefore, for some stars facing a short life cycle it may be better for the organization to harvest them, rather than committing further investment.

• Cash flow is only one factor on which to base investment decisions. There are others to consider, such as return on investment, market size, and competitors.

There are a number of models that use a range of weighted criteria in place of relative market share and growth in order to overcome some of the limitations of the growth share matrix. Two of these are discussed next.

The General Electric multifactor portfolio matrix

This model has two axes: market attractiveness and competitive strength. Industry/market attractiveness is assessed on a range of weighted criteria including:

• Market size
• Market growth rate
• Strength of competition
• Profit potential
• Social, political and legal factors

Competitive strength is also assessed on a range of weighted criteria such as:

• Market share
• Potential to develop differential advantage
• Opportunities to develop cost advantages
• Channel relationships
• Brand image and reputation

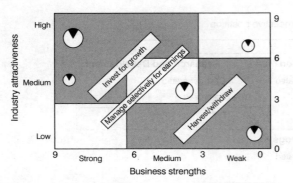

Figure 4.10   The General Electric multifactor matrix

	Prospects for sector profitability		
	Unattractive	Average	Attractive
Weak	Disinvest	Phased withdrawal	Double or quit
Average	Phased withdrawal	Custodial growth	Try harder
Strong	Cash generation	Growth leader	Leader

Enterprise's competitive capabilities (vertical axis label)

Figure 4.11   The Shell directional policy matrix (DPM)
(*Source*: Shell Chemical Co., 1975)

On the basis of these criteria and on an agreed weighting scheme, a SBU or product is then positioned on the matrix, which is divided into nine separate cells, three on each axis (see Figure 4.10). The SBU or product is represented on the matrix by a circle. The circle's area represents the sales volume of the business/product as a percentage of the overall business. On occasion the circle represents the size of the market and a slice of the circle is shaded to represent the business's share of that market.

The Shell directional policy matrix

This takes a similar approach to the General Electric multifactor matrix (see Figure 4.11). In both models the cells contain policy recommendations for businesses/products that fall within their boundaries. For instance, for products that fall in the cell that represents high industry attractiveness and strong business strength, on the GE multifactor model, the policy recommendation is to invest for growth.

In both the General Electric and Shell models the number of factors considered as important on either axis, and their relative weighting, are based on managers' subjective judgements. This is a major criticism of these more sophisticated portfolio models. However, this ability to use judgement based on their knowledge of their markets and industry does allow managers to adapt the model to an organization's specific situation. The models are also criticized as being more difficult for managers to use and more time-consuming than the BCG matrix.

There are also wider criticisms of portfolio models in general:

- They are based on an analysis of current areas of business and are therefore an inappropriate tool to employ in tackling the issue of new business development.
- They place too much emphasis on growth, either through entering high growth markets or through gaining high market share, whereas there are virtues to entering stable markets that have lower growth rates.
- They can require information that is difficult to obtain and are complex and time consuming to successfully execute.

In response to these criticisms, it should be pointed out that organizations should already be collecting much of the information required for portfolio analysis, to support strategic decisions.

The reality is also that all models have weaknesses – their role is to try and simplify relationships to foster understanding. Managers should be using a range of portfolio models along with other analytical tools in order to establish a rounded and comprehensive view of their organization's performance.

SWOT analysis

SWOT (strengths, weaknesses, opportunities and threats) analysis is another tool that is commonly used during the auditing process. The SWOT draws together the key strengths, weaknesses, opportunities and threats from the audit. This tool should be used to distil the critical factors that have been identified during the auditing process. It is a summary of the audit, not a replacement for it. The strengths and weaknesses of the organization have to be judged in relation to the opportunities and threats identified in the external environment. The list should therefore be limited rather than extensive. The aim of the SWOT is to highlight the critical issues in order to focus attention on them during the strategy development.

Summary

The internal analysis aims to identify the organization's key resources, its assets and competencies. Out of these arise organizational capabilities. There are a number of tools to help with this process. The aim at this stage is to identify these assets and competencies. Their current usage will already have been identified, and the next stage is to decide how they may be potentially applied. This requires managers to develop a view of future changes in the environment that these assets and competencies can effectively address. The next stage before developing a marketing strategy is to generate a view of the future.

References

Burnside, R., 'Improving corporate climates for creativity', in M.A. West and J.L. Farr (eds) *Innovation and Creativity at Work*, Wiley, 1990

Davidson, H., *Even More Offensive Marketing*, Chapter 2, Penguin, 1997

Hooley, G.H., Saunders, J.A. and Piercy, N.F., *Marketing Strategy and Competitive Positioning*, 2nd edition, Prentice Hall, 1998

Hurst, D.K., Rush, J.C. and White, R.E., 'Top management teams and organizational renewal', *Strategic Management Journal*, 10, pp. 87–105, 1989

Johnson, G. and Scholes, K., *Exploring Corporate Strategy*, 5th edition, Prentice Hall, 1999

Kim, C.W. and Mauborgne, R., 'Pioneers strike it rich', *Financial Times*, 11 August 1998

Kotler, K., Armstrong, G., Saunders, J. and Wong, V., *Principles of Marketing: The European Edition*, Prentice Hall, 1996

McDonald, M., Seminar Notes, Cranfield MBA Programme, 1985

Montanari, J.R. and Bracker, J.S., *Strategic Management Journal*, Vol. 7, No. 3, pp. 251–265, 1986

Morgan, G., *Imaginization, The Art of Creative Management*, Sage, 1993

Shell Chemical Company, *The Directional Policy Matrix: A New Aid to Corporate Planning*, Shell, 1975

Further reading

Davidson, H., *Even More Offensive Marketing*, Chapter 2, Penguin, 1997

McDonald, M., *Marketing Plans. How to Prepare Them, How to Use Them*, 4th edition, Chapter 5, Butterworth-Heinemann, 1999

Wilson, R.M.S. and Gilligan, C., *Strategic Marketing Management, Planning, Implementation and Control*, 2nd edition, Chapter 9, Butterworth-Heinemann, 1997

CHAPTER 5

Developing a future orientation

About this chapter

So far in Part 1 the strategic analysis has focused on establishing the current situation. Any strategy has to address the future, and therefore developing a perspective on possible developments is necessary. This chapter explores a range of forecasting techniques, trend extrapolation, modelling, intuitive forecasting, consensus forecasting and scenario planning. Information requirements and the make-up of teams undertaking forecasting are also covered.

Introduction

In Part 1 of this text we have been analysing the situation that any organization currently faces and identifying current issues that may have an impact on the company's operations. However, in order to make plans that are of a long-term nature an organization has to develop a view of the future in which it will have to compete. One of the major mistakes that an organization can make is to base decisions on the logic that explained yesterday's market. To quote L.P. Hartley (1953): 'The past is a foreign country: they do things differently there.' The future is not a replica-tion of the past and an organization cannot develop strategy based on a historical perspective. Over a five-year period there can be dramatic shifts in a whole range of areas that can have a major impact on an organization. Examples might be: aspects of consumer behaviour, distribution channel arrangements or advances in technology.

An organization that has anticipated these changes can take advantage of any opportunities they offer and establish a far stronger competitive position as a result. It is important that organizations are creative in the manner in which they address these changes. Yesterday's view of what worked is unlikely to be appropriate in the changed environment of the future. Drucker (1980) states: 'The greatest danger in times of turbulence is not the turbulence: it is to act with yesterday's logic.' The first step an organization has to take is to form a view as to what may occur in the future – the second step is to address the issues that arise creatively.

The role of forecasting is therefore crucial to developing strategy. New product development depends on forecasts of technological developments. Selecting target markets is reliant upon forecasts of their attractiveness on a range of factors. Plans have to be developed to address the future, not to suit the past. How then can organizations form this view of the future?

Forecasting

Forecasting the future is a different activity from market research. Market research can identify the current activities and perceptions of consumers. At an operational level relevant marketing information is likely to be readily available to support the activities that have to be undertaken. At the marketing management level, marketing information which is relevant to the supported activities will not be so easily available. At a strategic level, marketing information to support decisions is likely to be largely unavailable and the reliability of that information questionable (see Figure 5.1). On what basis can a manager judge the quality of marketing information relating to the future?

To give an example. Market research could be undertaken to establish consumers' current perceptions of the future. However, consumers' views of the future are based on what they currently know and they may not be in a position to take an informed view. Indeed, there is no reason to believe that the view of the average customer is relevant. Is this view any more realistic than the view of a single expert in the area?

More and more marketing information can be produced, but at a strategic level this is unlikely to be reliable. There is no useful benefit in acquiring more and more marketing information in order to support strategic decisions. Typically only 1–10 per cent of a company's resources and effort in gathering marketing information is useful in supporting the strategic decision-making process which is likely to generate 90–99 per cent of the value in an organization (Diffenbach, 1983).

What is critical is for managers to form a fully developed understanding of the market they are in and to establish the strategic issues that could have an impact on the business in the longer term. This will allow them to establish the key areas where changes in the environment could affect critical factors such as the industry's structure, market demand, or competitive reactions. Effectively this entails establishing the key questions that need to be answered in order to form a view of the future. These questions are unlikely to be important in terms of the day-to-day operation of the business but will be crucial to its long-term direction.

Forecasting can be an effective way of identifying these strategic questions. There are various forecasting techniques that can be used by an organization (see Figure 5.2).

Figure 5.1 Decision-making pyramid (*Source*: Adapted from Piercy, 1997)

Technique	% of companies reporting use of technique
Expert opinion	86
Trend extrapolation	83
Alternate scenarios	68
Single scenarios	55
Simulation models	55
Brainstorming	45
Causal models	32
Delphi projections	29

Figure 5.2 Forecasting techniques used by large industrial organizations (*Source*: adapted from Diffenbach, 1983)

Trend extrapolation

A simple forecasting technique is trend extrapolation. This technique simply takes a historical trend over time and extrapolates where the trend line will be if extended into the future. The general assumption is that whatever happened in the past will continue in the future.

In some areas this may be an entirely suitable way to establish what the situation will be. For instance, demographic trends are slow-moving and therefore more predictable. However, trend lines can mislead planners if they fail to understand the underlying nature of a market. Car ownership in the UK has been on an upward growth curve for years. The assumption is that this will continue, causing escalating problems in terms of congestion and pollution. However, it is unlikely these growth estimates will be fulfilled precisely because roads will become more overcrowded and less easy to use. Consumers will switch to other forms of transport.

Even where trends can provide reasonable forecasts it is usually in areas that are not of major strategic importance. Issues that have a major impact on the organization's strategy are likely to occur where a development in the future causes the trend line to change. Identifying these discontinuities is a critical activity, which this simple technique ignores.

Modelling

Modelling techniques have a generally more sophisticated approach to forecasting than trend extrapolation. Modelling tries to identify the key variables in a situation and how they interact with each other. In this way the key inputs to a particular market can be modelled. Once the model is created, variables such as quantity of supply or consumers' level of disposable income can be altered to see what effect this has on the market as a whole. These variables tend to be those that can be easily quantified. The problem with this approach, when applying it to futures forecasting, is that what appear to be key variables in the current market may not be the key variables in the market of the future. The relationship between these variables may also change in the future.

To enable managers to form a more challenging view of the future, other techniques have to be used that foster a more creative approach.

Individual forecasting

There can be some merit in an individual forecast or 'Genius' forecast. If an individual is an expert in a specialist area they are able to form a comprehensive overview of their area of activity. This can allow them to see potential patterns or relationships emerging that very few other individuals or groups have the perspective to contemplate.

In the 1930s military planners believed that any future war in Europe would be a repeat of the type of war fought between 1914 and 1918, with armies facing each other over fortified defences. However, one individual wrote a book called *The Army of the Future* in France in the early 1930s forecasting that any future war would be dominated by highly mobile tanks supported by aircraft. The British and French high commands rejected this forecast. The Americans believed they understood how a mobile war should be fought due to their experiences in the 'non-mechanized' American Civil War and rejected the book's view of the future. Adolf Hitler read this book and as we now know realized the strength of the ideas it contained. The book was written by a certain Charles de Gaulle, then a little-known French army officer. This is a dramatic illustration of the power of an individual genius forecasting the future.

However, the dangers of individual forecasts are obvious. An individual forecast is a personal judgement and is open to idiosyncratic interpretations of an individual's observations.

In reality, though, many company forecasts are reliant on an individual. This may be the owner of a small company or the marketing manager in a larger organization. Organizations also use forecasts published by an individual expert as the basis of their planning. The techniques we are going on to discuss try to address the weaknesses of this individual approach. However, it needs to be stressed that while there are obvious problems with relying on a single individual it has to be borne in mind that futures forecasting is largely more of an art than a science.

Consensus forecasting

To overcome the limitations of individual forecasting the obvious step is to involve a group of individuals in the forecast. These individuals will develop a forecast by reaching some sort of consensus. There are different methods available to reaching this consensus: a straightforward Jury system or the Delphi technique.

Jury forecasting

According to Dalrymple (1989) and Mentzer and Cox (1984) a jury of executive opinion is one of the most popular forms of forecasting used by organizations. Effectively a group of company executives (or it could be a panel of experts external to the company) are brought together to discuss their respective views of events that may occur in the future. A group forecast emerges that is the consensus view of the group. Any forecast will depend on the quality of the individuals within the group.

There are several problems with a jury method. Decisions about the composition of the jury will have a major impact on the judgements the group will derive. The consensus reached by a jury, as it attempts to

reach an accommodation all members can live with, may diminish the input of the more talented forecasters. An even greater threat is that persuasive individuals, or those with greater status, rather than those with the most knowledge dominate the group. The greater the cohesiveness of the group the more likely it is that they will be unwilling to listen to a dissenting individual within the group. This tendency is called 'groupthink' and can have major implications for management groups in general and jury forecasting in particular. Groupthink tends to occur with groups of individuals that know each other well, enjoy being together and belong to the same 'ingroup' (Janis, 1972; Janis and Mann, 1982). These ingroups are widespread in organizations.

Four key factors affect the way ingroups work and the level of groupthink that develops:

- *High cohesiveness.* Ingroups display the tendency to have a high degree of cohesiveness among their members. There is a great feeling of harmony among members of the group and a mutual self-support of fellow members. This results in members of the group increasingly conforming and complying to group norms. Members are less willing to show dissent during group meetings as a result.
- *Strong leadership.* Strong group leaders carry enormous influence within the group and this can lead to increased pressure for a unanimous group position to be taken in order to show solidarity with the leader.
- *Lack of objective search and evaluation.* Groups develop their own way of reaching decisions, which tends to be informal because of the level of trust between members. The result is that alternative courses of action are not explored. When alternative actions are identified they are only considered at a superficial level.
- *Insulation of the group.* As the group bonds increase, members tend to have fewer interactions with members outside the group.

Alternative viewpoints therefore are not heard on a regular basis. When they are heard they are largely rejected because the individual proposing them is not a member of the group and therefore not a reliable source.

Groupthink causes six different types of problem for jury forecasting:

- *Illusions of invulnerability.* Because the responsibility for a decision is shared in a group, individuals do not feel the same level of responsibility for the outcome. Groups therefore are more willing than an individual to take decisions that carry a higher level of risk. This is exacerbated by the fact that the individual group members have confidence in the combined wisdom of the group and feel the group's deliberations will have identified all the potential dangers. The reality is that ingroups tend to be over-optimistic and ignore warning signs, taking more risky decisions as a result. Research also shows that groups tend to become more extreme, whatever they are like, so for example conservative groups become more conservative.
- *Collective rationalization.* Ingroups tend to develop a collective rationale to discredit any evidence that may act as a warning or a threat. Elaborate reasons are developed to explain why events did not happen as predicted. The group will find a rationale that will allow it to defend itself from criticism, especially from outside individuals or groups. The overall effect is to reassure the group that its decisions are legitimate.
- *Belief in the inherent morality of the group.* All members of the group are presumed to have a set of high moral and ethical standards. Group decisions as a result are seen as unquestionably morally right. Ingroups therefore fail to pay rigorous attention to the moral consequences of their decision making.
- *Pressure on dissenters.* Both direct and indirect pressure to conform is applied to members of the group. A member who shows signs of dissent may be excluded from an exclusive

inner circle unless they return to the conformist view. Ultimately they may be ejected from the group altogether if their dissent continues.
- *The illusion of unanimity.* Individuals who may hold opposing opinions to other members of the group on an issue tend to practise self-censorship. They will give voice to mildly opposing views or keep quiet altogether as a way of avoiding the hostile reaction of the rest of the group. Group members may stay quiet merely because they believe that no-one else shares their views, which further reinforces self-censorship.
- *Self-appointed mind guards.* Members of the group take on the role of guarding against incoming information that may threaten the group's position. Thus information is effectively filtered to stop any opposing evidence from being considered during group discussions. The absence of any contradictory evidence reinforces the unanimity of view amongst group members.

Janis regarded decisions such as the Bay of Pigs invasion, escalation of the Vietnam War and the lack of preparation for an air attack on Pearl Harbor as illustrations of the effect of groupthink. A more contemporary example would be the disaster of the Challenger space shuttle. There are obvious commercial examples as well, including perhaps the Sinclair C5.

Ingroups cause obvious problems for organizations as they curtail critical evaluation, limit the serious reflection of alternative courses of action and foster acquiescent behaviour in individuals. However, they are virtually impossible to eradicate. Ingroups exist precisely because they offer security to individuals and a sense of belonging. There are, however, ways to minimize groupthink behaviour during forecasting and planning activities. The aim of these curtailing actions is to enforce a critical evaluation of the decision-making process without destroying the group. Fostering a critical evaluation can be facilitated by instituting several procedural measures (Makridakis and Wheelwright, 1989):

- A member of the group can be assigned the role of the 'Devil's advocate' when specific decision-making activities are taking place. The individual undertaking this role will obviously be rotated.
- The group leader is not allowed, at least at the early stages of the discussion, to advocate a particular point of view. They have to take an impartial role and allow the group to develop its own opinions.
- The group can invite outside independent individuals to attend group discussions when critical decisions are being made. Their role could be precisely to raise alternatives or to provide alternative evidence not considered by the group.

Given that group forecasting is prevalent in organizations it is crucial that companies recognize the dangers of groupthink in their forecasting and planning activities.

Delphi forecasts

One technique that has been developed to overcome the problem with group forecasts is the Delphi forecast. A Delphi forecast purposely keeps the panel of experts who are involved physically apart. In many studies they will remain unknown to each other. Communication is undertaken by letter or e-mail directly to each individual from the Delphi study co-ordinator. This approach is taken in order to remove the social pressures and other undesirable aspects of group interaction.

For example, if a study examining what technological breakthroughs are desirable and achievable in the next 20 years was commissioned the following procedures would be executed. Once a panel of experts has been formed by the co-ordinator the Delphi study will have at least four phases:

- *Phase 1*
  A letter is sent to each of the experts asking them to state the scientific breakthrough and

technological developments that they feel are, firstly, beneficial and, secondly, could be attainable in the next 25 years. Each expert will send his or her independent judgement back to the co-ordinator. From these lists the co-ordinator will create a comprehensive list or choose those items of particular concern to the organization undertaking the study.

- *Phase 2*
  In phase two each expert is sent the list and asked to judge for each item the probability of when each potential development will take place. The timescale would normally be broken down into five-year bands.

  One expert may reply to a question as follows:

Year	By 2005	2006–2010	2011–2015	2016–2020	2021–2025	Never
Probability	0.0	0.15	0.25	0.35	0.25	0.00

A second expert's judgement, however, may be different:

Year	By 2005	2006–2010	2011–2015	2016–2020	2021–2025	Never
Probability	0.05	0.10	0.15	0.25	0.45	0.00

The co-ordinator will then collate all the replies and draw up charts displaying the distribution of experts' responses for each potential development.

- *Phase 3*
  The co-ordinator will then write to each panel member enclosing the charts that have been developed as a result of stage two. These results will, however, be broken down into two areas. One set of results will have a very small spread of responses and therefore a near consensus. The other set will have a wide spread of responses and therefore be clearly non-consensus items. On each

question the expert can see how far they are away from the average. They are then asked to reassess their responses. Experts that are at an extreme position from the mean can be asked to give a rationale for their prediction if they continue to maintain their position.

- *Phase 4*

  This is a repeat of phase three except that the experts will now consider revised charts that have been developed as a result of the reconsideration that individuals have undertaken in the previous round. Panel members can adjust their judgements in the light of the previous round. In particular they may change their view once they have seen the reasoning given by the experts who took an extreme position.

Delphi forecasts aim to arrive at a consensus position and can go beyond a fourth phase in order to do so. Once a consensus has been achieved an organization can then begin to weigh up the impact the forecasted events will have on their operations.

There are several problems with this forecasting technique:

- The process consumes a lot of time, as there can be considerable delays waiting to receive a full set of replies every round.
- The time delays cause organizational problems as panel members begin to drop out or become less motivated.
- Delphi forecasts appear to be heavily influenced by the ideas in fashion at the time of the survey. This is recognized as a major problem.
- Experts on these studies have been shown to be invariably over-optimistic about the timescales involved in developments coming to fruition.

There are also issues about the membership of the panel in the first place. These relate particularly to how panel decisions, and those involved in making those decisions, can be subject to all the problems outlined in the jury method discussed earlier.

The advantages of the Delphi method should not be dismissed, however – it does attempt to remove some of the problems related to group decision making. The Delphi method also is a move away from striving to form a single view of the future. Although the aim is to narrow down the responses to as much of a consensus as possible, this may not be achieved. When the process does not reach a clear consensus it can still be useful as it has identified the spread of opinion among experts in the field. A planning team therefore can consider a series of potential outcomes.

Scenario planning

This idea of identifying a diverse range of potential futures lies at the heart of the scenario planning process. Scenarios are normally developed by a whole management group, although they can be undertaken by a cross-section of people from across an organization. They may also include specially invited outside guests who may be able to offer an alternative perspective. It is important that all members of the group are familiar with the environmental analysis that has already taken place.

There are several techniques available to develop scenarios, some much more sophisticated and thorough than others. Here we only explore the development of simple scenarios. There are four key stages in the development of simple scenarios:

- *Identify the critical variables.* The first step is to use a brainstorming session to establish the factors that will drive changes in the future environment. Longer-term time horizons should be used so that participants do not simply extrapolate from present trends. The focus is on the external environment, not the organization and its current relationships. Once these drivers for change have been identified they should be evaluated on the basis of their importance to the organization

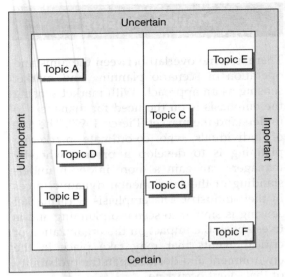

Figure 5.3 The importance/uncertainty matrix
(*Source*: Adapted from Van Der Heijden, 1997)

and the level of certainty associated with the manner in which that driver of change will actually develop (see Figure 5.3).
- *Develop possible strings of events.* The key drivers of change will be ones that are identified as being important but not predictable in which way they will develop. There will be more than one view or interpretation on which way these drivers will manifest themselves in the future. These will form the building blocks for the scenarios. The important drivers that are certain to develop may also appear in the scenario but these will appear in every scenario on the same timescale. The next step is to again have a brainstorming session that puts these drivers into alternative sequences of events over time. One way of operating is to write each driver of change on a separate piece of paper. These can then be moved to change their position as each alternative scenario is developed. The aim is to build scenarios that start from the situation today and develop into a future position that was not pre-planned by the planning group at the beginning of the scenarios' development.

- *Refine the scenarios.* Once a whole range of scenarios have been developed using the same key drivers for change they will need to be evaluated. Scenarios have to be challenging and have an internal consistency. A scenario would not, for example, be internally consistent if it had the UK government cutting interest rates dramatically below the rate of other European countries, while at the same time the Pound (Sterling) was dramatically strengthening against the Euro. Scenarios also should be credible and recognizable. Once the weakest scenarios have been discarded it is important to test the remainder for their robustness. One useful approach is to test the scenario from the perspective of organizations or individuals that are actors in the story line. Do their actions appear to be compatible with the logic of that actor's position?
- *Identify the issues arising.* The robust scenarios that have survived the evaluation process should then be reviewed to see whether any critical events or outcomes have been identified that would have a major impact on the organization.

There is no reason to assign a probability of the likelihood of a scenario actually happening. If the reasoning behind a scenario is sound then it is a potential future that could happen and management needs to be aware of the impact that future could have on their organization.

The technique was used to great effect by Shell in the early 1980s. Shell evolved a range of scenarios aimed at developing a view of economic development and the demand for oil that would accompany them covering the period 1980 to 1985. One scenario created a surprise result that demand for oil would fall as consumers began to implement conservation measures to lower energy use as a result of the second oil shock (OPEC's second oil price increase). The general consensus in the oil industry was that demand would be sustained at normal levels. At the time there were worries about the outbreak of the Iran–Iraq war, customer orders were strong, and the general feeling in the industry was towards expansion. Oil companies in 1980–1981 competed heavily to win supply contracts and increase drilling activity massively. However, early in 1981 there were the first signs that the scenario of less demand for oil was beginning to develop in the real economy. Further scenario work led Shell to refine this scenario to include more detail.

With the benefit of hindsight, in 1980–1981 oil companies clearly overestimated future demand. The scenario technique allowed Shell to see this early and to prepare appropriate plans in the event that this scenario actually started to develop. In 1981 Shell reduced oil stocks much earlier and at a greater level than the industry as a whole. This had the added benefit of allowing them to sell before prices decreased (Wack, 1985).

The scenario technique is obviously open to similar group dynamic problems as the jury method. It may also be open to the problem of currently fashionable ideas being given too high a profile. There are, however, clear benefits to the scenario planning process:

- It is a useful technique to help managers understand the critical issues that lie at the heart of the future of the organization. It can help create a framework within which to understand events as they evolve.
- It prepares managers for the possibility that there may be discontinuities in the external environment.
- Critically, it helps to place fundamental strategic issues on the management agenda.

The key dimension of scenario writing is not so much forecasting the future but helping managers to understand the factors that could have a major impact on their business. Graham Galer of Shell states: 'Accuracy has to be judged, I think, in terms of whether the scenarios got the right things on the management agenda' (Galer, 1998).

Market sensing

There is some overlap between the aims and operation of scenario planning and market sensing as an approach. With market sensing the emphasis is on the need for managers to understand the market (Piercy, 1997). The role of individuals who co-ordinate marketing planning is to develop a process whereby managers can gain a more in-depth understanding of the fundamental dynamic forces in their industry. The emphasis with market sensing is similar to scenario planning and is to establish the impact on the organization of critical events that may take place in the environment and decide upon the probability of that event occurring.

Strategic questions

Whichever approach is taken to developing a view of the future, one key feature is that the critical strategic questions facing the organization have to be identified.

There has been a range of studies by psychologists that show that in judgemental situations predictive ability does not improve as the amount of information increases (Alpert and Raiffa, 1982). The main effect of additional information is to lead to an overconfidence in the judgements made. In fact the studies show that the optimal amount of information reaches a plateau reasonably early in the process (Makridakis and Wheelwright, 1989). Once past this point additional information only increases the confidence of those involved in the judgement but does nothing further to enhance the quality of the forecast. Thus increasing amounts of marketing research beyond the threshold is wasting the resources of an organization.

Forecasting activities help identify the key factors underpinning an organization's position in the market. The follow-up is to monitor

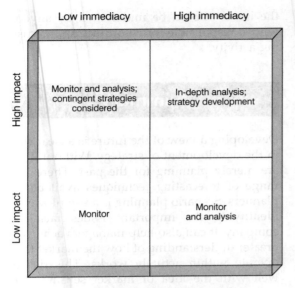

Figure 5.4   Categories of responses to strategic events forecasted in the external environment (*Source*: Adapted from Aaker, 1995)

and evaluate developments in those areas on an ongoing basis. This allows an organization to focus the marketing research requirements and planning efforts on the critical areas for strategic development (see Figure 5.4). Where an event has a high impact on the organization and the probability of it happening in the near future is high, then the company needs to undertake more in-depth analysis and develop a strategy that addresses the impact of the development. Where the impact of an event is high but the probability of it happening is low, or the event is only likely to happen far into the future, then the organization should monitor and analyse data and begin developing contingency plans. Events that only have a low impact will be given a much-reduced emphasis in terms of monitoring and analysis undertaken by the company.

People involved

The mix of people involved in the forecasting process will have an impact on the effective-

ness of the exercise. Part of the essence of the environmental analysis and futures forecasting is to build an understanding across the organization of the issues that it faces. Therefore this has to be a team activity that is widely spread. There are a number of issues that have to be considered when creating this team:

- *Ownership.* The managers who will be responsible for creating and delivering the strategy that flows from any analysis have to be involved in the process. If they are involved in developing the forecasts there is a higher likelihood that they will take ownership of resolving the issues that the process raises.
- *Subordinates' inputs.* A study by Aguilar (1967) illustrated that 23 per cent of information about the external environment came from subordinate executives. By contrast, only 9 per cent came from superiors and meetings. The clear implication is that lower status executives have to be involved in the process. Some forecasters also believe it is easier for younger people to envision the future because they have been brought up and socialized in the latest social, technical and political environment. Older individuals have come to the current situation holding values and beliefs developed when a different environment existed. Therefore an individual brought up with e-mail and CD-ROM technology may have a clearer perception of the technologies' potential than an individual whose formative education was based on paper-based information sources. These individuals again are likely to come from more junior executive positions in an organization. Although there should not be too much emphasis placed on this issue, having a group of individuals of mixed experience could help provide a more rounded perspective.
- *Challengers.* Creating a team who all have the same values and attitudes to the company is likely to develop a view of the future that does not challenge the status quo. Individuals who do not conform to the company

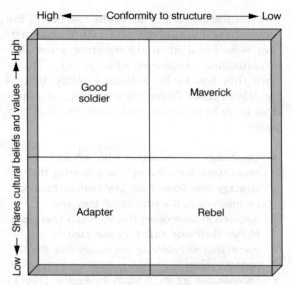

Figure 5.5 How individuals fit into corporate culture (*Source:* Adapted from Sathe, 1988)

stereotype are more likely to challenge and test the conventional attitudes and beliefs that predominate (see Figure 5.5). Mavericks and rebels are the type of nonconformists who will challenge conventional wisdom, and are of course the very individuals that ingroups tend to exclude.

- *Cross-functional teams.* Any team is obviously stronger if it is made up of individuals from across the company's operations. Not only does each individual bring an in-depth knowledge of their particular area of expertise but it also helps to build support for marketing plans within other functional areas.

- *Outsiders.* As has already been mentioned under scenario planning there can be advantages in including outside experts in any team. This can be widened to include representatives of both customers and suppliers.

Obviously there are likely to be weaknesses with any group that is formed. It is unlikely that all the above factors can be covered in any particular team. However, consideration of

the issues should be undertaken by anyone who is responsible for co-ordinating forecasting activity.

Summary

Developing a view of the future is a clear step in the development of strategy. Without it we are merely planning for the past. There is a range of forecasting techniques available to planners. Scenario planning is a useful way of identifying the important issues facing a company. It can also help managers achieve a greater understanding of how the market they operate within actually works. This ties in well with the idea of market sensing. The crucial step is then to motivate managers to develop creative approaches to deal with future issues the organization may face. Formulating elegant strategies to address the possible future that this part of the strategic analysis has identified is the next significant step in the planning process.

References

Aaker, D., *Strategic Market Management*, 4th edition, Wiley, 1995

Aguilar, F.J., *Scanning the Business Environment*, Macmillan, 1967

Alpert, M. and Raiffa, H., 'A Progress Report on the Training of Probability Assessors', in D. Kahneman *et al.* (eds), *Judgement under Uncertainty: Heuristic and Biases*, Cambridge University Press, 1982

Dalrymple, D.J., 'Sales Forecasting Practices from a United States Survey', *International Journal of Forecasting*, 3, pp. 379–392, 1989

Diffenbach, J., 'Corporate Environmental Analysis in Large U.S. Corporations', *Long Range Planning*, Vol. 16, No. 3, p. 111, 1983

Drucker, P., *Managing in Turbulent Societies*, Heinemann, 1980

Galer, G., *Shell Group Planning*, cited in D. Mercer, *Marketing Strategy: The Challenge of the External Environment*, Sage, 1998

Hartley, L.P., *The Go-Between*, Hamish Hamilton, 1953

Janis, I.L. and Mann, I., *Decision Making: A Psychological Analysis of Conflict, Choice and Commitment*, 2nd edition, Free Press, 1982

Janis, I.L., *Victims of Group Think*, Houghton Mifflin, 1972

Makridakis, S. and Wheelwright, S.C., *Forecasting Methods for Management*, 5th edition, Wiley, 1989

Mentzer, J.T. and Cox, J.E., 'Familiarity Application and Performance of Sales Forecasting Techniques', *Journal of Forecasting*, Vol. 3, pp. 27–36, 1984

Piercy, N., *Market Led Strategic Change*, 2nd edition, Butterworth-Heinemann, 1997

Sathe, V., *Culture and Related Corporate Realities*, Irwin, 1988

Van Der Heijden, K., *The Art of Strategic Conversation*, Wiley, 1997

Wack, P., 'Scenarios: Shooting the Rapids', *Harvard Business Review*, Nov/Dec, 139–150, 1985

Further reading

Mercer, D., *Marketing Strategy: The Challenge of the External Environment*, Chapters 2, 5–8, The Open University/Sage, 1998

Piercy, N., *Market Led Strategic Change*, 2nd edition, Chapter 10, Butterworth-Heinemann, 1997

Part 2
Formulation of Strategy

Strategic Intent
Strategy Formulation
Targeting, Positioning and Brand Strategy
Product Development and Innovation
Alliances and Relationships
The Strategic Marketing Plan

Part 1 examined the elements that make up a strategic analysis. This analysis is the foundation upon which strategic decisions are constructed. Part 2 explores the process involved in formulating strategy.

Chapter 6 examines the strategic intent of an organization. The influences on an organization's mission and the creation of a mission statement are explored. The development of specific goals and objectives are then discussed.

Strategy is formulated to achieve the mission and objectives of an organization. Chapter 7 explores the process of strategy formulation: competitor advantage, industry position and product/market strategies. A number of strategic models are also covered.

Chapter 8 explores the issues concerned with developing a specific competitive position, through targeting, positioning and branding strategy.

Chapter 9 examines the crucial areas of product development and innovation. Specifically, product development strategy and the new product development process are discussed. The chapter then examines management methods that can facilitate innovation in an organization.

Chapter 10 considers the increasing importance of alliances and joint ventures. Relationship marketing is also examined.

Chapter 11 examines the strategic marketing plan, and focuses on corporate and marketing planning. The analytical, behavioural and organizational aspects of planning which help overcome the barriers to success are also discussed.

Strategic intent

About this chapter

An organization has to have key objectives that define the aims that any strategy attempts to fulfil – this is the realm of strategic intent. This chapter explores the issues surrounding an organization's mission, goals and objectives. The hierarchy of objectives in an organization is discussed, as is the use of the balanced scorecard approach.

Introduction

Before an organization starts to make judgements about how it is going to compete, fundamental decisions about its overall method of operation and the areas it wishes to serve have to be articulated. A conscious statement of the primary direction and purpose of the organization has to be the key foundation upon which objectives and strategy are based. This rationale behind the company's existence usually comes in the form of a mission statement and is meant to act as a guiding light to all personnel within the organization.

Mission

The mission of the organization is the unique purpose that distinguishes it from other companies and defines the boundaries of its operations. The mission statement is a proclamation of the organization's primary objective that encapsulates its core values. The organization's aims and aspirations are the result of a series of influences (see Figure 6.1).

There are four major sources of influence acting upon the core meaning behind an organization's existence. Johnson and Scholes (1999) refer to these as:

- *Corporate governance.* To whom should the organization be accountable and within what regulatory framework should executive decisions be overseen and reviewed? With any organization these issues which relate to accountability will have an influence on the overall direction of the institution. Some groups that the organization is meant to serve, such as small shareholders, can be very removed from the managers actually running the company. Thus the regulatory framework acts to constrain management freedom and protect the rights of stakeholders.
- *Stakeholders.* Stakeholders in an organization include such groups as customers, suppliers, shareholders, employees, financiers, and the

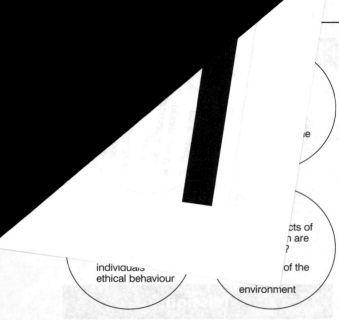

individuals
ethical behaviour

cts of
n are
?

of the

environment

Figure 6.1 Influences on an organization's mission and objectives (*Source*: Adapted from Johnson and Scholes, 1999)

wider social community. In reality, even when operating within the corporate governance framework, organizations may be inclined to further the interests of particular stakeholder groups according to the power and influence the groups actually wield.

- *Business ethics.* An ethical dimension also affects the mission and objectives that an organization should fulfil. This mainly relates to the corporation's social responsibility to stakeholder groups, in particular those whose power and influence is marginal, such as a local community. Although expectations of an individual's ethical behaviour have a significant influence, this ethical domain is subject to cultural attitudes and beliefs.
- *Cultural context.* The aspects of mission that are prioritized will reflect the cultural environment that surrounds the corporation. This influence will occur at several levels: at a broad level wider national cultures will be influential; individuals in functional areas will be influenced by the culture of their professional reference groups. There will also be internal subcultures operating at divisional or functional level within the company.

A mission statement then is subject to these influences and needs to address their interests in a manner that allows it to satisfy their diverse demands. In essence the mission statement ought to characterize the organization's principles and priorities and define the broad product, market and technologies that are core to the business. Missions can be framed with a very narrow view of the business or be given a much broader frame of reference:

- *Narrow focus.* Some organizations choose to frame a mission statement with a very narrow focus. An example is Newport News Shipbuilding (see below). The advantage is that it gives a very clear description of the organization's primary business. However, creating a narrow focus may set unnecessary constraints on the company's activities in terms of the markets served, the product/service offered or the technology employed.

Newport News Shipbuilding Mission statement – unchanged since the company was founded in 1886

We shall build good ships here – at a profit if we can – at a loss if we must – but always good ships.

(*Source*: Cosco, 1995)

- *Broad focus.* The use of a broad mission statement is fairly common and generally refers to all the various stakeholders in the business: shareholders, customers and employees as well as the area of business to be served. Scottish Power's mission statement has this broader focus, although it has a reasonably defined business scope. One noticeable stakeholder group not referred to in this mission statement is, surprisingly, the employees.

The Scottish Power Mission Statement

To be recognized as a highly rated utility-based company trading in electricity, other utility and related markets providing excellent quality and service to customers and above average total returns to investors.

In general, broad mission statements can address the problem of giving too narrow a focus on the business's area of operation, but can fall into the trap of failing to clearly define the market and product areas that are core to its operation. Richer Sounds is a company that retails hi-fi equipment; however, its

Mission Statement of Richer Sounds The Richer Way

In our business, our aim is to give customers friendly, efficient service and value for money second to none. We believe that by giving excellent customer service we will earn their loyalty and word of mouth recommendation to others. This is the only way to ensure our future success and so, looking after the customer must be an absolute priority at all times, and we really do expect our colleagues to give above average service.

We also believe that work should be fun. We believe that if people enjoy what they do, they will do a better job. We also believe at all times in aiming to be the best. This means that we expect and demand superior performance from our people with both quality of service, attention to detail in the presentation of our stores and in everything we do. We believe that if customer service is the top goal, this will create loyalty, and long term revenue and profitability will naturally follow.

(*Source:* Drummond and Ensor, 1991)

mission statement makes no reference to the product or market areas it is concerned with as a business. It does, though, engender a clear vision on the way that business should be undertaken.

Successful mission statements have to demonstrate the following characteristics:

- *Credibility.* The mission statement has to set realistic ambitions for the organization. In particular they have to be believable in the eyes of stakeholders, in particular the employees.
- *Uniqueness.* The mission has to relate to the particular organization. It should not be a statement that could be generically applied to a range of other organizations. The mission has to relate to the company and its stakeholders in a unique fashion.
- *Specific capabilities.* The mission should also embrace the core capabilities of the organization and emphasize their core role in the future of the organization.
- *Aspirational.* The mission needs to motivate individuals by giving them a statement that has significance to the work they undertake – a vision that is meaningful in terms of more than just making profits. It should engender a vision to which individuals feel they wish to contribute.

A mission statement should also define the boundaries of the business's ambitions. What is the territory that the business wishes to operate within? This is commonly referred to as the scope of the business or the competitive domain. There are several dimensions that have to be considered when defining the organization's scope:

- *Product scope.* This is defined in terms of the goods and services the enterprise supplies to customers. A critical aspect of defining product scope is deciding how to categorize the organization's products. Some products may fit into a collective category easily, some more important products may

be better served listed separately. The product could be defined in terms of its technology.
- *Market scope*. Market scope can be difficult to define but it is an important exercise. Market scope should depict the consumers and customers who utilize the company's products. There are a number of criteria that are helpful in defining market scope, such as:
  - Type of industry sector targeted
  - Channels of distribution
  - Demographics
  - Salient features of the consumer
- *Geographical scope*. This should be defined at an appropriate level of aggregation. Geographical scope may be defined in strictly local terms, for a small business, through to national and international regions for large organizations.

Definitions of the scope of the business based on markets are likely to be safer than a product definition. Particular products and technologies ultimately become obsolete but the consumer's needs addressed by those products or technologies may endure. There is a danger of marketing myopia developing (Levitt, 1960) if a business's competitive domain is defined solely according to a product type rather than a market need.

For example, pharmaceutical companies are beginning to redefine their competitive domain in terms of the customer benefits of 'good health' rather than purely product terms of 'drugs' (Green, 1995). SmithKline Beecham now sees the scope of its business covering four key areas of the healthcare market: prevention, diagnosis, treatment and cure, rather than just research and development of drugs. Products and services that address these primary market needs may change but the underlying market areas are likely to remain.

Stakeholders also have to be considered when developing a mission statement. Stakeholders are individuals or groups who rely on an organization to achieve some of their own personal objectives. At the same time the organization is reliant on these individuals (Johnson and Scholes, 1999). There are a number of different stakeholders that companies try to address and accommodate in a mission statement:

- *Internal*. These are the people most directly involved with the organization, therefore the values and attitudes of these groups are a key influence on the aims and objectives of the organization. Internal stakeholders include owners or shareholders, managers, employees and unions.
- *External*. These groups do not have the same close relationship with the organization as internal stakeholders do, nevertheless they can be a major source of influence over the direction of an enterprise. External stakeholders can be split into two groups:
  - *Primary external stakeholders*. These are external groups that have a direct relationship with the organization. They include crucial groups such as customers, suppliers, financiers and competitors.
  - *Secondary external stakeholders*. These have a less direct relationship with the company and include groups such as government agencies (local, national or international), political pressure groups, the financial community at large and society in general. These groups can exercise influence over the organization through such things as legislation and ethical campaigning.

Criticisms of mission statements are that many are too bland and ill-defined and therefore fail to give clarity to the business's endeavours. This could well be the result of the development of a statement that attempts to satisfy the interests of all stakeholders in the business. There are also some who feel mission statements are too brief to clearly depict the organization's strategic intent.

Statement of strategic intent

Some writers see strategic intent, or the corporate vision, as a concept separate from the mission. They would argue that a mission statement merely states what the organization is currently doing and that a statement of intent, or a vision statement, is also needed. A statement of strategic intent describes what the organization aspires to become. However, many companies strive to achieve both objectives within the single mechanism of the mission statement.

Nature of support for the mission statement

Mission statements can be put to use in different ways depending on which stakeholders have the dominant influence and what the nature of their support for the vision is. The dominant stakeholder will either be internal or external to the organization. Stakeholders' attitudes can be split into passionate campaigners for the mission and those who will afford more equivocal support (see Figure 6.2):

- *Faint support.* A mission statement is likely to be paid lip service where strategic decision making is dominated by internal managers that view other stakeholders and corporate governance in general merely as constraints. In these circumstances a mission statement has little influence on the strategic developments of the organization.
- *Passionate support.* Where the strategic process is dominated by internal managers who have a close identification with the values and philosophy of the organization, the mission statement will be central to their actions. These managers will use the mission statement as a vehicle to drive the corporate

Figure 6.2 Level of adoption of a mission statement (Source: Adapted from Johnson and Scholes, 1999)

aims and aspirations through the organization.
- *Dissipated mission.* If strategic decisions are the territory of external stakeholders whose overriding concerns are to do with corporate governance, then regulation and process will dominate the enterprise. The mission will become lost in the day-to-day routines of compliance with the regulations. Bureaucracies are classic examples of this type of organization, where the original mission of the organization is lost in the paperwork and strict regulations that have to be adhered to at all times.
- *Non-consensual mission.* The opposite of the previous situation is where external stakeholders who hold passionate ideological views dominate the strategic process. When this occurs it can become difficult to develop a mission statement that is acceptable to the different stakeholder groups. Alternatively the mission becomes a highly political one. One example is of state-owned industries that needed to shed production capacity and jobs in order to become competitive. These industries suffered because stakeholder groups, such as governments, could not support the organization's strategic decisions

because of their own political/ideological position. European governments and unions currently feel unable to support the closure of car plants even though there is clear over-capacity and therefore lack of profitability in the industry.

In summary, the mission statement, or mission and statement of strategic intent, operates as a guiding light that acts as a reference point when making strategic decisions in general and when forming objectives in particular.

Goals and objectives

The mission statement acts as a guide and leads to the development of a hierarchy of objectives. Objectives are the specific intended outcomes of strategy. There are differing views on the definition of goals and objectives. Some writers see goals as being less specific than objectives. Strategic goals are general aspirations that the organization needs to achieve but are difficult to measure or put within a specific timescale. Objectives therefore are more specific than goals and state what is to be achieved; they are given a quantifiable measure and a specific timescale. These objectives are seen as needing to be:

- *Specific*. Objectives that are specific should be set so that there is clarity throughout the organization as to what is to be achieved.
- *Measurable*. Objectives should be stated clearly, with tangible targets, what is to be achieved. Objectives can then be measured over time.
- *Aspirational*. Objectives should be set at a level that provides a high enough challenge to motivate individuals although not so high that it demoralizes them. Different groups or functions will have various perceptions of the level of challenge set by the objectives. One

way to address this problem is to set distinct objectives for each specific group.
- *Realistic*. Objectives should be achievable based on a thorough strategic analysis. Companies can fall into the trap of developing objectives that reflect an unrealistic, but desired for, position that does not reflect the current reality of their situation.
- *Timescaled*. A timescale should be put on the achievement of an objective. This again allows the organization to measure its performance against a set deadline.

These quantifiable objectives are normally referred to by their acronym SMART. Examples of SMART objectives are 3M's financial objectives:

Minnesota Mining & Manufacturing's Financial Objectives

- To achieve 10% annual growth in earnings per share.
- To achieve 20–25% return on equity.
- To achieve 27% return on capital employed.

(*Source*: Wheelen and Hunger, 1998)

Other writers, however, argue that both quantifiable and non-quantifiable objectives can be set. They would argue that some important objectives such as technology leadership might be impossible to quantify (Johnson and Scholes, 1999). Obviously with specific objectives it is easier for an organization to gauge whether those objectives have been achieved. However, a less specific objective, such as technology leadership, can still be assessed by comparing the organization's performance with the performance of its competitors. There are dangers, though, if all objectives are couched in such qualitative terms in that it becomes difficult to know whether they have been achieved or not.

Whichever perspective is taken on this matter, successful objectives also need to demonstrate the following characteristics:

- *Acceptability.* Internal managers are more likely to wholeheartedly support objectives that are in line with their own inclinations. As with the mission statement some of the organization's long-term objectives are drawn up to be acceptable to groups external to the organization.
- *Flexibility.* Objectives have to be flexible enough to be adaptable when discontinuities in the external environment occur (see Chapter 5). Here again is the issue of a trade-off between flexible and SMART objectives.
- *Comprehensibility.* Managers and staff at all levels have to understand what is to be achieved and know the main criteria by which their performance will be judged.

Drucker (1954) suggests that there are a number of key areas within which organizations should develop objectives:

- *Market standing.* This relates to the organization's success in the market. Objectives can be a statement of the total sales or the market share the organization seeks.
- *Innovation.* Targets can be set for innovation in: product and service development, cost reduction, financing, operational performance, human resources and management information.
- *Productivity.* Objectives can be set for the productive use of resources. A common approach is to state the number of items produced or the number of services performed per unit of input. Sometimes productivity can be stated in terms of decreasing inputs whilst retaining the same outputs. For example an objective could be to decrease overtime while at the same time maintaining production levels.
- *Physical and financial resources.* An organization can state objectives about the acquisition and use of resources.
- *Profitability.* A range of targets can be established for financial returns including earnings per share or return on equity.

- *Manager performance and development.* Objectives can be framed to set performance criteria for managers.
- *Employee performance and attitude.* Specific performance criteria can be set against which actual achievements can be measured. Objectives relating to aspects of employee relations are seen as beneficial in gaining employees' loyalty.
- *Public responsibility.* Objectives can be set for an organization's wider social responsibilities – in particular an effort could be made to be seen as responsible corporate citizens. They may establish objectives for contributions to charities, community action, urban renewal, or other forms of public and political activity.

There are dangers for organizations that see objectives in one of these areas as over-riding. Komatsu concentrated so much on competitive positioning objectives that its main concern became its position relative to its main competitor, Caterpillar. As a result Komatsu ignored emerging areas where there were opportunities for growth. This began to lead to a decline in the organization's profitability until corrective action was taken (Pearce and Robinson, 1997).

Hierarchy of objectives

Objectives are not only developed across a range of key areas, they also exist at a number of levels within an organization. Objectives cascade down through an organizational structure effectively forming a hierarchy. The fictitious Edinburgh Hotel is given as an example to illustrate this hierarchy of objectives (see Figure 6.3).

Edinburgh Hotel's objectives include:

- *Corporate objectives*
  Objectives at a corporate level relate to the organization's overall direction in terms of its general attitude towards growth. At this higher level, managers of the Edinburgh Hotel are likely to be concerned with long-term

Hierarchy of objectives: Edinburgh Hotel

	Objectives	Strategy
Corporate (over 3 years)	■ Increase gross operating profit by 30%	■ By becoming market leading luxury hotel in Edinburgh with 25% market share
Marketing (over 3 years)	■ Achieve 25% share of Edinburgh luxury hotel market	■ By providing best facilities for key market segments ■ By providing best standards of service ■ Promote it
Marketing mix (1–3 years) *Product*	■ Provide the best facilities for key market segments	■ Build more informal restaurant ■ Refurbish hotel to higher standard ■ Add fitness club ■ Improve bus facilities
Service	■ Provide best service standards	■ Retrain staff etc.
Promotion	■ Create awareness of improved facilities, service, etc.	■ Promote new restaurant ■ 'Relaunch' hotel

Figure 6.3   The Edinburgh Hotel's hierarchy of objectives (*Source*: Adapted from Revuelta, 1996)

profitability. (*Note*: In a not-for-profit organization the key objectives are more likely to relate to the efficient use of resources rather than profitability.) In this case the hotel management wishes to increase operating profit by 30 per cent over three years. The method proposed to achieve this objective is by growing market share to 25 per cent of the Edinburgh market. At this corporate level expanding market share becomes a strategy for achieving the organization's principal objective.

* *Functional objectives*
At a functional level expanding market share becomes an objective. Each functional area: finance, human resources, operations and marketing, will develop a strategy to support this objective. In terms of the marketing function it is concerned about which products/services should be sold into which markets. At a fundamental level marketing

strategy is about products and markets. In this example the strategy at the marketing function's level is to provide the best facilities in Edinburgh for key market segments, provide the best standards of service and ensure they are adequately promoted.

* *Operational objectives*
At this level the functional level marketing strategy becomes the objective. Strategies have to be developed for each element of the marketing mix to support these operational objectives.

This hierarchy ensures that at each level the objectives that are developed are consistent with the objectives that lie at the level above them. However, there has to be strong co-ordination between functional areas otherwise conflicting actions may be taken as each functional area conducts independent actions in order to fulfil their objectives. The key corporate objective could be to increase profitability by 10 per cent over the next three years. If independent actions are taken, marketing could develop strategies to increase sales in order to meet this objective. At the same time production could be operating at optimum capacity so any increase in throughput would increase its costs. Without co-ordination and communication functional areas can effectively be working against each other.

In many situations there will be more than three levels to this hierarchy, increasing the complexity of the situation even more:

* *Strategic Business Unit (SBU) objectives*
  In an organization with a divisional structure this hierarchy will have an additional level of the business (or SBU level) objectives that will be derived from the corporate level objectives and strategy and then feed into the functional level objectives.

Long-term versus short-term objectives

There is some tension between long-term and short-term objectives. Long-term objectives are an integral part of the planning horizons of up to five years ahead. Shorter-term objectives for12 months are more likely to drive the activities at the operational level. However, short-term objectives have to fall within the overall direction of the longer-term objectives. Budgets and targets generally are based on these short-term objectives and are essential for management control. But unless they are developed within a long-term framework they are not strategic in nature.

According to Aaker (1995) short-term financial measures such as sales, return on investment and market share are the dominant objectives in businesses. Even where other objectives exist they are eclipsed by these quantitative ones. This often leads to a bias in strategic choice towards squeezing a business

and starving it of investment in order to improve the short-term financial performance. One way to avoid this bias is to use the balanced scorecard approach – this would also have helped Komatsu to avoid their concentration on one key objective.

The balanced scorecard

Objective setting is not an isolated process. As has already been discussed there is a need for managers to know the key criteria by which their performance against objectives will be measured. There is a clear link between setting objectives and the setting of performance measures. The balanced scorecard (Kaplan and Norton, 1992, 1993) is an approach that more clearly links these two activities. Kaplan and Norton suggest that a balanced set of objectives should be created and at the same time a coherent set of performance measures should be developed alongside them.

At the core of the balanced scorecard approach is the belief that managers have to be able to look at a business from four key perspectives:

* *Customer perspective.* How customers see a business is critical, but financial measures alone do not provide this view. Customers are generally concerned with quality, performance, service and time. For each of these categories the organization should develop objectives and performance measures. Obviously how these categories are defined has to be from the customer's perspective. This will allow the organization to track how customers view the business over time.
* *Internal perspective.* Managers have to identify the critical internal processes that will allow them to satisfy customer needs. Identifying the processes that are important to customer satisfaction allows managers to identify the

functions and competencies in which they need to excel.

- *Innovation and learning perspective.* An organization's ability to create value is inextricably linked to its capacity to continually improve through innovation and learning.
- *Financial perspective.* This allows the organization to see how the business looks from the shareholders' point of view. This financial performance measures the success not only of an organization's strategy but also of its implementation.

The balanced scorecard widens the view managers have of the business rather than concentrating purely on financial criteria. For each of these perspectives the organization has to create distinct objectives and at the same time develop the accompanying performance measures. This process also forces managers to understand many complex relationships and to surmount some of the traditional functional barriers that hamper strategic development (Figure 6.4).

The balanced scorecard approach also addresses one other potential problem – that

	Strategic objectives	Strategic measures
Financial	F.1 Return on capital F.2 Cash flow F.3 Profitability F.4 Profitability growth F.5 Reliability of performance	⇨ ROCE ⇨ Cash flow ⇨ Net margin ⇨ Volume growth rate vs. industry ⇨ Profit forecast reliability ⇨ Sales backlog
Customer	C.1 Value for money C.2 Competitive price C.3 Customer satisfaction	⇨ Customer ranking survey ⇨ Pricing index ⇨ Customer satisfaction index ⇨ Mystery shopping index
Internal	I.1 Marketing ■ Product and service development ■ Shape customer requirement I.2 Manufacturing ■ Lower manufacturing cost ■ Improve project management I.3 Logistics ■ Reduce delivery costs ■ Inventory management I.4 Quality	⇨ Pioneer percentage of product portfolio ⇨ Hours with customer on new work ⇨ Total expenses per unit vs. competition ⇨ Safety incident index ⇨ Delivered cost per unit ⇨ Inventory level compared to plan and output rate ⇨ Rework
Innovation and learning	I.L.1 Innovate products and services I.L.2 Time to market I.L.3 Empowered workforce I.L.4 Access to strategic information I.L.5 Continuous improvement	⇨ Percentage revenue from pioneer products ⇨ Cycle time vs. industry norm ⇨ Staff attitude survey ⇨ Strategic information availability ⇨ Number of employee suggestions

Figure 6.4   The balanced scorecard (*Source:* Adapted From Kaplan and Norton, 1992, 1993)

of ensuring consistency between objectives. This can be difficult in practice because objectives are formed in a range of areas, at different levels and on different timescales (effectively objectives are formed both horizontally and vertically through the organization).

Gap analysis

The process of strategic analysis explored in Part 1 of this book effectively establishes the current situation that the company finds itself in and allows forecasts to be made of how the company will perform in the future. The objectives that are set by the organization allow it to project what the company's actual performance will need to be to achieve those objectives. It is at this point that the organization can calculate the gap between these two positions. This is commonly referred to as the gap analysis (see Figure 6.5).

The gap between these two positions represents the divide that the marketing strategy has to address. The rest of Part 2 of this book addresses how an organization can develop

strategy to allow it to meet its objectives by crossing this gap.

Summary

This chapter has explored the issues surrounding corporate mission, in particular influences acting upon the development of an organization's mission statement. The nature of strategic objectives was discussed, as well as the hierarchy of objectives and strategies. The possible tensions between functional objectives and strategies were highlighted. Strategies are developed to achieve the mission and objectives of the organization. The next step in the process is for the organization to formulate strategies to ensure that it can cross the gap between its current position and the fulfilment of its primary objectives.

References

Aaker, D.A., *Strategic Market Management*, 4th edition, Wiley, 1995

Cosco, J., 'Down To the Sea in Ships', *Journal of Business Strategy*, Nov/Dec, p. 48, 1995

Drucker, P., *The Practice of Management*, pp. 65–83, Harper and Row, 1954

Drummond, G. and Ensor, J., *Teaching Note for the Richer Sounds Case Study*, European Case Clearing House, 1991

Green, D., 'Healthcare Vies With Research', *Financial Times*, 25 April, p.34, 1995

Johnson, G. and Scholes, K., *Exploring Corporate Strategy*, 5th edition, Prentice Hall 1999

Kaplan, R.S. and Norton, D.P., 'Putting the Balanced Scorecard to Work', *Harvard Business Review*, Vol. 71, No. 5, pp. 134–147, 1993

Kaplan, R.S. and Norton, D.P., 'The Balanced Scorecard: Measures that drive performance', *Harvard Business Review*, Vol. 70, No. 1, pp. 71–79, 1992

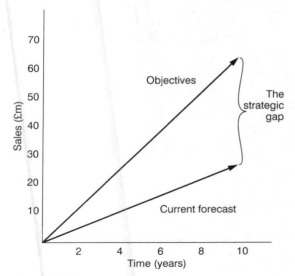

Figure 6.5   The gap analysis

Levitt, T., 'Marketing Myopia', *Harvard Business Review*, July/Aug, pp. 45–56, 1960

Pearce, J.A. and Robinson, R.B., *Strategic Management*, 6th edition, Irwin, 1997

Revuelta, J., Seminar, Napier Marketing Group, 1996

Wheelen, T.L. and Hunger, J., *Strategic Management and Business Policy*, 6th edition, p. 11, Addison Wesley, 1998

Further reading

Johnson, G. and Scholes, K., *Exploring Corporate Strategy*, 5th edition, Chapter 5, Prentice Hall 1999

McDonald, M., *Marketing Plans. How to Prepare Them, How to Use Them*, 4th edition, Chapter 6, Butterworth-Heinemann, 1999

CHAPTER 7

Strategy formulation

Marketing strategy aims to generate sustainable competitive advantage. The process is influenced by industry position, experience curves, value effects and other factors such as product life cycle. In any given marketplace, businesses must adopt defensive and attacking strategies. Such actions aim to maintain and/or increase market share. Organizations need to ensure their strategic position is relevant to current/future market conditions.

Strategy formulation – an overview

Chapter 6 outlined the basic principles of setting objectives. It is important to recognize that alternative methods of achieving objectives exist. The ability to identify and evaluate these alternatives forms the essence of strategy development. The goal is to obtain sustainable competitive advantage within predetermined markets. Figure 7.1 summarizes the process.

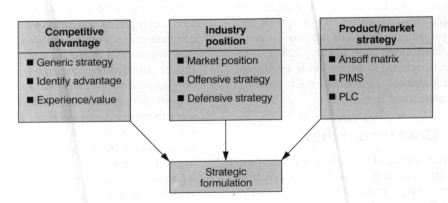

Figure 7.1   The formulation of strategy

Strategic advantage

Uniqueness perceived   Low cost position

	Uniqueness perceived	Low cost position
Broad Industry-wide	Differentiation	Overall cost leadership
Narrow Specific segment	Focused differentiation	Focused cost leadership

Strategic target

Figure 7.2   Competitive advantage (*Source*: Adapted from Porter, 1980)

Competitive advantage

The notions of competitive advantage and marketing strategy are intrinsically linked. Competitive advantage is the process of identifying a fundamental and sustainable basis from which to compete. Ultimately, marketing strategy aims to deliver this advantage in the marketplace.

Porter (1980) identifies three *generic strategies* – fundamental sources of competitive advantage. These are: cost leadership, differentiation and focus. Arguably, these provide a basis for all strategic activity and underpin the large number of marketing strategies available to the organization. Additionally, management needs to define the competitive scope of the business – targeting a broad or narrow range of industries/customers (see Figure 7.2), essentially either operating industry-wide or targeting specific market segments. Each generic strategy is examined in turn.

Cost leadership

One potential source of competitive advantage is to seek an overall cost leadership position within an industry, or industry sector. Here the focus of strategic activity is to maintain a low

cost structure. The desired structure is achievable via the aggressive pursuit of policies such as controlling overhead cost, economies of scale, cost minimization in areas such as marketing and R&D, global sourcing of materials and experience effects. Additionally, the application of new technology to traditional activities offers significant opportunity for cost reduction.

Difficulties can exist in maintaining cost leadership. Success can attract larger, better resourced competitors. If market share falls, economies of scale become harder to achieve and fixed costs, such as overheads, are difficult to adjust in the short-to-medium term. Additionally, cost leaderships and high volume strategy are likely to involve high initial investment costs and are often associated with 'commodity' type products where price discounting and price wars are common.

Remember, low cost does not need to equate automatically to low price. Products provided at average, or above average, industry price (while maintaining cost leadership) can generate higher than average margins.

The basic drivers of cost leadership include:

- *Economy of scale.* This is perhaps the single biggest influence on unit cost. Correctly managed, volume can drive efficiency and enhance purchasing leverage. Additionally, given large-scale operations, learning and experience effects (see later) can be a source of cost reduction.
- *Linkages and relationships.* Being able to link activities together and form relationships can generate cost savings. For example a 'just-in-time' manufacturing system could reduce stockholding costs and enhance quality. Forging relationships with external organizations is also vital. If industry partners were to share development and distribution costs, or activities were 'outsourced' to specialist operators, a substantial reduction in overheads is possible.
- *Infrastructure.* Factors such as location, availability of skills and governmental support greatly affect the firm's cost base. Given the

development of information technology and the global economy it is possible to have a worldwide infrastructure and selectively place activities in low-cost areas.

Differentiation

Here the product offered is distinct and differentiated from the competition. The source of differentiation must be on a basis of value to the customer. The product offering should be perceived as unique and ideally offer the opportunity to command a price premium. Will customers pay more for factors such as design, quality, branding and service levels?

The skills base for a differentiation strategy is somewhat different from a cost leadership strategy and will focus on creating reasons for purchase, innovation and flexibility. Remember, often it is the perception of performance as opposed to actual performance that generates differentiation.

There are several 'downsides' to this type of strategy. Firstly, it can be costly with associated costs outweighing the benefits. Secondly, innovation and other initiatives can be duplicated by competitors. Thirdly, customer needs change with time and the basis of differentiation can become less important as customers focus on other attributes. For example, in the car market, safety may now be seen as more important than fuel economy.

Common sources of differentiation include:

- *Product performance.* Does product performance enhance its value to the customer? Factors such as quality, durability and capability all offer potential points of differentiation. Performance is evaluated relative to competitors' products and gives customers a reason to prefer one product over another.
- *Product perception.* Often the perception of a product is more important than actual performance. Hopefully, the product has an enduring emotional appeal generating brand loyalty (see Chapter 8). This is commonly achieved via marketing communications (advertising, branding, endorsement, etc.) and direct experience of customer groups.
- *Product augmentation.* We can differentiate by augmenting the product in a way that adds value. For example, high levels of service, after-sales support, affordable finance and competitive pricing all serve to enhance the basic product offering. It is common for distributors, such as retailers, to provide the added-value augmentation. Product augmentation is dealt with in Chapter 9.

Focus

With this strategy, the organization concentrates on a narrower range of business activities. The aim is to specialize in a specific market segment and derive detailed customer knowledge. This focus, or niche, strategy can also generate the benefits of cost leadership or differentiation within a defined market segment (see Figure 7.2). For example, it may be possible to obtain cost leadership within a chosen segment or that segment may regard your product offering as differentiated.

Success within a specialist niche can attract competitors – perhaps much better resourced. Additionally, the narrow business base means more susceptibility to downturns in demand from key customer groups.

A focus strategy is based on factors such as:

- *Geographic area.* Using geographic segmentation allows a product to be tailored to local needs. The local association may offer the potential to differentiate the offering (e.g. Champagne comes from a specific French region) and protect the market from larger predators. Another rationale for such segmentation is to serve markets too small or isolated to be viable on a large scale (e.g. rural communities).
- *End-user focus.* It is possible to focus on a specific type of user as opposed to the entire market. Specialization offers the opportunity to get 'close' to customers and have a better understanding of their needs (e.g. specialist hi-fi manufacturer). Additionally, within a narrow segment the focused organization may

be able to offer the choice, service and economy-of-scale not available to more broadly based competitors. This strategy often works by selecting specific points on the price/quality spectrum within a given market (e.g. discount food retailer).

- Product/product line specialist. The organization focuses on a single product type or product line. Value is derived from the specialization in terms of skills, volume and range (e.g. industrial power supplies).

Consistency and the alternative view

The Porter (1980) view of generic strategy supports the need for consistency of approach. The organization needs to adopt a definite generic strategy. Attempting to mix the above strategies within a defined market-place may result in failing to achieve the potential benefits and result in the organization being 'stuck in the middle' of either low cost, differentiated or focused strategy. Figure 7.3 illustrates this.

Porter's concept of competitive advantage advocates pursuing one generic strategy and thus avoiding a low profit 'stuck-in-the-middle' position. However, alternative views exist. The adoption of common production, quality, marketing and management philosophies by industry competitors may mean that effective differentiation or absolute cost lead-

ership is rarely achieved. Additionally, which managers are not concerned with controlling costs? Therefore, differentiation strategies need a cost focus. It is also possible to follow 'hybrid strategies' aiming to offer added value and lower cost. Indeed, Fulmer and Goodwin (1988) point out that the two strategies (cost leadership and differentiation) are not mutually exclusive. For instance, total quality management programmes have resulted in superior quality and cost reductions.

The reality of modern business is that many successful organizations are 'stuck in the middle' within their competitive environments. This is not to decry the importance of establishing competitive advantage and consistency of approach. It merely serves to illustrate the competitive nature of modern business and the importance of uncovering and optimizing all available sources of competitive advantage. It is a question of how best to add value within the context of the strategic business environment.

Identifying sources of competitive advantage

Once the generic strategy is understood, it is possible to consider how it can be translated into specific competitive advantage. A prerequisite to competitive advantage is sustainability – the organization must be able to sustain its competitive advantage over the long term. In order to be sustainable the competitive advantage must be:

- Relevant. It must be appropriate to current and future market needs. Additionally, it must be relevant to the organization – achievable within the available resource base.
- Defensible. There must be barriers to replication, otherwise success will simply be duplicated by competitors. Such barriers tend to be: (i) asset based – tangible factors controlled by the organization, such as location,

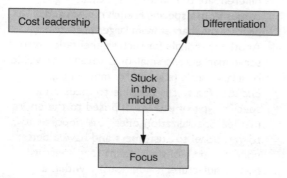

Figure 7.3   Inconsistent strategy

plant and machinery, brands and finance; (ii) skills based – the skills and resources required to make optimum use of the assets, such as quality management, brand development, product design and IT skills.

Clearly, competitive advantage must be appropriate to the strategic nature of the industry. An interesting template that evaluates the strategic competitive environment has been developed by the Boston Consultancy Group (Hooley *et al.*, 1998). This matrix identifies four types of industry (see Figure 7.4). The industries are classified in terms of: (i) size of competitive advantage and (ii) number of possible ways to achieve advantage.

- *Stalemate industries.* Here the potential for competitive advantage is limited. Advantages are small and there are only a few ways to achieve these advantages. Technological advances are commonly adopted by all industry 'players' and we see rapid convergence in product design/performance. Such industries tend to be mature, highly competitive and often akin to commodity-type products where price is the key buying criterion (e.g. manufacturing desktop computers).
- *Volume industries.* Here few but highly significant advantages exist. These industries are often capital intensive and are dominated by a few large players who achieve economies of scale (e.g. volume car manufacture).
- *Fragmented industries.* The market's needs are less well defined and numerous ways exist to gain advantage. The industry is often well suited to niche players and profitability may not be linked directly to size. Commonly, organizations grow by offering a range of niche products to different segments – a multi-segmentation strategy (e.g. computer software).
- *Specialized industries.* The potential advantage of differentiation is considerable and numerous ways exist to achieve this advantage. Profitability and size are not automatically related. Such industries include those developing customized solutions to specific problems (e.g. management consultancy) and

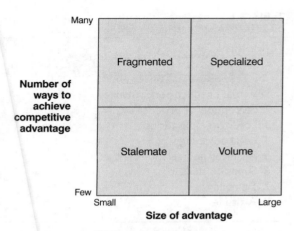

Figure 7.4   BCG strategic advantage matrix

firms involved in the development/application of innovative technology (e.g. biomedical engineering).

Understanding generic strategies and the application of competitive advantage to the business environment is fundamental to success. Davidson (1997) offers an alternative view and states that competitive advantage is achieved:

'. . . whenever you do something better than competitors. If that something is important to consumers, or if a number of small advantages can be combined, you have an *exploitable* competitive advantage.'

Instinctively, this view appeals to the industry practitioner. The most potent sources of competitive advantage can be summarized as shown in Table 7.1.

Such advantages are underpinned by the previously summarized generic sources of competitive advantage (Porter, 1980). Figure 7.5 illustrates this concept.

Experience and value effects

Perhaps it is to state the obvious to say that experience and ability to create value are

Table 7.1

Source of competitive advantage	Examples
1 Actual product performance	Robust, economic, easy to use
2 Perception of product	Brand image, product positioning
3 Low cost operations	Location, buying power
4 Legal advantage	Patents, contracts and copyright
5 Alliances and relationships	Networking, procurement and joint ventures
6 Superior skills	Database management, design skills
7 Flexibility	Developing customized solutions
8 Attitude	Aggressive selling, tough negotiation

(*Source*: Adapted from Davidson, 1998)

closely linked and are major factors in successful marketing strategy. In considering these factors, two useful models are presented here.

The experience curve denotes a pattern of decreasing cost as a result of the cumulative experience of carrying out an activity or function. Essentially, it shows how learning effects (repetition and accumulated knowledge) can be combined with volume effects (economy of scale) to derive optimal benefits (see Figure 7.6). With experience, the organization should produce better and lower cost products. The main influence of experience effects has been to promote a high volume/

low cost philosophy aiming at a reduction in unit cost. However, in today's competitive business world, organizations cannot simply rely on a 'big is beautiful' strategy based on economy-of-scale and market share. It is important to recognize the importance of learning effects on factors such as product quality and service levels. Such factors hold the key to future success and greatly influence the ability to 'add value' to product offerings.

Eventually, cost and learning effect will display diminishing returns and an optimum level is reached. However, the process never stops. The advent of new technologies may

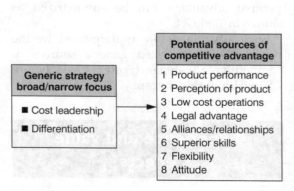

Figure 7.5 Generic strategy and potential competitive advantage

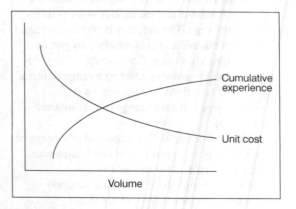

Figure 7.6 Experience curve

mark a shift in experience and offer new challenges. For example, the large monolithic market leader could be in danger as newer, more forward thinking competitors readily embrace new technology and the subsequent benefits it brings to today's business environment.

The concept of a *value chain*, developed by Porter (1980), categorizes the organization as a series of processes generating value for customers and other stakeholders. By examining each value-creating activity, it is possible to identify sources of potential cost leadership and differentiation.

The value chain (Figure 7.7) splits activities into: (i) *primary activities* – in-bound logistics, operations, outward logistics, marketing/sales and service; and (ii) *secondary activities* – infrastructure, human resource management, technology development and procurement. These secondary activities take place in order to support the primary activities. For example, the firm's infrastructure (e.g. management, finance and buildings) serves to support the five primary functions. While each activity generates 'value', the linkages between the activities are critical. Consider the interface between in-bound logistics and operations. A just-in-time logistics system, supported by computerized stock ordering (technology development – secondary activity), could reduce stock costs and enhance the quality of products manufactured in the operations phase of the chain, thus enhancing the overall

value generated by the process. The value generated is shown as the 'margin of value' in Figure 7.7.

The value chain provides an additional framework to analyse competitive advantage. It helps identify the key skills, processes and linkages required to generate success. Additionally, the concept can link organizations together. A series of value chains can be analysed as one overall process. For example, the value chains of a component manufacturer and equipment manufacturer could be merged into one system, with common support activities. This could have the effect of reducing overall costs and improving co-ordination between the companies.

Industry position

Clearly, strategy formulation must consider the position held within a given industry and the organization's resource base relative to competitors. Successful strategy amounts to implementing plans that meet customer need while effectively dealing with rival competitors. This section examines strategies relative to the competition.

Competitive marketing strategy draws heavily on military strategy. Indeed, many strategic principles can be traced to the analogy of the marketplace as a battlefield with competitors as enemy forces. It could be

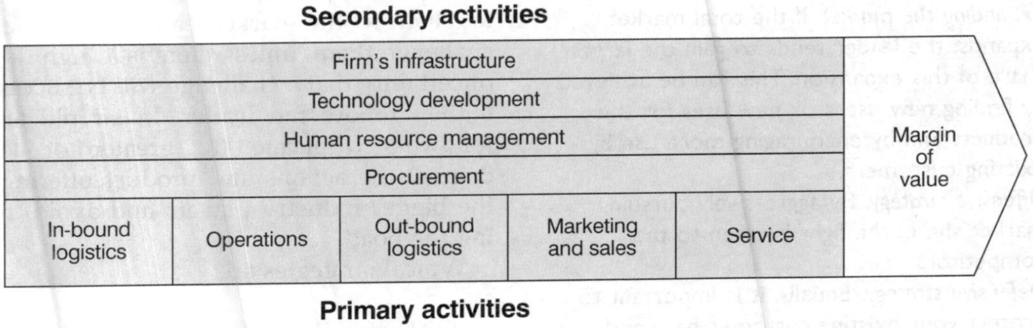

Secondary activities

Firm's infrastructure					Margin of value
Technology development					
Human resource management					
Procurement					
In-bound logistics	Operations	Out-bound logistics	Marketing and sales	Service	

Primary activities

Figure 7.7   The value chain (*Source*: Porter, 1980)

argued that Sun Tsu's *The Art of War* (a classic work defining ancient military tactics and philosophy) provides as much of an insight into the principles of modern day strategic marketing as it does to military campaigns.

Market position

The position of the organization (or product) within a given market will clearly influence the strategic options available. For example, when comparing the market leader with a smaller 'niche' competitor, it is likely that marked differences exist in: aims, capabilities and resources. When considering a market, competitors break down into four general categories: market leaders, market challengers, market followers and market nichers. Each will be examined in turn.

Market leaders

A market leader is dominant within the given industry or segment. This dominance is normally due to market share. However, some organizations may achieve 'leadership' via innovation or technical expertise. Additionally, the organization may only be a leader in a given segment (e.g. geographic area). Be careful how the term 'market' is defined when talking about market leaders.

The market leader will be a constant target for aggressive competitors and must remain vigilant and proactive. Common strategies include:

- *Expanding the market.* If the total market expands, the leader tends to gain the largest share of this expansion. This can be achieved by finding new users or new uses for the products and by encouraging more use by existing customers.
- *Offensive strategy.* By aggressively pursuing market share, the fight is taken to the competitors.
- *Defensive strategy.* Equally, it is important to protect your existing customer base and ensure that market share is retained.

Offensive and defensive strategies are applicable to all industry 'players' not just market leaders. These strategies are more fully discussed in the next subsection, Offensive and Defensive Strategies.

Market challengers

Market challengers will seek confrontation and aggressively pursue market share. Often, such organizations are large and well resourced. They are seeking market leadership and present a long-term sustained challenge to the current leader.

Strategies available to challengers include:

- *Selective targeting.* The challenger can target specific competitors. It may attack smaller (perhaps regional) competitors or firms that are equivalent in size and resources. Basically, the challenger is looking to attack weaker competitors – those failing to satisfy the customer in some way, or those under-financed or under-resourced. By picking-off weaker competitors, challengers enhance their market position.
- *Attack the leader.* The challenger can directly challenge the dominant player. This is often a long-term war of attrition and it is unlikely that market leadership will change overnight. Commonly, direct attacks sustained over time erode market share gradually.

Market followers

Being in second, third or even further down the rankings within an industry may still be an attractive position. Market followers tend to 'shadow' the market leader as opposed to challenge them, unless there is a high degree of certainty that a challenge will be successful – they follow the leader. In simple terms, followers duplicate (to greater or lesser degree) the actions and product offerings of the bigger industry players and avoid 'rocking the boat'.

Typical strategies are:

- *Duplication.* The product offering is duplicated in every possible way, even down to the packaging and promotion. Such strategies are potentially open to legal challenge in the areas of patents and copyright.

- *Adaptation.* Here we adapt the basic product offering. If we can improve on the concept, then the potential exists to differentiate ourselves. For example, we may sell the same/similar products but have a reputation for higher levels of customer service.

Market nichers

Niche players focus on specific market segments. They are more specialized in nature and seek to gain competitive advantage by adding value in some way appropriate to specific target groups.

Focus strategies adopted by niche players were outlined earlier in this chapter, in the subsection on Focus, and commonly involve geographic, end-user or product line specialization.

Offensive and defensive strategies

Two fundamentals exist in the battle for market share – the ability to gain market share and being able to retain existing market share. To achieve these objectives, organizations need offensive (attacking) and defensive strategies.

Kotler *et al.* (1999) identify a number of attacking and defensive strategies. Such strategies are used in combination by organizations in order to compete successfully in the modern business world.

Offensive strategies, designed primarily to gain market share, are shown in Figure 7.8. Each is summarized in turn here:

1 *Frontal attack.* This is an all-out attack on a competitor. Generally, such an attack requires a sustained effort. Attackers must be certain they have the resources to endure a long hard struggle and survive potentially heavy initial losses. They are likely to face a well-established competitor with broadly the same product offering. Therefore, the attacker needs a clearly defined advantage. For example, the attacker may have a cost advantage or its brands may be perceived more positively.

2 *Flank attack.* This draws on the analogy of the battlefield, where the flanks were always the weakest point of any army. Equally, this can be the case in the business world and 'flanking' is achieved by attacking selective market segments where the competitor is relatively weak. By concentrating resources on narrow areas it is possible to achieve superiority. The key to success is to identify worthwhile, under-served segments. For example, a computer manufacturer may feel a rival only offers a limited, and somewhat dated, range of laptop computers. This could be a weak 'flank' vulnerable to attack.

3 *Encirclement attack.* Here we aim to offer a range of products that effectively encircle the competitor. Each of these products will tend to stress a different attribute and leave the competitor's product facing a series of more focused rivals. For example, in marketing soap powder, the market leader could be encircled by three rival products each stressing a different attribute: cleaning power, low cost and environmental friendliness. The combined effect of the three rivals is to undermine the positioning of the market leader.

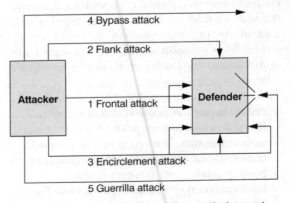

Figure 7.8 Attacking strategies (*Source*: Kotler *et al.*, 1999)

One obvious danger of this strategy is that it leads to a proliferation of products. These may compete with each other and are likely to drive up cost.

4 *Bypass attack.* This is perhaps more a policy of avoidance as opposed to attack. The attacker moves into areas where competitors are not active. This may involve targeting geographic areas, applying new technologies or developing new distribution systems. For example, a tour operator could bypass existing retail distribution outlets and sell direct to the public via mail-order.

5 *Guerrilla attack.* Tactical (short-term) marketing initiatives are used to gradually weaken the opposition. Sudden price cuts, bursts of promotional activity or other such tactics are used to create product awareness and slowly erode market share. Such attacks may be precursors to a longer, more sustained attack. Additionally, guerrilla attacks are not restricted to marketing – legal action such as law suits can be used to harass and restrict competitors. The key to success is the unpredictability of such attacks and their ability to destroy morale and deplete resources, such as management time or finance.

It is true to say that for every offensive move a defensive counter exists. Indeed, the 'backbone' of any marketing strategy must be to maintain market share. Regardless of market position, firms must continually defend their current business against competitors. A strong defence should deter, as well as repel, rivals and allow the organization to build on its strengths. Common defensive strategies are summarized by Kotler *et al.* (1999) in Figure 7.9:

1 *Position defence.* A position defence aims to strengthen the current position and shut out the competition. The aim is to use the distinct competencies and assets of the organization to build an unassailable position in the marketplace. If the defending firm can offer a differentiated, value-added product to customers its market position will be

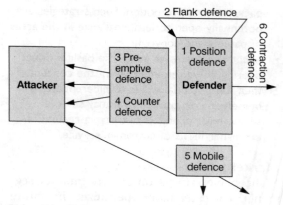

Figure 7.9 Defensive strategies (*Source*: Kotler *et al.*, 1999)

maintained, if not enhanced. Defending a market position is often dependent on brand management, service levels and distribution.

2 *Flank defence.* Not only do organizations need to protect their main areas of operation, but they must also protect any weak spots (flanks). Firstly, managers must identify weak areas and the potential impact of an 'attack' on the core business. Secondly, they need to be sure that the flank defence is sustainable. For example, a food retailer may see its flank as frozen products. Here it competes with specialist frozen food retailers. The flank could be protected by maintaining several 'loss leader' (sold at below cost) products.

3 *Pre-emptive defence.* This involves striking at potential competitors before they attack you. The aim is to pre-empt their actions and reduce the potential competitive threat. This may involve using, or threatening to use, the attacking strategies (e.g. guerrilla attack) shown in Figure 7.8. Large, powerful 'players' deter competitors by routinely threatening, but seldom actioning, price cuts or increased promotional expenditure. They warn others to back off.

4 *Counter defence.* When attacked, most organizations will respond with a counter-attack. The counter-attack may be immediate or a more considered response might be made once the situation has settled down. By nature, counter-defences are

reactive, and if the defensive position is strong enough no additional counter may be necessary. For example, a strong well-established brand loyalty may see off a price-cutting competitor.

5 *Mobile defence.* A mobile defence involves a flexible and adaptive response, allowing the defender to switch into new areas of interest as threats or opportunities materialize. It is achieved by broadening current markets or by diversifying into unrelated activities. To illustrate, an insurance company may broaden the range of financial services offered to customers or diversify into areas such as estate agency and property management. The key is to build a strategic presence in a range of lucrative areas/segments.

6 *Contraction defence.* It may prove impossible to defend all operational activities. Therefore, a selective strategic withdrawal could be the best option. By sacrificing some activities, resources are freed to defend core activities. For example, consider a computer company. It could withdraw from the high volume/low margin personal computer market and focus on more profitable areas, such as maintenance and software development.

Product and market strategies

Product/market strategies are detailed in nature. They address the specific market impact of a product or product line. This section examines three concepts useful in formulating such strategies: the product/market matrix, PIMS (product impact of market strategy) analysis and the product life cycle.

Product/market matrix

Ansoff (1975) developed a policy/market matrix (or 'Ansoff matrix') which provides a useful linkage between products and markets. The matrix (Figure 7.10) considers four combi-

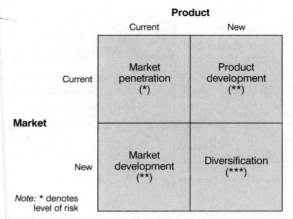

Figure 7.10   Product/market matrix

nations of product and market. Each combination suggests a growth strategy.

The organization's potential is determined by the combination of current and new products within current and new markets. Additionally, the element of risk must be considered. As organizations move away from existing markets and products the potential risk factors increase:

- *Market penetration.* The aim is to increase sales of existing products in current markets. An aggressive marketing drive, via factors such as competitive pricing, sales promotion or advertising, can expand the share of an existing market. Dealing with familiar customers and products is low risk and provides a starting point to planned growth. However, the potential for market penetration is often limited and strategic plans may require additional options to be pursued.
- *Market development.* Referring to Figure 7.10, market development aims to find new markets for existing products. This could involve new geographic markets (e.g. exporting), adding distribution channels or finding new market segments. For example, a manufacturer of sports clothing may try to position its products as fashion items and target a different set of retailers.

Product

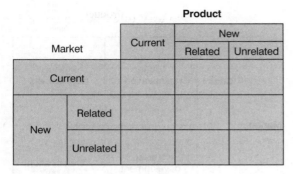

Figure 7.11   Expanded product/market matrix

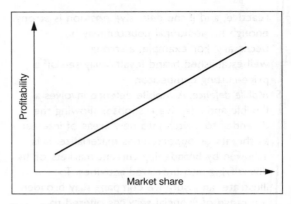

Figure 7.12   Profit related to market share

- *Product development*. Organizations must update their product portfolio to remain competitive. Ideally, a balanced product portfolio should exist, with established products generating funds for product development.
- *Diversification*. This involves moving beyond existing areas of operation and actively seeking involvement in unfamiliar activities. Diversification can be related (having linkages to existing activities), or unrelated (venturing into totally new activities). While unrelated diversification may spread risk, it can be difficult to achieve.

The product/market matrix can be expanded to consider the degree to which new activities are related or unrelated (Figure 7.11) to the core business. As previously stated, it is more difficult to achieve success in unrelated activities. Hence, unrelated diversification of products and/or markets is often tackled via joint ventures, mergers and acquisitions (see Chapter 10).

PIMS analysis

Many influential marketing studies have examined the link between profit and marketing strategy. These PIMS (profit impact of market strategy) studies aimed to identify the key drivers of profitability and have recognized the importance of market share as such

a driver. Generally speaking, profits will increase in line with relative market share. This relationship (Figure 7.12) has influenced marketing thinking, promoting actions aimed at increasing market share as a route to profitablity.

While such a relationship is often true, it is not universal, and some industries display a 'V-shaped' relationship. Here, profitability can initially fall until a critical mass, in terms of market share, is reached. The effect of the 'V-curve' is polarization – industries with small niche players and large dominant companies. Medium sized firms see profits fall until critical mass is reached. This makes it very difficult for small/medium companies to grow. Figure 7.13 shows the relationship.

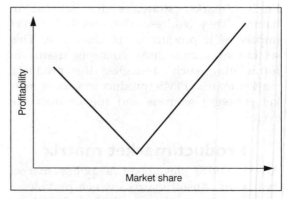

Figure 7.13   'V-shaped' profit/market share relationship

Clearly, the marketing strategist must consider the nature of these relationships and not blindly pursue market share. It should be possible to determine the optimal market share/profitability position.

Product life cycle

The product life cycle (PLC) has been described as the most quoted but least understood concept in marketing. Any strategy considering products and markets will be influenced by the PLC. Organizations are advised to ensure they fully understand the product life cycle for their products *and* industry segments.

The basic concept (Figure 7.14) can be summarized as products passing through four stages: introduction, growth, maturity and decline. Sales will vary with each phase of the life cycle:

• *Introduction*
It takes time for sales to grow and the introductory phase sees awareness and distribution of the product increasing. Some organizations will specialize in innovation and aim consistently to introduce new products to the marketplace. Common strategies include: (i) *skimming*, where a high price level is initially set, in order to capitalize on the product's introduction and optimize financial benefit in the short term; or (ii) *penetration*,

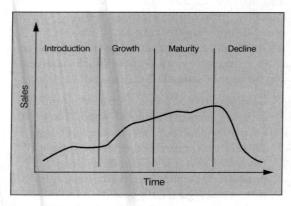

Figure 7.14   Product life cycle

with pricing being used to encourage use and build market share over time.

• *Growth*
This phase sees a rapid increase in sales. Additionally, competition begins to increase and it is likely that prices will be static, or fall, in real terms. The growth stage sees the product being offered to more market segments, increasing distribution and the development of product variations.

• *Maturity*
Here product sales peak and settle at a stable level. This is normally the longest phase of the PLC, with organizations experiencing some reduction in profit level. This is due to the intense competition common in mature markets. As no natural growth exists, market share is keenly contested and marketing expenditure is increased. Marketers may try to expand their potential customer base by encouraging more use or finding new market segments.

• *Decline*
The decline stage can be gradual or rapid. It is possible to turn around declining products and move them back into the mature phase of the cycle. The alternative is replacement. A residual demand will exist, with current users needing parts, services and ongoing support. Often the decline phase offers a choice: reinvesting (turn-around/replace) or a 'harvesting' strategy that involves maximizing financial returns from the product and limiting expenditure.

To fully utilize the PLC, managers need a detailed understanding of the concept. The following points merit consideration:

• *Industry and product line.* The product life cycle concept can also apply to overall industry sales. Clearly, the PLC for individual product lines needs to be considered in relation to this. For example, if an industry is entering the decline phase of its PLC, it may be unwise to launch new product lines. Currently, high technology industries, such as telecommunications, are in the growth phase. However, individual product lines have very short PLCs as they are rapidly

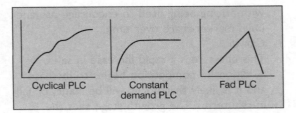

Figure 7.15 Variation in product life cycle shape

replaced by more advanced technology. It is important to understand where the industry is in terms of the overall PLC and how the organization's portfolio of products fits into this pattern.

- *Shape of the PLC.* While the PLC normally conforms to the classic 'S-shaped' curve (see Figure 7.14), it is not always the case. Product life cycles can take different forms. They can display: (i) cyclical/seasonal trends; (ii) constant demand, where a steady level of sales is reached; or (iii) rapid growth and fall, common to fashion or fad products (see Figure 7.15).
- *Volatility.* Sales levels will fluctuate over time. The reality of the PLC is that sales will vary and the smooth graph shown in most textbooks will in fact display considerable volatility. This makes predicting the product's exact position in the life cycle difficult. Does a fall in sales mean that the point of decline has been reached or is it a temporary blip? Only time will tell. Figure 7.14 shows the variation in the curve.
- *Duration of stages.* Some would argue that the length of each PLC phase is closely related to marketing decisions and not simply a natural cycle. Effective marketing should be able to extend and sustain the growth or maturity of a product offering. Equally, ineffective marketing would hasten its decline.

Strategic wear-out

The adage 'nothing lasts for ever' is certainly true of marketing strategy. Care must be taken to avoid strategic wear-out. This occurs when the organization no longer meets customer

needs and the pursued strategy is surpassed by competitors. Davidson (1998) summarizes the causes of strategic wear-out:

1 Changes in customer requirements
2 Changes in distribution systems
3 Innovation by competitors
4 Poor control of company costs
5 Lack of consistent investment
6 Ill-advised changes in successful strategy

Future business requires active steps to ensure that the organization's strategy does not 'wear out' and the role of strategy formulation is to develop/maintain a marketing orientation. This is based on the premise of defining customer need and prospering through customer satisfaction and loyalty. Sound general and financial management should underpin this orientation and the entire corporate focus should relate to the key asset of any business – customers.

Difficult market conditions

Marketing strategy is often linked to a premise of favourable market conditions. For example, strategies tend to work well when we are experiencing incremental growth – the market demand grows annually. However, many industries (arguably the majority of industries) are now experiencing static or declining demand. Such markets are hostile in nature and feature factors such as volatility, over-capacity, price discounting, reduced profit margins and 'downsizing'.

Given these conditions, Aaker (1995) advocates a number of strategic options for declining and/or hostile markets:

- *Generate growth.* Can we revitalize the industry by finding growth? This could be possible via: (i) encouraging existing users to increase usage; (ii) developing new markets for products; and (iii) finding new applications for existing products or technologies/skills. The Ansoff matrix (see Figure 7.10) provides a useful analytical framework for this purpose.

- *Survival.* Organizations can survive by effectively managing costs and clearly signalling their commitment to the industry and its customers. Obviously, there is a need to manage cost structures, with experience effects and economy of scale becoming vital. Organizations may rationalize their product portfolios and focus on larger, more profitable customers. Conversely, perhaps correctly, organizations may actually expand their product range, aiming to cover the maximum number of customers by offering a wide range of price points. We may witness take-overs, mergers and acquisitions, as organizations aim to reduce cost and generate economies of scale. A portfolio approach can be taken, with 'cash cows' supporting operations/products which are currently struggling but are deemed to have long-term potential. A useful strategic option is to reduce industry exit barriers by selectively buying-out elements of competitors' current business – for example, take over their commitment to supplying spare parts and maintain existing products. This 'shake-out' inevitably leaves the industry with fewer but larger competitors.

- *Exit strategy.* If business conditions are particularly unfavourable, prudence may dictate that the organization withdraws from the industry. Such action will involve overcoming exit barriers such as the costs associated with downsizing (redundancy, legal costs of breaking contracts, etc.) and handling commitments to existing customers. Exit strategy can be rapid – withdrawing immediately – or a slow phased withdrawal with activities being gradually run down. Exiting a market may have repercussions for other activities and products, as it affects goodwill and customer confidence.

Summary

Strategy formulation offers alternative methods of achieving objectives. The process has three components: (i) competitive advantage, (ii) industry position and (iii) product/market strategies. The importance of having constant and sustainable strategies cannot be underestimated.

Three generic (fundamental) strategies exist – cost leadership, differentiation and a focused approach. Porter (1980) stresses the importance of adopting one generic source of competitive advantage and thus avoiding the strategic equivalent of being 'stuck in the middle'. These strategies can be expanded upon to generate specific sources of competitive advantage. For example, superior products, perceived advantage or scale of operation are all exploitable competitive advantages. Additionally, it is important to understand the effects of experience curves and value chains within the industry. The primary and secondary activities of a value chain, coupled with experience effects, should support the organization's strategic thrust.

Companies need to examine their position within the market place. They can occupy the role of market leader, challenger, follower or niche player. Marketing strategy needs to be appropriate to the position occupied, relative ambition and resource base. All organizations actively pursue offensive and defensive strategies. The need exists to protect the core business and flanks (weak areas), while taking the fight to competitors via appropriate offensive options (e.g. bypass or guerrilla attacks).

Ansoff's product/market matrix provides a useful summary of product and market strategies. Organizations can consider market penetration, market development, product development or diversification as key marketing initiatives. Much product/market strategy focuses on gaining market share. PIMS analysis has proved highly influential and has linked market share to profitability. While this relationship is often true, market share should not be blindly chased as the relationship is not universally applicable.

Additionally, an awareness of the product life cycle (PLC) is important. The strategist needs to understand the PLC shape and how the marketing mix varies in the introduction, growth, maturity and decline phases.

Organizations need to be watchful and avoid the pitfall of strategic wear-out. Strategies need to address hostile and declining markets.

References

Aaker, D., *Strategic Market Management*, 4th edition, Wiley, 1995

Ansoff, I., 'Strategies for Diversification', *Harvard Business Review*, 25(5), pp. 113–125, 1975

Davidson, H., *Even More Offensive Marketing*, Penguin, 1997

Fulmer, W. and Goodwin, J., 'Differentiation: Being with the Customer', *Business Horizons*, 31(5), 1988

Hooley, G.H., Saunders, J.A. and Piercy, N.F., *Marketing Strategy and Competitive Positioning*, 2nd edition, Prentice Hall, 1998

Kotler, K., Armstrong, G., Saunders, J. and Wong, V., *Principles of Marketing*, 2nd European Edition, Prentice Hall, 1999

Porter, M., *Competitive Strategy: Techniques for Analysing Industries and Competitors*, Free Press, 1980

Further reading

Aaker, D., *Strategic Market Management*, 4th edition, Chapter 14, Wiley, 1995

Wilson, R. and Gilligan. C., *Strategic Marketing Management*, 2nd edition, Chapters 9, 10, Butterworth-Heinnemann, 1998

CHAPTER 8

Targeting, positioning and brand strategy

About this chapter

The subject of targeting and positioning builds on the segmentation techniques that were covered in Chapter 3. This chapter now explores criteria by which the attractiveness of a market segment can be judged. The targeting process is then examined before a discussion on a range of product positioning techniques is undertaken. Central to this discussion is the issue of brand strategy.

Introduction

At a fundamental level marketing strategy is about markets and products. Organizations are primarily making decisions about which markets to operate in and which products/services to offer to those markets. Once those essential decisions have been taken the company then has to decide on what basis it is going to compete in that chosen market. Segmentation is therefore at the heart of strategic marketing decision making. In essence it is a strategic rather than an operational issue and has to be treated as such.

The previous chapters have been concerned with establishing the organization's strategic intent and formulating the organization's overall strategic approach. Initially any organ-ization has to identify how it can, in general, gain competitive advantage. The stage that we will now explore is concerned with creating a specific competitive position. The first crucial step is to decide in which specific market segments to operate. Chapter 3 examined the criteria that can be used to identify discrete segments within a market. Once segments have been identified they then have to be evaluated in order that an organization can decide which particular segments it should serve. Target marketing, or targeting, is the common term for this process.

Once target markets have been chosen an organization then has to decide how it wishes to compete. What differential advantage can it create that will allow the company's product or service to hold a distinctive place in the chosen market segment? This process is normally called positioning. Targeting and positioning are critical processes that require the attention of senior management.

Evaluating market segments

To evaluate different market segments effectively it is necessary to systematically review two issues: the market attractiveness of the competing segments and the organization's comparative ability to address the needs of that segment. There are a number of criteria that can be used to judge the attractiveness of a market segment. These fall under three broad headings: market factors, the nature of competition and the wider environmental factors. At this point it is important to stress that marketers need to recognize that many of the criteria that can be used to evaluate the attractiveness of a market segment are qualitative rather than quantitative in nature. This has implications for the manner in which the process is managed. We will return to this topic later in the chapter. Firstly we need to review the criteria themselves.

Market factors

When assessing market attractiveness the particular features of a market will affect any evaluation:

* *Segment size.* A large segment will generally have greater sales potential. This in itself will make it more attractive but it may also offer the potential of gaining economies of scale because of the larger volumes involved. Large segments with their potentially larger sales can justify the higher investments that may be necessary for organizations wishing to operate within them. However, large segments may not always be the most attractive. Large segments can be more competitive as their very size will attract other companies into them. Smaller organizations may not have the resources to address a large market and therefore may find smaller segments more appropriate for their attention.
* *Segment's rate of growth (measured in terms of real revenue growth after inflation).* Segments that are growing are normally seen as being more attractive than segments where growth has peaked or even begun to decline. Segments in growth are seen as having a longer term potential and therefore justify any investment necessary. Once again, however, these segments are likely to be

more competitive as other companies also recognize their potential.

* *Segment's profitability.* What is the total profitability of the segment? If an organization is already operating in this segment it is not that organization's profitability alone that should be reviewed. In order that all segments are evaluated on a consistent basis it is the profitability of all companies operating in the segment that should be calculated. This will have to be an estimate based on analysing competitors' activities.
* *Customers' price sensitivity.* Segments where consumers have low price sensitivity are likely to be more attractive as higher profit margins can be gained. Consumers will be more concerned about quality and service rather than price alone. Price-sensitive segments are more susceptible to price competition, which leads to lower margins.
* *Stage of industry life cycle.* Entering a segment that is in the early stages of an industry's life cycle offers the advantages of potentially high growth in the future. In the early stages there are also likely to be fewer competitors. However, the early stages of the industry life cycle are characterized by the need for high investment in new plant, promotional activities and securing distribution channels. This occurs at a time when there may only be modest sales revenue. There will be a drain on cash into the new area of business that the company has to be able to fund. Businesses that are more interested in cash generation or profits in the short term may consider mature markets more favourable. These markets are likely to require a more modest level of investment.
* *Predictability.* The potential value of a market will be easier to predict if it is less prone to disturbance and the possibility of discontinuities. In the long term a predictable market is likely to be more viable (see Chapter 4).
* *Pattern of demand.* The attractiveness of a segment will be affected by any seasonal or other cyclical demand patterns it faces. A large percentage of sales in the gift and card

market take place at Christmas in western countries. An organization has to be able to withstand the cash flow implications of this skewed demand. The same problem occurs in other industry sectors such as travel and tourism.

- *Potential for substitution.* In any market there is the potential for new solutions to be developed that will address consumers' needs. An organization should review markets to establish whether new innovations could be used in the segment. Where substitutions are likely an organization may decide not to enter, on the basis that it makes the segment less attractive. If, however, the organization has the ability to deliver that innovatory approach it may make the segment a prime target as the company has the skills to change the nature of competition to their advantage.

Nature of competition in the target market and the underlying industry structure

- *Quality of competition.* Segments that have weak competition are more attractive than segments where there are strong and aggressive competitors. It is not the number of competitors operating but the nature of their competition that is critical in judging an opportunity.
- *Potential to create a differentiated position.* A segment will be more attractive if it contains unsatisfied customer needs that allow the company to create a differentiated product or service and gain a higher margin by charging a premium price. If it is a commodity market then competition is likely to be driven by price and the segment will be less attractive.
- *Likelihood of new entrants.* Segments that currently have limited competition may appear attractive. However, the potential for other companies to enter this market has to be taken into account.
- *Bargaining power of suppliers.* An organization will be in a stronger negotiating position where there is a range of potential suppliers.

If, however, supply is in the hands of a few dominant companies the balance of power in negotiations will lie with the suppliers, making a segment less attractive.

- *Bargaining power of customers.* Customers may be the end customer, but they can also be a customer in the channel of distribution, e.g. a major supermarket. If customers are in a strong negotiating position they will try and push suppliers' prices down, reducing margins. A market segment will be less favourable when a few major customers dominate it or the channels of distribution.
- *Barriers to entry into the market segment.* There may be entry barriers to a segment that will reduce its appeal. These can be in the form of patents, new specialized plant or machinery necessary, or the need for high promotional expenditure. It may be that the overall level of investment necessary to successfully enter an area may be unrealistic for some companies. These same barriers may also put off other potential entrants. Therefore if a company calculates that it can overcome these barriers it may be able to enter a segment where there is little direct competition.
- *Barriers to exiting the market segment.* There may be barriers that make exiting a segment difficult. Expensive facilities may have to be built that can only be used in servicing a particular market segment. Therefore withdrawing from this segment would leave redundant expensive plant. Other barriers could include service agreements to provide spare parts to customers for a number of years into the future, or plant and machinery that would be expensive to decommission. Organizations would have to anticipate the potential barriers to exit when they are initially evaluating a segment's attractiveness.

Environmental factors

- *Social.* Social changes can lead to newly emerging segments that are not currently served by any organization. There can be a significant advantage to companies that are the first to move into these areas. Organizations also need to review the impact that any likely changes in social trends will have on a particular segment.

- *Political.* Changes in the political environment can create new segments in a market. For example, the deregulation of the utilities market in the UK created several new market segments that organizations could address. The political environment may also make certain segments less attractive. Segments that are located in particular geographic areas may be affected by political instability. There may also be regulatory changes that will affect a sector such as pharmaceuticals.
- *Economic.* Economic trends may make segments more or less attractive. The growing affluence of older people in western economies is making them a much more attractive group than twenty years ago.
- *Technological.* Technological changes have to be taken into consideration when evaluating a segment. A judgement will have to be made as to whether new entrants will be able to

enter a segment competing on a different basis by using technology to create innovative ways of delivering a product or service.

- *Environmental.* Consumers' and governments' concerns about environmental issues have become much more important in recent years. Therefore an evaluation of the environmental issues that may affect an organization's ability to service a segment will have to be considered.

Establishing organizational capability

Companies will not be capable of supplying every attractive segment that is identified. Having analysed a segment's market attractiveness it is then necessary to compare the needs of that group of consumers with the organization's capabilities. An organization's

Scale advantages	■ Market share ■ Relative and absolute media weight ■ Leverage over suppliers	■ International presence ■ Sales/distribution service coverage ■ Specialist skills due to scale
Production processes (plant, machinery and information systems)	■ Level of contemporary practice ■ Level of flexibility	■ Economics of scale ■ Capacity utilization ■ Unique items
Customer franchises	■ Brand names ■ Brand franchises ■ Databases	■ Customer relationships ■ Unique products/services ■ Patents
Working capital	■ Quantity ■ Ready access	■ Location ■ Access to credit
Sales/distribution service network	■ Coverage ■ Relationships with external distributors	■ Size ■ Quality
Relationships with other organizations	■ Suppliers ■ Financial institutions ■ Joint ventures	■ Joint exploitation of assets (technology or distribution)
Property	■ Type ■ Location	■ Ability to expand ■ Quality

Figure 8.1 Examples of assets that create a competitive advantage (*Source*: Adapted from Davidson, 1997)

strengths can be judged by analysing its assets and competencies.

The key areas to identify are where the organization is superior to the competition. A full discussion of identifying corporate assets and competencies is undertaken in Chapter 4.

In summary, assets are organizational attributes, tangible or intangible, that can be utilized to gain advantages in the market (see Figure 8.1).

Obviously assets should not be viewed in isolation – it is also important to establish any competencies that give the organization advantages. The value chain is a useful framework to use to identify these areas of unique competence (see Figure 7.7 in Chapter 7). Key competencies may lie in primary activities. These include activities such as inbound logistics (e.g. inventory control), operations (e.g. manufacturing), out-bound logistics (e.g. global delivery), marketing (e.g. brand development) and service (e.g. installation). Other key competencies may lie in support activities such as procurement, technology development, human resource management and the organization's infrastructure (refer to Chapter 7 for more detail).

When trying to identify these competencies, rather than using the generic value chain it may be more effective to develop a value chain that reflects the specific operations that face a particular business sector. The primary activities for an organization offering management consultancy are outlined in Figure 8.2.

An organization's key competencies, once identified, will normally fall into the areas of marketing, selling or operations (see Figure 8.3).

Strategic alignment of assets and competencies (targeting)

The critical stage in the segmentation process is matching the capabilities of the organization to attractive market segment opportunities. At a largely operational level, management analyse organizational assets and

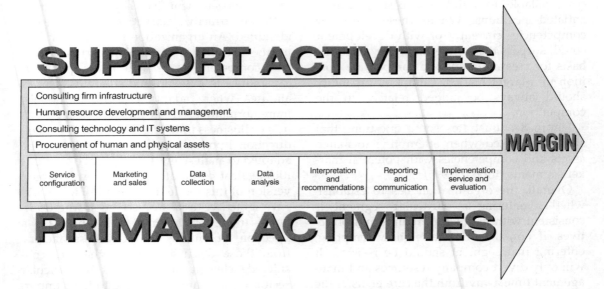

Figure 8.2   The value chain of a management consultancy practice (*Source*: Adapted from Buckley, 1993)

Marketing	■ New product development ■ Business analysis ■ Category management ■ Brand extension ■ Brand equity measurement ■ Unique market research techniques ■ Planning skills ■ Database management	■ Advertising development ■ Customer service ■ Marketing process ■ Spending efficiency ■ Customer relationships ■ Customer targeting ■ Testing design
Selling	■ Supply chain management ■ Account management ■ Relationship development ■ Customer service ■ Building partnerships ■ Motivation and control ■ Planning	■ New account development ■ Merchandising ■ Presentation skills ■ Space management ■ Negotiation ■ Pricing and promotion ■ Trade marketing
Operations	■ Motivation and control ■ Process engineering ■ Industrial relations ■ Inventory control ■ Cost management ■ Productivity improvement ■ Planning ■ Health and safety ■ New facility development ■ Management training and development	■ Speed of response ■ Flexibility ■ Total quality management ■ Purchasing ■ Payment systems ■ Capacity utilization ■ Commercialization of new products or services ■ Method of supplier management ■ Property skills ■ Global operation

Figure 8.3 Examples of competencies that create a competitive advantage (*Source:* Adapted from Davidson, 1997)

competencies to identify the skills and resources available to build low cost or differentiated positions. Where these assets or competencies currently, or with development could, surpass the competition, they form the basis for creating a specific competitive position in a target market. Company capability should always be judged relative to the competition.

Figure 8.4 illustrates some questions that should be asked when attempting to match assets and competencies with potential market segments (Jobber, 1995).

Overall, the organization has to establish whether entering a particular segment is consistent with its long-term aims and objectives. If not, then no matter how tempting, entering that segment should be resisted. It will only divert company resources and management time away from the core goals of the enterprise.

Once the key areas of a company's capabilities have been identified they can be aligned with the attractive market segments already identified. An organization should enter segments that allow it to exploit current assets and competencies, or will allow potential capabilities to develop into strengths. This is an area where adapting portfolio models, more normally used to evaluate current products or business units, can be useful. The Shell directional policy matrix, for instance, can be adapted to analyse market segment opportunities against corporate strengths. An adapted version of this model is shown in Figure 8.5.

Weighted criteria are used as in the traditional usage of the model. In this case a selection of market attractiveness factors, from those discussed earlier, that are considered relevant in evaluating a particular sector are weighted according to their importance as judged by the organization's

Marketing assets
Does the market segment allow a company to take advantage of its current marketing strengths? Successful situations are more likely to occur where a company's current brand identity, or method of distribution, is consistent with those required to enter the new target market.

Cost advantages
Does the market segment allow the company to take advantage of its cost base? Entering a price sensitive segment would be consistent with the capabilities of an organization that has a low cost base.

Technological strengths
Where the organization has access to superior technology is its use compatible with the market segment, and will it allow the company to gain any advantage?

Managerial capabilities and commitment
Does the company have the technical and managerial skills necessary to successfully enter a market segment?

Figure 8.4 Examples of assets and competencies matching with potential market segments

management. The same exercise is then undertaken of selecting a range of assets and competencies deemed relevant to this particular sector. These are again weighted. Choosing factors in relation to the specific area being considered ensures that the model is custom-made to the particular situation and organization under review.

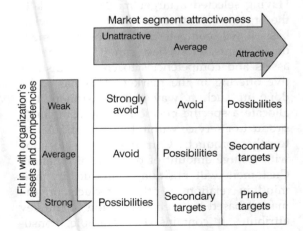

Figure 8.5 Adapted Shell directional policy matrix applied to target market selection (*Source*: Shell, 1975)

Every potential market segment is then evaluated on a rating scale, normally of 1 to 10 (1 = poor, 10 = excellent), on each of the criteria. The overall position of the segment on each axis is established by multiplying the ratings by the weighting given to each factor (see Chapter 4 for full details). The result of such an exercise for an imaginary situation and organization is shown in Figure 8.6.

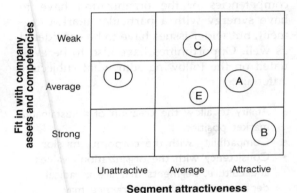

Figure 8.6 Evaluating market segments for an imaginary organization/situation

The most attractive segment is B as it lies in the box that is attractive on the horizontal axis representing segment attractiveness and has a strong fit with the company's assets and competencies as represented on the vertical axis. This segment should be a priority for the company. Segment A is an attractive market but has only an average fit with the organization's assets and competencies. This may have potential and would be a higher priority for the organization than segment E. Segment E has medium attractiveness and medium fit with the organization's and should be selectively managed. The model suggests that targeting segments C and D is likely to be a poor investment.

This example illustrates how an adapted portfolio model can act as a screening device for identifying market segments that should be targeted.

The strategic nature of making target segment choices

However, as has already been stated, segmentation is a strategic process where qualitative and creative judgements have to be taken. Opportunities have to be evaluated on their strategic fit. Not only do the assets and competencies of the organization have to have synergy with a particular market segment, but wider issues have to be considered as well. Opportunities have also to be evaluated on the following somewhat subjective criteria:

• Ability to allow the creation of a sustainable market position.
• Compatibility with the corporate mission.
• Consistency with the organization's values and culture. Segments that are a radical departure from current practice may challenge the prevailing values in the organization and the established status quo. The new segment may challenge the current power structure within the organization, which will create influential barriers to implementation.
• Ability to provide a focal point for action and future development in the organization.
• Ability to facilitate an innovative approach to market entry.
• Ability of the current organizational structure to service the target market. Does this opportunity lie between two areas of responsibility in the current organizational structure? This may lead to the opportunity never being seriously addressed.
• Compatibility with current internal information flows and reporting lines. Difficulties will arise where a segment does not sit easily with the current data collection or distribution systems. Segments in an innovative area may cause managers problems in terms of how to allocate

targets and monitor progress. If this is linked to the problem already discussed under organizational structure, it may complicate issues such as areas of responsibility and reporting lines even further.

These factors of compatibility with the internal practices of an organization are likely to prove critical to the successful implementation of a new segmentation strategy. The newly entered segment has to have clear departmental ownership. Reporting lines and information flows have to be able to monitor its progress. In short, individuals within the organization have to wholeheartedly embrace the development of the new segment or failure will follow no matter how attractive the segment or how well the organization's overt assets and competencies might fit.

A successful selection process will have identified a market segment or segments that are in alignment with the company's assets and competencies and is also compatible with the wider organizational issues.

Positioning

Having selected a target market or markets the organization then has to decide on what basis it will compete in the chosen segment or segments. How best can it combine its assets and competencies to create a distinctive offering in the market? This has to be done in such a way that consumers can allocate a specific position to the company's product or service within the market, relative to other products. Consumers have to cope with a huge amount of product information. Customers will position a product in their mind in relation to other products on the market based on their perception of the key attributes it contains. For example, consumers will see the key attributes of Volvo as safety and durability. BMW's main attributes are based on performance, hence the 'The Ultimate Driving Machine' advertising slogan. When consumers consider the car market these two companies' products will be positioned relative to each other based on these perceptions. Companies can attempt to associate various qualities to their product as a way to help shape consumers' perceptions of their position in the market. A brand can be positioned using a range of associations such as (Kotler, et al., 1996):

- *Product attributes*. Heinz positions its products on the attributes of no artificial colouring, flavouring or preservatives.
- *Product benefits*. Volvo positions itself using the product benefits of safety and durability.
- *Usage occasions*. The convenience store SPAR eight-till-late shops are positioned on the usage occasion. Customers use the shops when they need to shop out of normal hours or near to their home. Kit Kat ('Have a Break, Have a Kit Kat') links the brand to tea and coffee breaks in the UK market.
- *Users*. Ecocover cleaning products are positioned as environmentally friendly products for the green customer.
- *Activities*. Lucozade is positioned as an isotonic drink for sporting activities.
- *Personality*. Harley Davidson motorbikes are positioned as a macho product with a free spirit.
- *Origin*. Audi clearly illustrates its German origins in the UK market by the use of the 'Vorsprung durch technik' slogan. The hope is that the product will be linked to the German reputation for quality engineering.
- *Competitors*. Pepsi-Cola is positioned as the choice of the next generation reflecting the fact that in blind tasting tests younger people preferred Pepsi over competitors' offerings.
- *Product class*. Kellogg's Nutrigrain bars are positioned as 'morning bars', a substitute for the traditional breakfast.
- *Symbol*. Esso petrol has used the symbol of the tiger to position itself in the market.

These are the various ingredients that can be used by an organization endeavouring to influence consumers' perceptions of the product offering. Companies have to decide which of these they can use and, more importantly, how they wish to position their product in the market *vis-à-vis* the competing options.

Four factors are of critical importance for successful positioning (Jobber, 1995):

- *Credence*. The attributes used to position the product have to be perceived to be credible by the target customers. It would be very difficult for a nuclear power generator to position itself as environmentally friendly.
- *Competitiveness*. The product should offer the consumer benefits which competitors are not supplying. Clairol launched a new shampoo Herbal Essences in the USA in 1995 which emphasized the brand's wholesome ingredients. By 1997 this was the fastest growing brand on the market and ranked number two behind Pantene.
- *Consistency*. A consistent message over time is invaluable in helping to establish a position against all the other products and services fighting for a share of the market. An organization that changes its positioning on a regular basis causes confusion in the consumer's mind. This will mean they have an unclear perception of exactly what are the key characteristics of the product.
- *Clarity*. The positioning statement an organization chooses has to create a clearly differentiated position for the product in the minds of the target market for example. A distinct message such as 'Bread wi' Nowt Taken Out' underlines the wholemeal old world nature of Allison's bread.

Perceptual mapping

Mapping consumer perceptions can allow an organization to see where it is currently

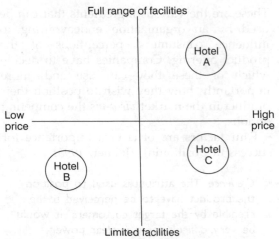

Figure 8.7 A perceptual map of various hotels

placed compared with competitors' offerings. A simple perceptual map is based upon two axes representing key attributes in a particular market. These attributes are identified through market research and are determined by consumers' perceptions of the important factors in the market. This could for example be price and quality, or style and performance, or a range of other issues. Products/companies, or more particularly brands, can then be placed according to their position on these attributes (see Figure 8.7).

In the case of Figure 8.7, in the hotel market the key attributes are deemed to be the price and the facilities. Hotel A on this map is seen as expensive but with a full range of facilities. Hotel B is perceived to be inexpensive but with limited facilities. Both of these are reasonably consistent offerings. Hotel C, however, is seen as expensive but with intermediate level of facilities. This position does not offer any unique aspects. There may of course be more than two key attributes in a market. Figure 8.7 does not map out quality – Hotel C may be seen as having high service quality, for instance. To gain a fuller picture, obviously more than one positioning map can be developed. There are also more sophisticated three-

dimensional mapping techniques available for marketers to use.

Through the use of perceptual maps marketers can establish the current situation in a particular market. There will then be a number of alternatives from which to choose.

Positioning alternatives

In a seminal work, Ries and Trout (1981) claim that when considering positioning there are three principal alternatives open to an organization:

- An organization can build on a current position to create a distinctive perception of the brand by consumers. Avis famously uses the 'We Try Harder' slogan to make a virtue out of being number two in the market.
- Having established the attributes that are most important to the consumer, the organization can see if there are any unoccupied positions that are desirable in consumers' minds and therefore viable opportunities. IDV Ltd used this approach when it launched Croft Original Sherry. The key product attributes in the sherry market from a consumer's perspective were the colour and the taste of the product. Consumers favoured a sweet taste; they also perceived that a light coloured sherry was more sophisticated than the traditional, darker coloured sherries (see Figure 8.8). There was at the time no sherry that had a light colour and a sweet taste and yet this combination was highly desirable to consumers. Croft Original entered the market with this unique positioning and now is the best selling sherry brand in the UK market.
- Due to changes in consumer behaviour, or where perhaps there has been a failure of the original positioning, a third alternative can be considered which is to reposition the brand. Campari has recently been

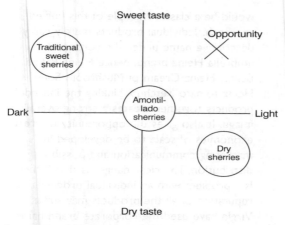

Figure 8.8 Perceptual map of the sherry market

relaunched in an effort to shake off its 1970s image as endorsed by Lorraine Chase. The new repositioning has a more macho feel, and even includes a notorious London underworld character 'Mad' Frankie Fraser in the advert. Both the soft drink Tango and the snack Pot Noodle have successfully been repositioned in recent years. However, repositioning can be difficult to achieve and there are several examples of brands that have been less successful at moving their position. Babycham abandoned the famous deer symbol and the trademark green bottle for a more masculine image in 1993. By May 1997 it had revived both the bottle and the Babycham deer and went back to its original more female orientated positioning.

There are alternative views on the correct approach to successful product/brand positioning. One view is that an organization should identify one unique selling proposition (USP) for a product and concentrate purely on that aspect. The whole focus of this approach is to be seen as the brand leader on that key attribute. For example, Gortex fabric is seen as the leading fabric for breathable, waterproof, lightweight clothing material. The most effective USPs are based on quality, service, price, value or advanced technology (Ries and Trout, 1981).

An alternative approach to stressing a USP, based on a functional aspect of the product, is to concentrate on an emotional selling proposition (ESP). The product can be distanced from functionally similar rivals by appealing to unique emotional associations. An example of this is Alfa Romeo's positioning on the heritage and image of the traditional Italian sports car.

Both these approaches stress one key aspect of the product; however, there is a view that more than one factor can be used to position a product. As has been mentioned earlier, Volvo is positioned on safety and the compatible factor of durability. Whichever approach is taken, there are a number of positioning mistakes that can be made by an organization:

- *Underpositioning.* In this situation consumers have only a very limited perception of the brand and are unaware of any distinguishing features.
- *Overpositioning.* Consumers have a perception that the brand is only active in a very focused area, when in fact the brand covers a much broader product range.
- *Confused.* Consumers have an unclear view of how the brand relates to competitive offerings.

Positioning is concerned with establishing an organization's product in the mind of a customer, in a position relative to other products in the market. Inevitably, therefore, making decisions about branding strategy will be a crucial aspect of this process.

Creating brand equity

The overall aim of branding decisions is to create an identity for the product or service that is distinctive and also in line with the targeting and positioning decisions already taken. Organizations should strive to produce a brand equity that delivers value to the

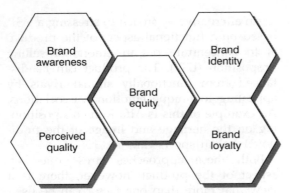

Figure 8.9 The constituents of brand equity (*Source:* Aaker, 1995)

consumer. This will result in either the customer showing greater brand loyalty or being willing to pay a premium price for the product. Brand equity according to Aaker is 'a set of assets and liabilities linked to a brand's name and symbol that add to or subtract from the value provided by a product or service to a firm and/or that firm's customers' (Aaker, 1991).

Brands that contain high equity have strong name awareness, strong associations attached to the brand, a perception of quality and have high levels of brand loyalty (see Figure 8.9). To create a brand that exhibits these characteristics takes time and investment. A successful brand will, however, become a valuable asset in its own right to an organization.

Brand strategy

At a strategic level an organization has to decide its policy for branding across all its products and services. Branding decisions for any new products can then be taken within this framework. There are several options open to an organization considering an overall brand strategy:

- *Corporate brand*
  Organizations following this approach use one corporate name across all its products. Heinz would be a classic example of this unified approach. Individual products merely carry a descriptive name under the corporate umbrella Heinz brand, hence Heinz Baked Beans, Heinz Cream of Mushroom Soup, Heinz Tomato Ketchup. Linking the individual products together creates a strong overall image. It also gives the opportunity to create economies of scale to be developed in marketing communication and possibly distribution. The clear danger is that if there is a problem with an individual product the reputation of all the products may suffer. Virgin have used the corporate brand name across their entire product portfolio. Their high-profile problems with the Virgin rail franchise in the UK may over time have a negative impact across their other operations. The fact that this does not yet appear to have happened is a testament to the strength of the core brand name.
- *Multi-brand*
  Multi-branding or discrete branding is the complete opposite of the corporate branding approach. With multi-branding each product is given its own unique brand name. The aim is to build completely separate brand identities. This is appropriate if the organization is competing in a number of different segments and the consumers' perceptions of a product's position in one segment may adversely affect the consumers' perceptions of another product. A classic example of this approach would be Procter & Gamble, who produce a range of washing powders such as Daz, Ariel and Bold aimed at discrete sectors of the market.
- *Company and individual brand (endorsed approach)*
  Unilever used to take a multi-brand approach with their washing powders but have been moving closer to the strategy of linking a company name to an individual brand name. Their products now have Lever Bros as a high profile endorsement on the individual brands such as Persil, Radion and Surf. This can be used in different ways. Endorsing a product with the corporate

name gives a new product credibility whilst at the same time allowing the new brand some degree of freedom. A fixed endorsed approach entails the corporate brand name being given a consistent profile against each individual product's brand name in the range. For example, all Kellogg's products give individual product brand names the prominent position on the pack, while the same secondary weighting is given to the company brand name. (*Note:* this is different to Heinz where the prominence of the corporate brand is paramount.) Cadbury's take a more flexible approach to the corporate endorsement – it is more or less prominent depending on how independent they choose to make the brand.

- *Range brand*
  Some organizations use different brand names for different ranges of product – in effect creating a family of products. Ford has done this to an extent using Ford for its mass-market car range and Jaguar for the up-market executive car range. Volvo, Ford's latest acquisition, has its own distinct brand values that appeal to a particular market segment and therefore will become another brand family for the Ford group.

When companies develop new products the branding decision will be taken according to the general branding strategy of the organization. Multi-brand orientated companies will tend to always create a new brand for the new product. For other companies the decision will depend on the nature of the target market. If it is very different from the organization's current markets they may decide to introduce a new brand. Toyota did this when they entered the up-market executive car market, introducing the Lexus brand. This is a rational approach where the target market is large enough and has the potential profitability to justify investing in creating a new brand. Companies may, however, choose to use a current brand name and opt for a brand extension or brand stretching policy:

- *Brand extension*
  There are occasions where an organization will try to extend the use of a brand name to new products in the same broad market. Brands that carry high brand equity are candidates for brand extension as they have the ability to increase the attractiveness of the new products. The Pretty Polly hosiery brand has been extended into the wider but related lingerie market (Tucker, 1998). The Pretty Polly brand is seen as fashionable, young, exiting and innovative – all qualities Sarah Lee, its holding company, feels can be extended to other markets.
- *Brand stretching*
  Brand stretching takes place when an organization stretches a brand into new unrelated markets. Virgin is an obvious example of this, moving from the record industry to airlines, railways, financial services and cola drinks. Marks and Spencer and Tesco have both moved from mainstream retailing into financial services. Both are examples of brand stretching. This policy is more likely to be successful where the original brand values are compatible with the aspirations of the new target group.

Summary

Targeting aims to align an organization's assets and competencies to attractive market segments. Once these market segments have been identified an organization has to decide how it will position its product in the market, relative to the competition. One key aspect of this positioning process is branding.

An organization's assets and competencies can be used to create new products and services, to unlock the potential in market segments that are not currently served, either by the company in question, or by companies in general. Product development and innovation are critical areas that have to be considered in any strategic plan and will be addressed in Chapter 9.

References

Aaker, D., *Managing Brand Equity*, The Free Press, 1991

Aaker, D., *Strategic Market Management*, 4th edition, Wiley, 1995

Buckley, A., *The Essence of Services Marketing*, Prentice Hall, 1993

Davidson, H., *Even More Offensive Marketing*, Penguin, 1997

Jobber D., *Principles and Practice of Marketing*, McGraw Hill, 1995

Kotler, P., Armstrong, G., Saunders, J. and Wong, V., *Principles of Marketing: The European Edition*, Prentice Hall, 1996

Ries, A. and Trout, J., *Positioning: The battle for your mind*, McGraw-Hill, 1981

Shell Chemical Company, *The Directional Policy Matrix: A New Aid to Corporate Planning*, Shell, 1975

Tucker, J.. 'Pretty Polly Set for Lingerie Push', *Marketing*, 23 April 1998

Further reading

Davidson, H., *Even More Offensive Marketing*, Chapters 9 and 10, Penguin, 1997

Doyle, P., *Marketing Management and Strategy*, Chapter 6, Prentice Hall, 1994

CHAPTER 9

Product development and innovation

About this chapter

Product development is a strategic necessity. In terms of product development, organizations can modify, imitate or innovate. A rigorous NPD process is essential to avoid marketing failures. Additionally, managers must address the concept of innovation across the entire organization.

The strategic agenda

It is essential that all organizations develop products. Product development and innovation are the 'life blood' of any business. By definition, development and innovation are strategic activities that shape the future. The creation of an acceptable product offering involves many strategic decisions. For example, building on core competencies, matching resources to market opportunity and co-ordinating activities across functional boundaries are all accepted strategic activities which normally determine the success or failure of our products. Given that many organizations now face difficult commercial conditions – static/declining demand and intense competition – innovation and product development should top the agenda of today's (and tomor-

row's) successful organizations. In essence, all organizations must evolve or they will perish. Product development and innovation allow organizations to evolve.

It is important to define 'product' in its broadest sense. What counts is the total product offering – this provides benefits to the customer. Hence, the process of product development involves not only innovation of the core product, but also innovation in areas such as support services and production processes. Business cannot afford to view innovation in the narrow sense of technical/scientific development, but rather as a management process. Such a process focuses creative effort with the intention of developing products perceived as delivering superior benefits. Innovative projects require the right balance of creative, technical and managerial skills. Blending these factors together fosters an organizational culture that embraces innovation, product development and strategic success.

The nature of products and product development

As stated above, products must be considered in terms of the total product offering. Remember, the term 'product' covers goods, services, ideas and information. In reality, most products are combinations of these items. Service-based products tend to be intangible in nature. Above all, products must meet needs and deliver benefits to the user.

Kotler *et al.* (1999) defines a product as having three levels. Firstly, a *core product* defines the fundamental need being meet. Fundamental needs are generic in nature (e.g. transportation, data storage or self-esteem). Secondly, the *actual product* is the specific offering aimed at meeting a core need. This includes attributes such as styling, branding, performance features and packaging. Finally comes the *augmented product*, which enhances the actual product by offering additional services and benefits, making the product a more attractive proposition to the consumer. Examples include factors such as after-sales support, maintenance and affordable finance.

It is important to consider product development at each of the above levels. Organizations must fully understand their core product(s) – what need does it meet? Then they must develop actual and augmented product offerings that are attractive to specific customer groups. As an illustration, consider Orange plc:

Core	Actual	Augmented
Communications	Mobile phone network	Voice mail
	Hand-set	Insurance against loss
	Brand image	

One school of thought suggests that in certain markets, advances in quality management, manufacturing systems and information technology will tend to generate competitive products indistinguishable from each other. Therefore, the only way to differentiate products is at an augmented level – who offers the best service and support? Indeed, the augmentation may become such a vital part of the product offering that it is absorbed into the actual product. It becomes an integral, essential part of the product. For example when buying a new car, the warranty package is an integral part of the product offering.

Fundamentally, a product delivers a set of benefits to a customer, in order to meet a need. Organizations must strive to fully understand this process and be certain their product offering best matches not only need but also customer expectation.

Product development strategy

There is much debate relating to product development strategies. For example, how is the term 'new product' defined? The reality is that few products are 'new' in the sense of being innovative, unique or novel. Most 'new' products are updates and revamps of existing goods and services. Jain (1997) views new product strategy in terms of three categories (see Figure 9.1):

- *Product improvement and modification.* Unless products are to be replaced by completely new entities, they must be upgraded and enhanced as a matter of necessity. The process can have two possible aims: (i) maintaining the competitive position in an existing market; and/or (ii) adapting the product in order to appeal to other market segments. Major changes may result in the need to reposition a product offering within a given market. Conversely, organizations may only make minor changes aimed at ensuring the products remain up-to-date.

■ Product improvement and modification

■ Product imitation

■ Product innovation

Figure 9.1   Product development strategy

- *Product imitation.* This strategy involves capitalizing on the initiatives of others and suits organizations that are risk averse and/or have limited funds to invest. Clearly, there are potential ethical and legal problems with this option and organizations must define the line between imitation and copying. The strategy is most effective when the 'new' version of the product brings some additional dimension of added-value.
- *Product innovation.* This involves bringing new and novel ideas to the market place. Product innovation may be aimed at: (i) replacing existing products with new approaches and items which enhance customer satisfaction; or (ii) providing diversification in order to target opportunities in new markets. Clearly, organizations should expect a correlation between risk and diversification.

Booz *et al.* (1982) classified 'new' products using the categories shown in Table 9.1. Again this demonstrates that truly original, innovative products represent only a small proportion of total development.

New product development process

Regardless of whether we are developing a 'new to world' product, a new product line or simply aiming to reduce cost, we need a new product development (NPD) process. All organizations require some mechanism, or process, which enables ideas to be evaluated and, when appropriate, translated into commercial products. Such a process provides a vital ingredient in the fight for commercial success. Indeed, Davidson (1997) cites lack of rigorous process as a factor commonly contributing to the failure of new products.

NPD processes take many shapes and forms. It is vital that any process is driven by an overall NPD strategy, otherwise development activities will lack co-ordination and focus. This concept is expanded upon later in the chapter.

Stages commonly found in a NPD process include:

Table 9.1 Type of 'new' product

Type of product development	Nature
1 New to world	Often scientific or technical development high risk/return activities which can revolutionize or create markets
2 New product lines or line additions	Such products can be: (i) new to the provider as opposed to the market place; or (ii) be additions to the product ranges already on offer
3 Product revision	Replacements and upgrades of existing products. This category is likely to cover the largest single number of new product developments. Additionally, this may cover changes aimed at generating *cost reductions* – no perceived change in performance but more economic product/provision of the product
4 Reposition	Aiming to diversify away from existing markets by uncovering new applications, uses or market segments for current products

1 *Idea generation*
New product ideas have to come from somewhere. This may be via a formalized technical research and development process or from systems that scan the business environment, enabling the organization to identify trends, customer requests and competitors' intentions. Market research certainly has a role to play in this process. Equally, management needs to encourage staff to suggest product development ideas and have systems to enable and reward such activity.

2 *Idea evaluation*
Next, ideas must be screened in order to establish what is feasible and where opportunities exist. Ideally, ideas are screened against strategic objectives by demonstrating how they are likely to contribute to such objectives. It is important to establish criteria against which all ideas are evaluated. This provides a consistent approach to decision making and provides the safeguard of rigorous testing. Evaluation is likely to include marketing and operational/production criteria.

3 *Concept development*
Having passed through a screening process, ideas are developed into product concepts. This stage involves initial technical and marketing evaluations. Having established the technical/operational feasibility and resource requirements, marketing (often using secondary data – general industry trends, key competitor profiles, etc.) evaluates the potential for the product. A marketing strategy needs to be outlined – target segment(s), product positioning and marketing goals such as market share.

4 *Business evaluation*
The aim is to evaluate commercial potential and investment requirements. Sales volume, revenue and cost projections will establish the viability of the project. Clearly, this is more difficult when dealing with diversification or highly innovative products. Often organizations have predetermined returns on investment, which projects must demonstrate they will meet.

5 *Product development*
This stage turns the concept into an actual product. The stage tends to be dominated by technical and operational development. There is a need to examine both the development of the product (styling, features, performance, branding, etc.) and the means of its production/delivery (manufacturing, administration, after-sales support, etc.). The stage may see the building of a prototype and the use of market research to establish the final product offering. To gauge marketplace reaction, products may be test marketed with groups of actual consumers.

6 *Product launch*
Using the knowledge and targets generated in the previous processes, a final plan is developed. This includes all the other elements of the marketing mix. For example, a final price is set, a promotion campaign is designed and the build-up of stock begins within the distribution channels. It is vital that the product has the correct marketing, operational and logistical support to make it a success. Competitor and customer reaction should be monitored and the product offering 'fine-tuned' if required. Where resources are limited, or where high degrees of uncertainty exist, the product may be introduced using a 'roll-out' strategy. This entails a phased launch, gradually building market coverage.

Given the importance of new product development, managers must endeavour to make the process as rigorous and objective as possible. Only in this way can organizations maximize the likelihood of success and minimize the chances of progressing with poor ideas. However, there is a dilemma: while a robust development process has its advantages, there is increasing commercial pressure to do things quickly. This may result in 'corners being cut' and ultimately mistakes being made in the new product development process. So, the reality of business life means management has to develop the right products in an increasingly shorter time-frame. How can we enable this? Adhering to the following principles should optimize the entire process:

1 *Multi-functional teams*
There is much evidence to suggest that projects go more smoothly when a multi-functional team is in control. By taking people from different functional backgrounds (e.g. production, marketing, design and finance) a balanced viewpoint is obtained. For example, problems relating to the manufacture/provision of the product are addressed early in the project. Additionally, the multi-functional approach promotes 'ownership' of the project and staff can be more committed and motivated.

2 *Completeness and evaluation*
NPD can be viewed as a six-stage process (see above). The simple process of completing all these steps can increase the likelihood of product success. Undertaking each stage in a systematic manner and building an ongoing evaluation into the process may not guarantee success, but it will reduce the chances of failure. So-called 'evaluation gates' at the end of each stage can review the potential product and whether the NPD process has been properly conducted.

3 *Customer involvement*
Often market research is used to evaluate possible ideas and to review products after launch. It may be advisable to integrate the 'voice of the customer' into the entire project. This is possible by having an ongoing process of market research that takes place during each development stage or by having customer representation on the multi-functional team.

4 *Parallel processing*
Traditionally, NPD has been viewed as a sequential process – activities follow each other in sequence. It may be possible to conduct some activities concurrently, in other words undertaking a process of parallel development. Encouraging functional areas, departments and individuals to work more closely has a number of advantages. Firstly, this overlapping, parallel approach reduces overall development time. Secondly, as activities are being undertaken at the same time, they can share information and a more interactive approach can be taken. This can improve the overall quality of the process. To illustrate, a technical and marketing feasibility assessment could be conducted as one process, generating a more vigorous product/market specification.

5 *Strategic direction*
NPD requires a strategic focus and clear links must be established between overall corporate strategy and the NPD process. As previously stated, strategic objectives can be used as a template against which new product ideas are evaluated.

Additionally, the process of strategic analysis and audit should provide valuable information (external and internal) relating to the development of product offerings. The aim is to integrate into one coherent framework: (i) technical development – improving the technical capability of the product; (ii) process development – improving the provision/production of products and services; and (iii) marketing strategy (see Figure 9.2).

6 *Knowledge management*
This concept is closely related to strategic direction. Increasingly, organizations are developing knowledge management strategies. Mobilizing and managing the knowledge base of the organization is rapidly becoming a

Figure 9.2   Strategic direction of NPD

management priority. The collective experience and accumulated learning within the organization can be vital to successful NPD. The organization needs to facilitate the development of, and access to, information. Enabling technologies and methods include benchmarking, brainstorming, computer networks, 'groupware' – software products enabling work and knowledge to be shared (e.g. Lotus Notes) – and data warehousing. O'Connor and Galvin (1997) define data warehousing as constructing a high-level database of all operating and customer data, and making such a database available to support decision making.

Why do products fail?

It is reasonable to suggest that an understanding of the pitfalls of product development can help us avoid them. When addressing this question, managers need to consider the nature and background to NPD, as some types of development activity are inherently more risky than others. Additionally, the organization's attitude to risk and investment has a bearing on the situation.

Common reasons for failure can be summarized as follows:

- *Under-investment*, where the project is short of funds and lacks the investment required to establish/sustain it in the marketplace.
- The product fails to deliver any *customer benefit*. This can happen with technical or scientific advance. While the technology may be innovative, it must be perceived as innovative by the marketplace, otherwise it is unlikely to be adopted. Additionally, the product must perform to the required performance parameters. Remember, quality is defined as 'fit for purpose'. There needs to be a clear definition of the market segment and how the product offering is positioned.
- *Forecasting errors*. It was once said: '. . . forecasting is difficult, especially if you're

forecasting the future'. This is certainly true! Often, forecasting errors relate to over-optimistic forecasts of demand and/or under-estimates of costs. Managers need to examine the assumptions supporting forecasts as well as the forecasting techniques used. Also, timescales for planned development have to be realistic.
- *Internal politics*, trade-offs and compromise can result in problems. The project may lack the support and commitment of staff and vested interests may conspire against its success. Equally, trade-offs, and other such factors, may result in the project drifting from its original target, as internal conflict distracts management. Internal conflict has been the graveyard of many good product ideas.
- *Industry response* is vital. For example, success may be completely dependent on retailers stocking products or on the response of competitors – what happens if they drastically cut price? Such factors are less controllable, but good quality market research and competitor intelligence can lessen the negative effects.

While some factors are unpredictable, and projects are a 'hostage to fortune', most issues are simply a matter of management and marketing. Applying a sound structured approach to NPD and having effective project management should move the odds in your favour. Products need a product champion – a leader/manager who gets things done. In turn, this leader needs the support of the organization.

Managing innovation

The term 'innovation' means different things to different people, with common definitions relating to scientific advance and the development of high-technology products. However, the reality is that innovation is a far broader activity. Essentially, innovation is about changing established products, processes and practices. Innovation must blend creativity, clear thinking and the ability to get things done into one process. Ultimately, the market-place will judge innovation. New ideas need support, commitment and resources if they are to be effectively implemented.

Organizations cannot remain focused on the past. The static organization that believes 'the old ways are the best' will flounder. Innovation means change. Such changes are not normally single events, but are complex combinations of actions and functional activity. Note that innovation and invention are not one and the same, as innovation is concerned with the commercial application of ideas.

Senior management should address the issue of innovation and create a culture and infrastructure to support the process. After all, organizations that continue to learn and effectively translate this learning into product offerings are the ones who will prosper.

Innovation creates the environment for successful product development. Product improvement and modification, product imitation and product innovation (where the product is truly new or novel – see Figure 9.1) all stem from the overall process of innovation.

Having established the importance of innovation, how do organizations facilitate the process? Figure 9.3 summarizes common enablers. *Teamwork* is vital, as successful innovation requires a combination of skills and functional activity (e.g. marketing, research and design). Innovation tends to flourish where frequent contact and good working relationships exist among groups. The *exchange of information* and ideas should be encouraged, as this not only facilitates innovation but also enhances teamwork. Information flow and effective communication contribute greatly to creativity. However, it is important to recognize that more information is not necessarily better – information overload should be avoided. There is a need to be focused on the external environment. *External inputs* relating to market trends, customer perception, technological development and competitor activities are vital inputs into the

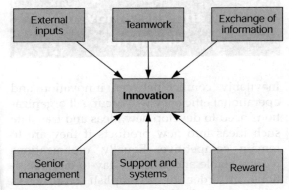

Figure 9.3 Generating innovation

overall process. The organization must be receptive to new ideas/change and have the capacity to evaluate such concepts. Clearly, *senior management* has a role to play in the process. They need to develop appropriate strategies and act as facilitators to the process. This normally involves taking calculated risks and allocating required resources (see the following section). Consequently, senior managers need to be committed to long-term growth as opposed to short-term profit. If it is to work properly, innovation requires the correct systems and support. Frequently, this relates to organizational culture. Creating the right organizational climate is important, as the wish is to challenge existing practice and generate creativity. *Systems*, such as communications networks, computer-aided design and project management structures, need to be in place.

The organization must foster and exploit innovation. Group and individual motivation are important. *Reward* and recognition for innovation helps generate ideas and foster a collaborative atmosphere. Additionally, the role of the individual must not be neglected in the discussion of innovation. While the organization can facilitate and foster innovation, individuals have to take ownership. People need to have the courage, skill and motivation to make things better. Only this type of commitment will see the process to completion.

Risk and the innovation dilemma

Inevitably, conflict between innovation and operational efficiency will occur. All organizations need to develop new ideas and translate such ideas into new products if they are to remain competitive. Equally, organizations require stable and efficient day-to-day operations in order to accomplish basic tasks effectively. Indeed, many views of management, and management techniques, tend to focus on eliminating waste, reducing cost and optimizing the use of assets. Figure 9.4 illustrates the principle.

So, should management focus resources on generating innovation or ensuring optimal efficiency? This is a dilemma to which there is no easy answer. The answer may be a hybrid solution attempting to balance innovation with operational effectiveness. A key maxim is that innovation should be fostered, but never allowed to disrupt activities. Clearly, the nature of the industry and/or product life cycle is important. So-called 'sun-rise' industries which are research and design led (e.g. telecommunication, biotechnology) will have a different innovation profile from more mature industries, or service sector industries. Such industries tend to be affected more by process and customer service based innovations.

Innovation and operational effectiveness cannot be seen as mutually exclusive. They are interlinked, with one supporting the other. Given these factors, innovation should lead to

operational effectiveness – however this is defined. Remember, innovation is invention plus commercial exploitation, and there is little point in pursuing innovations that do not lead to operational effectiveness. The question is not should we innovate, but rather how we support and resource the process, given other often more immediate demands.

Assuming organizations have the right factors in place (as outlined in the previous section) it can be argued that innovation will eventually pay for itself several times over. However, in order to stimulate the process, forward-looking organizations allocate funds to such activities. A number of methods are commonly used for this purpose:

- Gap analysis can be used to establish the difference between desired and projected future revenue requirements. Management then examines how much of the 'gap' can be closed by innovation. This provides an 'innovation target'. Resources can then be allocated to the new product development areas and innovations most likely to close this gap.
- An alternative is to allocate a percentage of sales revenue to an 'innovation fund' and request internal bids for this money. These bids are then evaluated and screened, with funding being given to the strongest.
- Additionally, the organization can seek collaborative ventures, partnerships and external funding (e.g. government grants, venture capital).

Organizations, and individuals, need to balance the risk associated in innovation with the potential return. Higher risk projects invariably need to demonstrate greater potential returns. Pearson developed the concept of an uncertainty map (Henry and Walker, 1991), which helps in the understanding of the concept of risk and uncertainty in innovative projects. Pearson identifies two key variables. Firstly, uncertainty about the endpoint – what is the project likely to result in? Secondly, uncertainty about process or approach – how

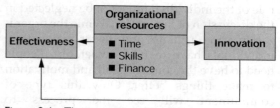

Figure 9.4   The innovation dilemma

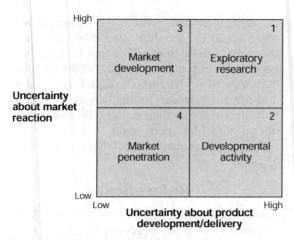

Figure 9.5   Marketing uncertainty map

will the endpoint be achieved? The model is adapted (see Figure 9.5) to reflect the importance marketers attach to market reaction and product development issues. High degrees of uncertainty relating to market reaction tend to exist when organizations are: (i) dealing with innovative new technologies, with the potential to create markets; or (ii) diversifying away from core customers/markets in order to find new applications/markets for their existing products. In terms of product development it is important to consider product development issues and the infrastructure required to deliver the product (distribution, after-sales support, etc.).

This gives four possible situations with varying degrees of uncertainty and helps management convert ideas and concepts into workable solutions:

- *Quadrant 1 – Exploratory research.* Here there is much uncertainty. Innovation needs to be nurtured over time and immediate commercial gain cannot be expected. Typically, this involves state-of-the-art technical research and development of new technologies. Risk relates to two factors: (i) the work may be resource-intense and divert resources away from more commercial activities; and (ii) no actual exploitable benefits may be generated. While activities in this area may require to be

shielded from commercial pressure, this cannot be done indefinitely. Such activities require to be evaluated and either further developed or dropped. This requires a clear focus in terms of likely commercial outcomes and overall strategic goals. Given the right management structures risks can be kept to acceptable levels.

- *Quadrant 2 – Developmental activity.* This situation sees clear marketing goals and a well-defined market reaction, but uncertainty as to how such outcomes can be achieved. Many NPD projects fall into this category. For example, marketing has defined a specific need, but there is a debate as to the means of satisfying such needs. Given the high degree of uncertainty over how to achieve outcomes plus a requirement to commit (often substantial) resources, risk factors can be high.
- *Quadrant 3 – Market development.* The method and technologies are proven and well understood and uncertainty of outcome relates to applying such methods to new opportunities. The process of market development aims to find new applications and target new markets or market segments. As businesses move away from core markets, uncertainty will increase. Innovation revolves around the creative use of market information, creative segmentation and positioning.
- *Quadrant 4 – Market penetration.* The uncertainty pertaining to outcomes and method is low, and there appears to be an immediate opportunity. The organization needs to align its assets and competencies in order to capitalize on this. The problem is often one of speed of response. Here, innovation relates to flexibility, recognizing opportunity and adaptation of product offering.

Summary

Product development and innovation are strategic activities. Given the increasing competitiveness of the business world, organizations and their product offering must evolve to survive. It is vital that management understand the true nature of their core, actual and augmented products. It is often the augmentation – enhancing the actual product via additional services – that generates commercial success.

Product development falls into three categories: product improvement/modification, product imitation and product innovation. It is product innovation that brings new and novel ideas to the market place. Regardless of the degree of innovation, a new product development (NPD) process is required. Essentially, this is a six-stage process covering: (1) idea generation, (2) idea evaluation, (3) concept development, (4) business evaluation, (5) product development and (6) product launch. The NPD process can be enhanced by using factors such as multi-functional teams and customer involvement to instil a market focus and ensure operational problems are resolved in advance of launch. Additionally, it is important that all product development has a strategic direction, with the process integrated into overall business strategy. To successfully develop products we must understand the pitfalls of NPD. Such pitfalls relate to factors like investment, failing to deliver customer benefit, forecasting errors, internal conflict and competitor response.

Innovation is effectively a management process aiming to bring together creative thought, technical/process development and commercial exploitation. Organizations need the right climate to promote innovation. They need to encourage teamwork and the ongoing exchange of information, coupled to support and reward systems. In this way, it is possible to innovate across their entire field of business operations. Managers need to consider the risks and returns associated with such activity.

References

Booz, Allen and Hamilton, *New Product Management for the 1980s*, New York: Booz, Allen and Hamilton Inc., 1982

Davidson, H., *Even More Offensive Marketing*, Penguin, 1997

Henry, J. and Walker, D. (eds), *Managing Innovation*, Open University/Sage Publications, 1991

Jain, S., *Marketing Planning and Strategy*, 5th edition, South-Western, 1997

Kotler, K., Armstrong, G., Saunders, J. and Wong, V., *Principles of Marketing*, 2nd European Edition, Prentice Hall, 1999

O'Connor, J., and Galvin, E., *Marketing and Information Technology*, Pitman, 1997

Further reading

Davidson, H., *Even More Offensive Marketing*, Chapter 11, Penguin, 1997

CHAPTER 10

Alliances and relationships

About this chapter

Increasingly, businesses have recognized the importance of alliances and joint ventures to future success. In marketing, vertical marketing systems (VMS) demonstrate the benefits co-operation can bring. Additionally, organizations need to build relationships with a range of 'markets'. Therefore, a broader definition of marketing is required.

Introduction

The saying 'no man is an island' could easily be adapted to 'no business is an island'! No organization can exist in isolation. All organizations depend on establishing and developing relationships. In short, they must develop relationships with other organizations (suppliers, distributors, etc.) and, even more critically, with customers. Indeed, this latter relationship provides the fundamental basis of all marketing activity.

Alliances, joint ventures and other co-operative strategies are now widely recognized as effective strategic solutions to the challenges of the commercial world. Many commentators predict that the future of many organizations depends on their ability to successfully enter,

and manage, collaborative ventures. The coming decade will be one of strategic collaboration.

Marketers readily acknowledge the importance of building relationships with customers. We have seen the emphasis move from transaction marketing (focusing on single sales) to relationship marketing (focusing on customer retention and building meaningful customer relationships).

When considering inter-organizational relationships, or relationships with customers, increasingly there are moves away from conflict and towards collaborative-based strategies and philosophies. In this chapter, we examine the role of alliances within marketing strategy and principles of relationship marketing.

Alliances

At a strategic level, managers aim to 'add value' by ensuring the organization has the optimal level of assets and competencies. Increasingly, strategic thinking recognizes that it is neither wise, nor feasible, to attempt to exclusively provide/own this optimal level of assets and competencies. Rather than do everything themselves, it may be more feasible to enter into partnership arrangements with other organizations. For example, two manufacturers could set up a joint distribution system and both benefit from economies of scale. Telecommunications and computer manufacturers could combine their technical expertise to produce a range of integrated products. While the concept of alliances is now more common, it is hardly new. The history of business is littered with good, and bad, examples of collaborative ventures.

What motivates an alliance? There is no single answer to this question. Any number of factors can initiate such action. Common factors include:

- *Globalization*. Businesses are increasingly able, or indeed compelled, to compete on a world scale. Alliances and joint ventures are a means of responding to this challenge. Shortening product life cycles, the globalization of technology and political change mean the world is becoming a smaller place with more opportunity/necessity for collaboration. For example, parts and components can be sourced worldwide, or organizations can now more readily seek partners to distribute their products in previously inaccessible markets. Joint initiatives give access to expertise and contacts in local markets and greatly help the process of market entry. It should be noted that while world markets are increasingly open, some less developed economies (e.g. China) may insist on joint venture agreements as a condition of market entry, thus ensuring inward investment.
- *Assets and competencies*. As previously stated, there is a recognition that organizations cannot be truly effective at all activities. The move towards downsizing has seen organizations concentrate on core activities and contract out non-essential activity. Additionally, the cost (plus shortages of skills) associated with product development may facilitate joint activity. This allows market opportunities and new technologies to be developed at a relatively lower cost. Complementary activities and/or management skills can lead to inter-organizational synergy – the combined

effect of two, or more, organizations working together is greater than their individual effect. To illustrate synergy, consider the following example. In-House Cuisine provides a restaurant delivery service – customers order, via In-House Cuisine, from a directory of top restaurants and In-House's uniformed waiters collect the meal and deliver it to the customer. The scheme has now been extended to hotels, with the Scottish Tourist Board allowing hotels with limited restaurant services to retain their three-star status by using In-House Cuisine as a form of room service.

- *Risk*. Collaboration is often born from the need to reduce risk. The sheer financial commitment may be so great that a consortium approach is required to spread the financial risk across a number of participants. A 'go-it-alone' strategy may incur other risks. Co-operative ventures can promote industry standards and common practice. For example, JVC's alliance with Sharp and Toshiba helped establish VHS as the industry standard for video recorders. Thus, 'go-it-alone' firms risk being isolated from accepted industry practice and technical standards. Additionally, joint activity can reduce the time taken to develop products, thereby reducing the risk associated with launching products.
- *Learning and innovation*. Collaborative ventures are great opportunities to learn and innovate. Technology and skills transfer are often essential in generating meaningful commercial benefit. Indeed, Morrison and Mezentseff (1997) attribute sustainable competitive advantage (generated via collaborative ventures) directly to learning and knowledge transfer. Consider the alliance between Rover and Honda. When active, this collaboration enhanced Rover's expertise in total quality management. The expertise and skills gained during the venture proved more durable than the alliance.

When examining the concept of alliances, it is important to consider the various forms such ventures may take. The scope of alliances ranges from highly formalized agreements involving ownership, to informal co-operation based on little more than a handshake. Johnson and Scholes (1999) summarize alliances in terms of four main categories.

Firstly, *acquisitions and mergers* involve taking formalized ownership. This includes co-operative or hostile take-overs. Commonly, this is driven by: (i) possible efficiency gains which lead to lower operating costs in areas of activity: procurement, transaction processing and operational scale; and (ii) synergy effects, where combined activity leads to greater 'added value' than the two organizations could hope to generate separately. Acquisition strategies normally look to benefit from eliminating duplicated activities. For example, the merger of the Leeds and Halifax Building Society (subsequently converted into a bank) has seen the rationalization of the branch network.

Secondly, *consortia and joint venture* activities involve independent organizations entering into specific project agreements or setting up jointly owned ventures. Consortia are groups of companies in partnership, normally to develop large-scale projects. For example, the 'Euro-fighter' project brings together a Europe-wide consortium of defence, electronic and aerospace companies developing the next generation of military aircraft.

Thirdly, *contract and licensing* agreements are legal, contractual agreements whereby the right to a product/activity is assigned to an independent operator. Common forms include subcontracting and franchising arrangements. Such agreements can allow organizations to focus on core activities, while contracting-out work to specialist operators. For instance, the prison service in the UK has experimented with contracted-out transportation and custodial services to Group-4 – a private security firm.

Finally, *networks* are informal agreements of co-operation built on working relationships and mutual benefit, as opposed to contractual agreement or ownership. Networks can also take the form of opportunistic alliances that,

while informal, focus on specific opportunities. For example, a group of independent local retailers may join together and launch a customer loyalty card, as a response to increased competition from national retail chains.

For any alliance to stand the test of time, there needs to be a strategic and cultural fit. *Strategic fit* essentially means that the core assets/competencies of the partners are configured in such a way as to complement each other and offer more effective pathways to strategic goals than generic internal development. As previously stated, strategic fit relates to efficiency, synergy and, on occasions, legal necessity. Strategic fit needs to be clearly defined and must offer sustainable competitive advantage. *Cultural fit* is vital if organizations are going to work together. For any partnership to be successful, there is a need for the partners to have similar aspirations, goals and attitudes. For example, joint ventures between a fast-moving entrepreneurial company and a highly risk-averse conservative organization could be difficult to achieve. The question of cultural fit is pivotal in the selection of a partner and type of alliance.

A marketing perspective on alliances can be illustrated by examining the development of *vertical marketing systems* (VMS). A VMS approach offers an alternative to the traditional view of distribution channels. Traditional distribution channels involve a chain of independent companies, each pursuing individual goals. Each channel member aims to optimize its position, normally at the expense of other channel members. The resultant tension and conflict between the buying/selling organizations within the channel tends to lead to distrust, erosion of margins, higher costs and other lingering problems. A VMS approach aims to integrate channel members into one cohesive unit, with common objectives and distribution being actively managed across all channel members. Such an approach has the advantages of: (i) reducing overall cost by avoiding repetition and reducing administration; and (ii) enhancing quality and

Traditional channel structure **VMS channel structure**

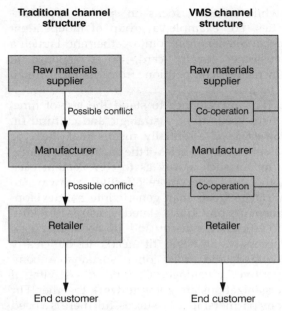

Figure 10.1   Traditional and VMS marketing channels

effectiveness by means of joint problem solving and shared expertise. Figure 10.1 illustrates both activities.

VMS ventures tend to operate in one of the following ways. They can be *corporate* – all parties in the VMS having common ownership. Alternatively, it is possible to have an *administrative* VMS – independent organizations agreeing to conform to common standards and compatible interlinked systems, normally determined by the dominant partner. For example, Ford car dealerships, although independent, conform to service, stock holding and marketing criteria set by the Ford Motor Company. Finally, there are *contractual* VMS agreements which have legally binding obligations. For example, the SPAR retail chain is a group of independent retailers who sign up to a centralized buying agreement.

To examine a practical VMS example, consider Marks & Spencer (M&S). M&S has remained at the forefront of British retailing for longer than most commentators can remember. Although the mighty M&S has

recently experienced troubled times, its enduring appeal and acknowledged strengths flow from its relationships with suppliers. Over decades, it has developed innovative and mutually beneficial supplier partnerships. Close working relationships enable the company to effectively manage the entire supply chain. Indeed, supply chain management will prove increasingly vital as M&S faces future challenges.

Relationship marketing

The concept of relationship marketing takes marketing back to basic principles. It recognizes the fundamental importance of sustaining customer relationships in order to generate customer loyalty and repeat business. Additionally, relationship marketing acknowledges a broader view of marketing, and defines a number of 'markets' which must be addressed in order to optimize customer relationships. Christopher *et al.* (1994) identify a six-market model relating to the organization's relationships (see Figure 10.2).

Undoubtedly, customer markets should be the primary focus of any organization. Previously, marketing has tended to focus on

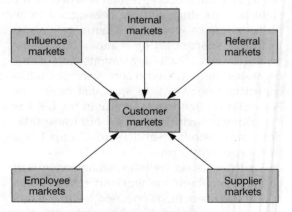

Figure 10.2   The six-market model (*Source:* Christopher *et al.*, 1994)

finding new customers and winning new business. Modern marketing practice (relationship marketing) now recognizes the importance of retaining customers and generating repeat business. Relationship approaches aim to develop customer alliances, whereby the customer not only sees the organization as their preferred provider, but actively recommends others to use their products and services. This 'elevated status' is more achievable when a broader view of marketing is taken. Such a view recognizes the role of 'markets', other than the direct customer, in developing customer relationships.

Supplier markets are important, as strong supplier links and joint innovation enable the overall supply chain to be optimized. This leads to reduced cost and potentially enhances the overall quality of the customer experience. *Employee markets* recognize the importance of recruiting and retaining the right staff. Ultimately, it is staff who, directly or indirectly, deliver the desired levels of customer satisfaction. Closely related to the employee market is the concept of *internal markets*. The idea of internal markets and internal marketing is examined in Chapter 12. The concept uses marketing principles (segmentation, targeting and the 'mix') internally. By treating employees, departments or functions as customers, we can deliver internal services and support more effectively, thus motivating staff, improving effectiveness and, ultimately, enhancing the external customer experience. External groups can have a significant influence on the organization and its customer base. Marketing strategies may need to consider such *influence markets*. For example, management may need to build relationships with financial analysts, the media, local communities and campaign groups. Finally, *referral markets* lead to new business. Organizations that deliver high degrees of customer services are well placed to receive customer referrals. Additionally, referrals may come via other parties (e.g. trade groups, distributors) and relationship marketers must strive to establish a wide referral network.

The process of relationship marketing is summarized by Kotler *et al.* (1999) in terms of creating and further developing 'value laden' relationships with stakeholders.

Developing relationships

There is a strong body of evidence supporting the economic case for relationship marketing. For example, Reichheld and Sasser (1990) illustrate that relatively minor improvements in customer defections can generate significant improvements in profit. As relationships are built on mutual benefit, what benefits does relationship marketing bring to customers? The approach typically benefits customers in that: (i) it requires marketers to have a much closer understanding of customer needs and therefore provide more appropriate solutions to customer problems; (ii) it may result in schemes rewarding customer loyalty; and (iii) it fuses together all aspects of the business, making the entire entity more customer-focused and responsive to customer need.

Having clearly established the benefits of a relationship approach, organizations must consider how they can move from transaction-based marketing (focusing on single sales) to sustainable relationship-based strategies. Common principles of relationship marketing are:

- *Use appropriately.* Like any technique, relationship marketing works better in certain situations. Not all transactions are relational in nature. For example, impulse buys or one-off purchases generally do not require, or offer, scope to develop relationships. Indeed, attempts to install a relationship approach in such circumstances may simply agitate potential customers. Relationship strategies work well in high-involvement purchases categorized by: (i) complex decision making, (ii) a degree of risk associated with purchase, (iii) a requirement for ongoing support, and/or (iv) regular purchase. To be

worthwhile, the additional revenue generated needs to exceed the cost of any relationship programme. Organizations may well prioritize customers in terms of relationship potential, with higher priority being given to certain segments or type of customer.
- *Establish relationship drivers.* If a relationship strategy is feasible, what are the key components driving success? Market research techniques facilitate an understanding of what is important to building/maintaining relationships. By identifying how customer expectations are set and evaluated, organizations are more able to generate positive interactions. For example, if it is found that key customer service attributes are accurate order processing and delivery time as per agreed schedule, it is possible to allocate resources to ensure such expectations are met (or hopefully exceeded).
- *Build customer value.* Businesses need to adopt a value-building approach to relationships. There are three basic approaches to generating customer value. Firstly there are *financial benefits*, where the relationship has some economic benefit to the customer. For example, Tesco was the first major supermarket chain to introduce a customer loyalty scheme. 'Tesco Clubcard' points can be exchanged for goods or discounts. The firm now plans to enhance the scheme by creating three classes of loyalty points – gold, silver and bronze – with higher spending customers receiving bigger awards. Secondly, there are *social benefits*. Here, relationships are based on social contact, belonging, support and personal interaction. For example, friendly relationships with clients may provide the basis of a hairdressing business. Brand loyalty may also be based on this concept. In the fashion market, people adopt brands as a symbol of lifestyle and group identity. Thirdly, *structural benefits* stem from close operational association. For instance, manufacturers and retailers could implement automated stock control/replenishment to facilitate a just-in-time approach to inventory management.

- *Retain customers.* It is a normal fact of business life that long-established customers tend to be more profitable than new or occasional customers. They tend to be larger, more frequent consumers and major sources of referral business. Therefore, organizations need not only to measure retention, but also to guarantee that all employees are aware of its importance. The ideas outlined above all have a role to play in retaining customers, but organizations must actively seek to strengthen ongoing business relationships. Common methods include corporate hospitality, sending referral business to customers and briefing clients on new developments. A key step in many retention programmes is to establish a relationship management structure within the organization. This involves: (i) identifying which customers (or customer groups) merit special attention; and (ii) assigning account/relationship managers to develop and implement a relationship plan. Such a plan requires specific objectives and strategies aimed at enhancing the organization's business position with that target group.

Amazon – the Internet bookshop – offers a practical illustration of relationship marketing. Obviously, as a virtual bookshop Amazon has no direct, face-to-face contact with its customers. However, its website allows customers to write book reviews, read what others thought of a given text, and track the progress of individual orders. The process engenders a feeling of belonging – a social benefit.

Summary

Increasingly, businesses need to recognize the importance of alliances and joint ventures. A collaborative approach has much to commend it, and is being driven by factors such as globalization, risk reduction and the need to share learning and generate innovation.

Alliances can range from acquisitions and mergers through to networks based on informal co-operation. To be successful, organizations need to seek partnerships where strategic fit exists. Strategic fit relates to factors like economy of scale, synergy benefits resulting from complementary assets/competencies and, on occasion, legal necessity. Cultural fit is also important as it sustains relationships.

Relationship marketing is a vital component of business success. To be truly effective, organizations must recognize that they serve a range of 'markets'. They need to consider a broader definition of marketing, one that embraces 'markets' such as employees, suppliers, internal function, referral sources and influences. However, relationship marketing is not applicable in all cases. When applicable, organizations must strive to identify the key relationship drivers, build customer value and do everything reasonable to retain customers.

References

Christopher, M., Payne, A. and Ballantyne, D., *Relationship Marketing*, Butterworth-Heinnemann, 1994

Johnson, G. and Scholes, K., *Exploring Corporate Strategy*, 5th edition, Prentice Hall, 1999

Kotler, K., Armstrong, G., Saunders, J. and Wong, V., *Principles of Marketing*, 2nd European Edition, Prentice Hall, 1999

Morrison, M. and Mezentseff, L. 'Learning alliances: a new dimension in strategic alliances', *Management Decision*, 35(5/6), May/June, 1997

Reichheld, F. and Sasser, W. 'Zero defections: quality comes to services', *Harvard Business Review*, Sept./Oct., pp. 105–111, 1990

Further reading

Hooley, G.H., Saunders, J.A. and Piercy, N.F., *Marketing Strategy and Competitive Positioning*, 2nd edition, Chapter 8, Prentice Hall, 1998

CHAPTER 11

The strategic marketing plan

Planning is an integrative, co-ordinating activity that gives focus to the organization. Strategic and tactical decisions are made at corporate and functional levels. Addressing the analytical, behavioural and organizational aspects of planning can help overcome the many barriers to success. While the format and presentation of marketing plans may vary, a common purpose exists – to identify, select and implement appropriate marketing activities.

Corporate and marketing plans

Marketing managers plan in order to complete tasks on time and without exceeding pre-set resource limits. It is likely that objectives, targets and budgets will be set as part of the overall corporate planning and budgeting process. The task is to translate these factors into a workable marketing plan.

When developing a plan, the process involves choosing certain courses of action and ruling out other possible options. Planning should be systematic, structured and involve three key components: (i) objectives –

what has to be achieved; (ii) strategy (or actions) – defining how the objectives are to be achieved; and (iii) resource implications – the resources required to implement the strategy.

Clearly, it is important to understand the interface between marketing and corporate strategy. This is best illustrated by considering the hierarchical structure of an organization. Senior management formulates objectives and strategy for the entire organization (or a strategic business unit – SBU). Managers in various functional areas, such as marketing, contribute to the process by developing specific functional strategies and ultimately tactics to achieve these corporate objectives. Effectively, the process involves a hierarchy of plans, with strategy at one level becoming the objective(s) at the next. Additionally, this process provides feedback on the success/failure of any strategy. Figure 11.1 illustrates the concept.

Corporate planning

The corporate plan will define objectives for the entire business and should co-ordinate the various functional strategies (marketing, operations, human resource management, finance, etc.) to deliver the overall corporate objectives. It is important that functional strategies are interrelated (see Figure 11.1). For

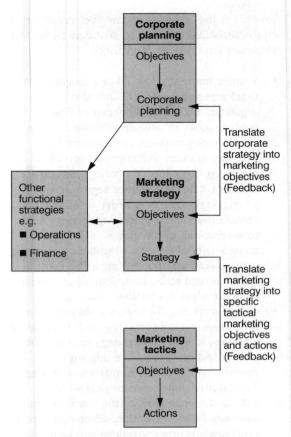

Figure 11.1   Corporate and marketing planning hierarchy

and markets served. This *strategic direction* allows functional areas to develop appropriate strategies and tactics.

- *Important.* By its very nature, corporate strategy is the process of making major business decisions. It defines business direction over the *long term* and is critical in setting the overall resource profile available to the organization.
- *Matching.* There is a need to match the organization's activities and resource base to the current and future business environment.

A useful summary of corporate strategy management is provided in Figure 11.2. This model takes a top-down view of the overall strategy process. It identifies the five components vital in achieving corporate success:

- *Vision.* Senior management and other stakeholders must establish an overall vision of what the corporation should be. This defines the basic need they fulfil and establishes the generic direction of the business.
- *Corporate objectives and strategy.* Collective goals and strategy define the benchmarks for success, and ways of achieving success. This level co-ordinates corporate activity and initiates activities to achieve desired results.
- *SBU/functional objectives and strategy.* Corporate strategy translates into objectives and plans for individual elements of the

example, if the marketing strategy focused on developing high levels of customer service in order to retain key customer groups, both the operations and human resource management functions would have a role to play in delivering this. Corporate strategy can be summarized as:

- *Integrative.* The process *co-ordinates functional activity* towards a common goal and takes a 'whole organization' view of the corporation. By defining corporate targets, normally in financial terms, collective targets are set for the functional groups.
- *Providing focus.* Strategy defines the scope of the business – the general nature of activities

Figure 11.2   The strategic process

business. This may take the form of SBUs (Strategic Business Units – divisions within a company) or functional activities. For example, a hotel chain could divide its business into three SBUs – accommodation, food/beverage, and conferences/leisure.

• *Resources.* For a given strategy, the need exists to match resources to strategic intent. This process normally involves annual budgeting.

• *Structure.* Management must develop the appropriate organizational and staffing structures to facilitate success.

Successful businesses ensure these factors are aligned in order to turn strategic intent into business reality.

Marketing plans – strategy or tactics?

There are two types of marketing plan – strategic and tactical. This distinction generates much confusion and debate: is it a strategy or a tactic? This question may be academic when faced with the reality of the business world, as the distinction between the two will vary from organization to organization and manager to manager. However,

much of the confusion can be removed if characteristics common to strategic plans and tactical plans can be identified.

• *Strategic marketing.* This takes a longer term timeframe and broadly defines the organization's marketing activities. The process seeks to develop effective responses to a changing business environment by analysing markets and segmentation and evaluating competitors' offerings. Strategy focuses on defining market segments and positioning products in order to establish a competitive stance. Marketing strategy tends to embrace all of the mix, or significant components of the mix (distribution strategy, communications strategy, etc.). Problems in this area tend to be unstructured and require external, often speculative, data.

• *Tactical marketing.* This takes a shorter term timeframe and concerns day-to-day marketing activities. It translates strategy into specific actions and represents the ongoing operational dimension of marketing strategy. Tactical marketing tends to deal with individual components of the marketing mix elements (sales promotion, advertising, etc.). Problems are often repetitive and well structured with data being internally generated.

Table 11.1 examines the differences between strategic and tactical marketing.

Table 11.1   Strategic and tactical marketing

	Strategic marketing	Tactical marketing
Timeframe	Long term	Short term
Focus	Broad	Narrow
Key task(s)	Defining market and competitive position	Day-to-day marketing activity
Information and problem solving	Unstructured, external, speculative	Structured, internal, repetitive
Example	New product development	Price discounting

Why does planning matter?

The organization needs a strategic marketing plan in order to adapt to a changing business environment. Given the basic business premise of 'success through effectively meeting customer needs' it is clear that organizations must continually adapt and develop to remain successful. Strategic marketing facilitates this process and provides robust solutions in an increasingly competitive world. Essentially, the plan should provide a systematic framework with which to analyse the marketplace and supply a well-defined way to pursue strategic goals.

However, the truly successful plan goes further than the simple process of planning. It is a vehicle to communicate, motivate and involve staff in fundamental business activities. Too often planning is viewed as a restrictive process based on programming events and generating paperwork. Remember, plans need employee commitment and 'ownership' to achieve results.

The key reasons for planning are summarized as follows:

- *Adapting to change*. Planning provides an opportunity to examine how changes in the business environment have affected or will affect the organization. It enables management to focus on strategic issues as opposed to day-to-day operational problems.
- *Resource allocation*. Planning allows us to deploy resources to effectively meet opportunities and threats. No plan can succeed without appropriate resources. When a strategic perspective is taken, organizations are better placed to marshal the resources required to meet strategic 'windows of opportunity'. Doyle (1994) defines strategic windows of opportunity as changes that have a major impact in the marketplace. Strategic windows include factors such as: (i) new technology; (ii) new market segments; (iii) new channels of distribution; (iv) market redefinition – where the nature of demand

changes; (v) legislative changes; and (vi) environmental shocks – sudden unexpected economic or political change. Essentially, the process involves aligning marketing activities with opportunities in order to generate competitive advantage.
- *Consistency*. By providing a common base to work from (e.g. techniques and assumptions) the overall decision-making process can be enhanced. Additionally, common methods and formats should improve internal communication.
- *Integration*. As a strategic process, planning should facilitate the integration and co-ordination of the marketing mix. By providing a strategic focus it should be possible to generate synergy from the individual elements of the marketing mix.
- *Communication and motivation*. The plan should clearly communicate strategic intent to employees and other stakeholders. Clear objectives and an understanding of the individual, or group, contribution to the process serves to generate 'ownership' and motivation.
- *Control*. All control activities are based on some predetermined plan. The planning process should set meaningful targets, thus defining the criteria by which success is measured.

Barriers to successful planning

Few would argue with the concept of planning. In any activity, a plan provides a fundamental basis for success. Marketing plans should offer exactly what is required – optimizing the use of marketing techniques and resources in order to make the most of marketing opportunities. However, even the most charitable of marketing managers would view this statement as naive and unlikely to be fully achieved. If managers view planning as 'fine in theory' but failing in practice to deliver its full potential, where does it go wrong?

Clearly, barriers must exist to successful planning. Often, these barriers are more to do with the human aspects of business management. They involve people, politics, skills and culture to a greater degree than formal systems, methodology, and data.

Common barriers to successful planning are:

- *Culture.* The prevailing culture may not be amenable to marketing plans. If the fundamental principles of marketing are not accepted by the organization, any move towards being market-led and customer-orientated could be dismissed as 'not the way we do it'. Often we see considerable resistance to change and gradual regression back to old work practices.
- *Power and politics.* All organizations are subject to internal politics. The development of strategic planning becomes a battlefield where vested interests fight each other's proposals and squabble over status and resources. This process absorbs much management time and can result in ill-advised compromise and unnecessary delay.
- *Analysis not action.* Much time and energy can be wasted by the process of analysing data and developing rationales for action, as opposed to simply acting. While a rigorous process is commendable, it should not displace action. This 'paralysis-by-analysis' barrier tends to substitute information gathering and processing for decision making. Perhaps surprisingly, many planning systems do not promote action and are more concerned with reviewing progress and controlling activity, rather than tackling strategic issues.
- *Resource issues.* In any planning situation, the potential exists to negotiate over resources. Indeed, a major aspect of the process is to match resources to strategic aims. Managers must take a realistic view of the resource position and endeavour to ensure that resources are not over-committed or needlessly withheld.

- *Skills.* In some instances, managers do not have the skills (e.g. project management, forecasting) required to make the best use of the planning process. Here, planning takes on a ritual nature – a meaningless but 'must-do' annual task. Often, planning is reduced to incremental increases/decreases in annual budget and fails to examine opportunities for business development.

Many of these barriers relate to the implementation of plans rather than the planning process itself. Chapter 12 deals with the issue of implementation in detail. However, sound management practice would advocate the inclusion of implementation as part of the planning process. Indeed, Piercy (1997) suggests a multi-dimensional model of planning. This considers the analytical dimension, the behavioural dimension and the organizational dimension of any plan. Figure 11.3 summarizes the model.

- *Analytical dimension.* Analytical tools, techniques and models are important, as they provide a framework to tackle issues and identify/solve problems. While formalized planning systems have the advantage of offering a common (corporate-wide) systematic approach, to be truly effective they must address behavioural and organizational issues.

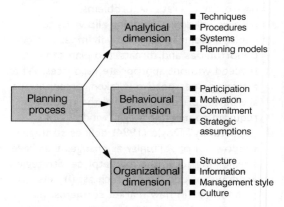

Figure 11.3 A multi-dimensional model of marketing planning (*Source*: Piercy, 1997)

- *Behavioural dimension.* Here we focus on the people aspects of the planning process. Plans only become successful because of the support, participation, motivation and commitment of people. There is a need to understand and fully communicate the strategic assumptions underpinning the strategy. Plans must address behavioural factors in order to gain the support so vital to smooth implementation.
- *Organizational dimension.* Strategic planning takes place within the context of a given organization. Therefore, it will be influenced by organizational factors, such as culture and style of management. Remember, organizational structures determine the flow of information, as well as defining responsibilities and reporting lines. Major strategic initiatives may require radical organizational changes.

By taking this 'multi-dimensional' approach to planning and actively considering behavioural and organizational issues within the planning process, it is possible to enhance the overall likelihood of success.

The structure of a strategic marketing plan

What does a strategic marketing plan look like? While the answer to this question will vary from organization to organization (in terms of structure and presentation), marketing plans perform a common function and have common components. Indeed, McDonald (1999) views marketing planning as a systematic way of identifying, selecting, scheduling and costing activities in order to achieve objectives. Such definitions focus on the purpose, as opposed to the structure, of planning.

Regardless of precedent and planning formats, strategic plans tend to have common elements. Marketing managers, would expect a strategic plan to cover:

- Industry analysis
- Internal analysis
- Opportunity identification
- Objective setting
- Formulation of strategy
- Proposed marketing programmes and actions
- Implementation and control – including financial forecasts

Figure 11.4 presents an annotated example of a strategic marketing plan. Note that this figure does not attempt to portray the definitive marketing plan, but merely illustrates the component parts common to such plans.

Strategic marketing plans take on many different guises. The content, structure and complexity of a plan will vary. While planning formats and conventions are largely a matter of historic precedent within the organization, the key imperative is to generate action. Plans should address critical issues in a way that is relevant to the organization – for example, promoting decisive marketing initiatives within a limited timescale.

Approaches to marketing planning

The development of a marketing plan is a significant and time-consuming activity. All planning is essentially objective-driven – objectives are translated into actions. A number of schools of thought exist as to how the task is best approached, though the standard approaches to planning are:

- *Top-down.* Senior managers develop objectives and strategy. Managers at an operational level are then required to implement these strategies. This approach is said to encourage professionalism and promote a corporate strategic view of marketing activity.

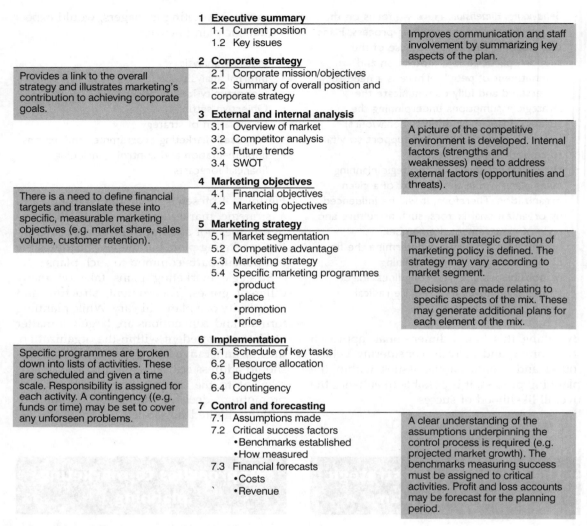

Figure 11.4   Illustrative example of a strategic marketing plan

- *Bottom-up.* Here, authority and responsibility for formulation and implementation of strategy is devolved. Senior marketing managers approve, and then monitor, agreed objectives. It can be claimed that this approach encourages ownership and commitment.

Hybrid systems are also common, where objectives are top-down and responsibility for the formulation/implementation of strategy is devolved.

Summary

Strategic planning offers a systematic and structured approach to choosing and implementing certain courses of action. Corporate plans define overall business objectives, while providing focus and co-ordinating functional activities. Such plans need to align the stakeholders' vision to the objectives, strategy, resources and structure of the strategic business units.

There is a need to differentiate between marketing strategy and marketing tactics. Essentially, strategic marketing focuses on defining segments, establishing competitive positions and co-ordinating all the elements of the mix. Tactics translate strategies into action and deal with day-to-day marketing transactions.

Planning allows organizations to adapt to a changing business environment and provides a framework for resource allocation. Additionally, sound planning promotes a consistency of approach and facilitates integration of activity, communication, motivation and control of activities. In order to achieve these benefits, the organization must overcome the numerous barriers to successful planning. These include culture, internal politics and lacking the requisite skills to make planning a successful activity. Truly successful plans make use of analytical techniques but also address the behavioural and organizational dimensions of the process.

The structure and content of a strategic marketing plan will vary. However, plans tend to have common elements – industry analysis, internal analysis, opportunity identification, formulation of strategy, marketing programmes/actions and implementation/control.

Formulating marketing plans can take a top-down, bottom-up or hybrid approach.

References

Doyle, P., *Marketing Management and Strategy*, 2nd edition, Prentice Hall, 1994

McDonald, M., *Marketing Plans*, 4th edition, Butterworth-Heinemann, 1999

Piercy, N., *Market-Led Strategic Change*, 2nd edition, Butterworth-Heinemann, 1997

Further reading

Aaker, D., *Strategic Market Management*, 4th edition, Chapter 17, Wiley, 1995

Piercy, N., *Market-Led Strategic Change*, 2nd edition, Chapter 11, Butterworth-Heinemann, 1997

Part 3
Strategic Implementation

Strategic Implementation
Control

Part 3 examines issues relating to implementation and control. Any strategic activity must address two basic issues – selecting a competitive strategy and putting it into practice. Implementation and control address the second issue. Managers should never underestimate the importance, or indeed complexity, of 'putting it into practice'.

Chapter 12 assesses the general issues pertaining to implementation and how to build effective implementation approaches within the context of marketing projects. Chapter 13 is concerned with the application of financial measures, performance appraisal and benchmarking as control mechanisms. The concept of control loops applied to marketing is also examined.

CHAPTER 12

Strategic implementation

About this chapter

Implementation is critical to the success or failure of any venture. Basic generic management principles (e.g. leadership, team building and delegation) contribute to the process. Marketing managers must evaluate the ease, or otherwise, of implementation and deploy project management techniques to achieve desired goals. Additionally, 'internal marketing' can ease the process of implementation.

Implementation – stressing the importance

A key maxim in business is: never acquire a business you don't understand how to run. Equally, it would be true to say: never adopt a strategy you don't understand how to implement.

It can be said that, in terms of strategy, planning is the easy part. With a basic grounding in marketing, most managers could sit down with a blank sheet of paper and develop an outline marketing plan. This plan may contain all the correct 'buzz-words'.

Ideas relating to market penetration, segmentation, globalization and competitive advantage would fill the page and a clear concise way forward formulated. However, it is not that simple. While many managers could produce such an outline, how many could implement it? Without implementation, the plan remains simply some ideas on a piece of paper.

In the context of marketing the goal will be to achieve and/or maintain a marketing orientation – success by a process of understanding and meeting customer need. It is doubtful if a marketing strategy can be implemented where this orientation does not exist. Achieving such a goal is dependent on the quality of management and their understanding of marketing as a business philosophy.

It is reasonable to suggest that implementation is often a key determinant in the success or failure of any strategic activity. Therefore, it should be an integral part of any marketing strategy. This view is supported by examining the history of corporate strategy. Recent times have seen a move away from corporate planning to the concept of strategic management. The main difference is that strategic management addresses the issue of implementation.

Success vs. failure

Two dimensions determine the success of a strategy: the strategy itself and an organization's ability to implement it. A useful starting point in considering success or failure is outlined in Figure 12.1. Bonoma (1984) examines the appropriateness of the strategy and the effectiveness of execution skills, thus establishing four general positions:

- *Success.* The ideal situation, an appropriate strategy and a strong ability to execute such a strategy. This should present little or no problem.
- *Chance.* Here the strategy is poor, perhaps lacking detailed analysis or not building on existing strengths. However, it may be saved by effective execution. This may be such that we can adopt and adapt from a weak opening basis and, with luck, do what is required. Clearly, the degree of 'inappropriateness' is highly significant. Is the strategy saveable? Notwithstanding this question, this position always brings a high degree of risk.
- *Problem.* We are doing the right things badly. The strength of strategic planning is dissipated by poor execution. Often the true value of the strategy is not fully recognized and it is

dismissed as being inappropriate.
- *Failure.* A no-win situation. With failure on all levels there is a danger of struggling on with implementation and simply 'throwing good money after bad'. Organizations should try to learn from such situations. Do not make the same mistake twice.

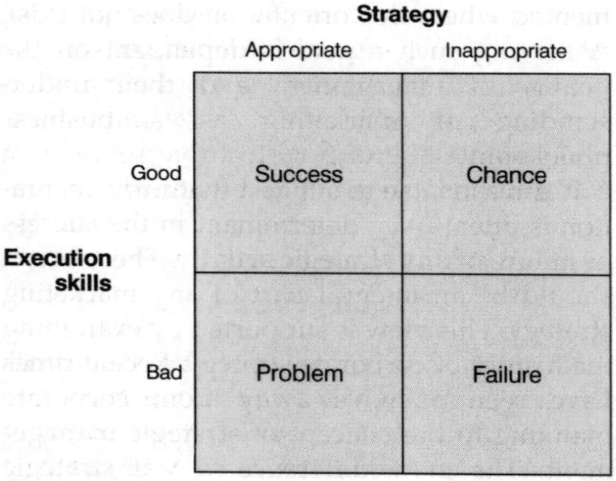

Clearly, there is an issue of subjectivity within defining good/bad and appropriate/inappropriate and it is all too easy to be wise after the event. It is simple to classify a strategy as inappropriate after it is deemed to have failed. The key quest is to ensure strategies fall into the 'success' category. Formulating an appropriate strategy has been dealt with in the preceding chapters of this book and we will now focus on the execution of strategy – in other words implementation.

Effective implementation can be viewed in terms of:

1 Understanding the fundamental principles of implementation.
2 Assessing the ease, or otherwise, of implementing individual projects.
3 Applying project management techniques.

Fundamental principles

Having stressed the importance of implementation we turn to the issue of what factors are required for success. These are summarized as:

- Leadership
- Culture
- Structure
- Resources

- Control
- Skills
- Strategy
- Systems

Any successful strategy must be supported by each of these components. They cover the human aspects of business and a more objective process approach to management. Note that these factors can have either a positive or negative effect on a given project.

Figure 12.1   Strategy and execution (*Source:* Adapted from Bonoma, 1984)

Leadership

The role of the leader is to get the best out of people and deal with the unexpected. They should be viewed as facilitators. This is achieved by creating an environment where actions can take place. Leaders require effective people skills such as negotiation and delegation. Often leaders acquire their leadership position by means of technical expertise. This can be dangerous, since their primary function is to facilitate rather than undertake the work themselves. The leader needs transferable management skills in addition to technical and marketing competence. Adair (1984) summarizes leadership as:

1 Task needs – aiming to complete the project.
2 Group needs – developing team spirit and morale.
3 Individual needs – harmonizing the above with the needs of the individual.

Depending on circumstances, the leader will emphasise task, group or individual needs (see Figure 12.2).

Leaders need to adopt an appropriate style of management. If a crisis looms then a more direct autocratic style may be called for. However, under different circumstances a participatory style may be best suited. Hence leaders can move from task, individual or group orientation depending on the circumstances.

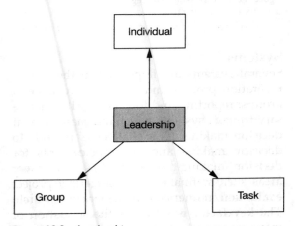

Figure 12.2 Leadership

Culture

Much management theory relates to corporate culture. Culture can be defined as a combination of shared values and beliefs. These are commonly reinforced with corporate symbols and symbolic behaviour. For example, a company may wish to pursue a culture of openness and accessibility. The symbol of this may be to encourage all staff to dress informally on a Friday, to promote a more relaxed atmosphere.

Great care must be taken when implementing strategy. If the strategy goes against the dominant culture it is likely to fail unless a major effort is made to develop and maintain support. This could be achieved via staff training, appraisal and restructuring. The strategist needs to be sensitive to the shared values that exist within the organization. Normally it is best to work with, as opposed to against, such values.

Structure

The structure of any organization, or project, has two primary functions. Firstly, it defines lines of authority denoting levels of responsibility. Current management thinking promotes a move towards flatter structures with more devolved authority. Secondly, structure is a basis for communication. Structures can filter out information making senior management remote from the customer. In the area of implementation, consideration should be given to how communication occurs.

In relation to developing marketing strategy, it can be advisable to have multi-functional teams. A group with a diverse range of backgrounds can promote ownership of projects, identify operational problems in advance and enhance overall quality.

Resources

Any project needs to be properly resourced. Leaders have the role of obtaining and making optimum use of resources. The resourcing of projects is often more to do with internal politics than actual need. In many organizations there needs to be a more objective process of resource allocation. Resources will ultimately relate to finance and staff.

Resourcing is normally budget driven. However, there is now a recognition of the importance of being time focused. For example, a three-month time delay is likely to be more serious than a minor budgetary overspend. The concept of 'time-to-market' is dealt with in a later section.

Remember, implementation never takes place in a vacuum – things change and it is important to be flexible and build in an acceptable degree of contingency (additional resource to be called on) within any implementation strategy.

Control

Control is simply a way of making sure that what is supposed to happen actually happens. The term itself – control – often appears to have negative connotations and is seen as limiting and coercive in nature. This should not be the case. Astute management can develop effective control systems.

The basic approach is a simple feedback loop. You measure progress, compare against some pre-set standard and if required take action. Given the importance of control the concept is expanded upon in the next chapter.

Skills

The appropriate skills mix is required in order to achieve any aim or goal. Within the context of implementing marketing strategy, 'softer' human resource management (HRM) skills can be lacking. It should be remembered that project management is a skill in its own right. To summarize, successful implementation requires skills such as:

*   Technical/marketing skills, e.g. design, market research, industry analysis.
*   HRM skills, e.g. delegation, performance appraisal, training.
*   Project management skills, e.g. budgeting, resourcing, forecasting.

Strategy

To state the obvious, there must be a strategy to implement. However the fact that a strategy exists may not be apparent to everyone. Additionally, the strategy may not be seen as appropriate by all staff. The project leader must ensure that people are aware of the strategy, the reason for it and their role in making it work.

Potential strategy should be screened to ensure that it is appropriate to current circumstances. For example, what is the basis of competitive advantage? What organizational changes need to take place?

The development of strategy is an ongoing activity. During and after the implementation phase, management should review and adapt policy as required. While the overall objectives remain intact, there may be changes in how we set about achieving such targets (see Figure 12.3).

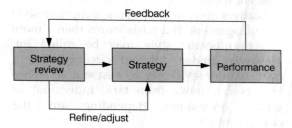

Figure 12.3   Reviewing strategy

Systems

Several systems are important in the implementation process and fall into two general groups: reporting and forecasting. It is necessary to have systems which aid management decision making. Note that these are aids to decision making and not replacements for decision making. Such systems will cover areas such as finance and budgeting, project evaluation/refinement and market research. The key factor is often the interpretation of information rather than the system itself.

The seven S's

The 'Seven-S' model developed by McKinsey & Co. provides a useful summation of these ideas. The model can be adapted as seen in Figure 12.4 and split into: (i) human resource management (HRM) – dealing with the people-based aspects of implementation; and (ii) process – the policy, procedures, reporting and systems aspects of implementation.

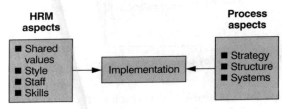

Figure 12.4   The seven S's

Assessing ease of implementation

It is now possible to test and evaluate the likely ease of implementation. Firstly strategic fit – how easily will the strategy fit into current activities? Unsurprisingly, the easier the fit the less likely implementation problems are to occur. However, it must be recognized that an easy fit does not guarantee success. The strategy must be right for the business environment.

Primarily, the concern is with the level of change associated with the implementation. The greater the change, the greater the management challenge and the greater the perceived benefit of the change needs to be. Hence there is a need to consider the potential pay-off and the amount of change required to achieve this. Figure 12.5 illustrates the relationship between change and importance:

- *Overhaul.* Here implementation will have a significant impact and face significant challenges. Given that a high degree of change is likely, one must expect increasing levels of resistance and

risk as the strategy has only a limited fit with current activity. There needs to be compelling strategic reasons and significant support for this strategy's implementation. The strategy is likely to involve activities such as restructuring, downsizing, mergers and overhauling business culture.
- *Synergy.* The word can be defined as 'working together'. The combined effect of high importance and relatively limited change offers a potentially 'easy ride'. Problems should be limited and risk of failure is reduced. However, great problems occur when a strategy is deemed to fall into this category, only to find it is not the case and far more change is required. The organization needs to be doubly sure it has the required synergy before embarking on this route.
- *Limited impact.* Low levels of change affecting relatively unimportant areas of activity. Often a series of such activities can yield incremental change. This could represent a stage-by-stage approach to change, where relatively minor changes are introduced over a period of time. This option of incremental activity can be used where resources are limited or a phased consolidated approach is deemed appropriate.
- *Overkill.* This has high risk and limited impact importance. Questions have to be asked. Why are we doing this and what is the pay-off? Care is needed in order not to alienate staff and

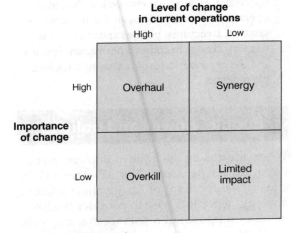

Figure 12.5   Strategic fit

disrupt activity. Such projects often occur as a result of political manoeuvring and compromise.

Successful management requires an appreciation of the nature of change and its subsequent impact on the organization and individuals. The process starts with an awareness of the need to change, then progresses to a transition phase and finally reaches some predetermined state. Normally, the transition stage is the most critical as it is fraught with risk and uncertainty.

Management must assess the level of change associated with a project and deploy strategies relating to the management of change. For example:

- *Justification.* Have supportive evidence in the form of facts and quantitative/statistical data. Hard data often proves a powerful ally.
- *Commitment.* Try to involve others via group problem solving, participation and communication. Such factors tend to generate commitment to change.
- *Learning.* Change is often difficult to achieve and mistakes will be made. Learning from mistakes is important. Remember, experience is the name we like to give our mistakes.
- *Incrementalize.* It may be better to have an overall strategy that can be broken down into a series of smaller ongoing changes, as per the 'limited impact' strategy.
- *Operations.* Ensure that change is reflected in operational activities through the appropriate systems, structures, policies and monitoring. In this way, change becomes a permanent feature and the organization avoids slipping back into old practice.

People, power and politics

When addressing the issue of implementation there are no panaceas. Not all staff will be equally supportive of a given marketing strategy, hence it is wise to consider the likely levels of support and resistance that may exist relative to a given project. Piercy (1997) sets out

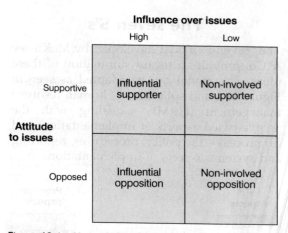

Figure 12.6   Key players matrix

general categories into which staff can fall (see Figure 12.6).

Those with influence, often the appropriate decision-making unit (DMU), need careful consideration. Common tactics include:

- Converting or isolating opposition.
- Upgrading the status of influential supporters.
- Recruiting the active involvement of non-involved supporters.
- Negotiate and trade-off with vested interest.

In short, the success of any programme requires sufficient influence and support. This becomes more complex when the project generates high levels of change.

The issue of supporters and their influence tends to relate to the dreaded, but vital, concept of internal office politics. Within the organization, political behaviour can be either desirable or undesirable. Often this depends on your perspective. Good strategies can flounder on the rocks of political self-interest and behaviour.

Kakabadse (1983) identifies seven common approaches to playing the political game:

1 Establish who the interested parties are – the stakeholders.
2 Consider their comfort zones. What do they value, fear or tolerate?
3 Work within these comfort zones.
4 Use networks – those interested or influential.

5 Identify 'gatekeepers' and adhere to the norms of the network.

6 Make deals for mutual benefit.

7 Withhold and withdraw. Consider withholding information and know when to withdraw from areas of conflict and dispute.

Arguably, political behaviour is an essential part of strategy implementation. This view requires management to identify key players and consider their potential reaction to strategic initiatives. Remember, the art of politics is about influencing people when you cannot rely on direct authority. By considering the political dimension related to the project it is possible to gauge resistance and support, develop justification and counter argument in advance of critical decisions.

Additionally, it may be possible to develop influence via various power bases. For example controlling resources, having access to people and controlling the flow of information. These can all assist in playing the political game.

Internal marketing

No discussion relating to the ease, or otherwise, of implementation would be complete without considering the potential use of internal marketing. Internal marketing focuses on the relationship between the organization and its employees. Berry and Parasuraman (1991) define the process in terms of viewing employees (or groups of employees) as internal customers.

Definitions of this type encompass the work traditionally within the remit of personnel/human resource management function (recruitment, training, motivation, etc.). Few would argue with the importance of staff in relation to implementation. Therefore, can marketing techniques be used to motivate employees and ease the path of project implementation?

By applying the marketing concept internally, it may be possible to enhance the likely success of a project. Factors such as internal segmentation and application of the 'mix' may well have a role to play. Consider the following:

- *Segmentation.* This is the process of dividing groups into subgroups with similar characteristics and is perfectly feasible within any organization. For example, senior managers may have different training needs from other staff. By grouping like types together more effective training and communication is possible.
- *Product.* This may well be the strategy and accompanying process of change. Equally, the individual's job or function could be viewed as an 'internal product'. The internal product, service or task is a component in delivering the overall strategy.
- *Promotion.* Clear communication has a vital role to play in establishing success. The project manager could design a 'promotional campaign' stressing the benefits of a new strategy. In all cases, communication is an issue that must be considered when planning implementation.
- *Place.* How to get the 'product' to the internal customer. Channels of distribution for information, services and training can be developed and optimized. These could include team briefings, seminars and day-to-day business interactions.
- *Price.* This is a complex issue. While it is relatively easy to cost factors like training, communications, vehicles and other associated tangible costs, it is worth remembering that a price is also paid by the group and/or individual. This 'psychological' price is difficult to measure, but is important. It takes the form of uncertainty, loss of status, stress and loss (hopefully short-term) of operational efficiency.

In its simplest form, internal marketing offers a framework (the 4 P's) which can lay the foundations of successful policy implementation. It offers the marketing concept as a way to achieve specific strategic goals. Figure 12.7 illustrates how the concept could be applied to an organization . Here we segment by level of

Organization		
Segment 1	Segment 2	Segment 3
Influential supporter	Influential opposition	Non-involved supporter
Internal mix I	Internal mix II	Internal mix III

Figure 12.7   Internal marketing

support. However, other criteria (e.g. department or management level) could be applied.

Applying project management techniques

The ability to manage a project is a skill in its own right. Such skills are 'transferable' and can be applied to any situation. Therefore, they adhere to general principles which can be learned by the marketing strategist.

Essentially, project management involves achieving unity of purpose and setting achievable goals within given resource and timescale parameters. Efforts tend to focus on integrating activity, building teamwork and monitoring progress. Marketing projects are rarely simple and often have to be achieved while overcoming unforeseen problems and barriers. Effective project management deals with such problems as and when they arise. Common tasks in project management are:

- Objective setting
- Planning
- Delegation
- Team building
- Crisis management

Objective setting

An overall strategic objective will be broken down into a series of sub-objectives. It is important that these are clear, concise, understood and accepted by team members. A useful acronym is to develop SMART objectives. These add focus and relate to the task(s) required.

S   *Specific*. They should be clear and task orientated.

M   *Measurable*. Objectives must be measured in order to establish progress.

A   *Action*. They should be task related and promote activity.

R   *Resourced*. A realistic resource base has to be allocated to enable progress.

T   *Time*. There is a need to make the objective time focused. How long will it take?

Planning

Having established what is to be achieved, planning involves breaking an activity into a series of structured manageable tasks, co-ordinating these tasks and monitoring progress.

Tasks can be carried out in series or parallel. So-called 'parallel processing' – running several tasks simultaneously– has several advantages. Namely, it can reduce the overall timescale for the project and reduce the risk of a delay in one task delaying the entire project (see Figure 12.8).

Increasingly there is an awareness of being time-focused. Business is now adopting a Time-to-Market (T-t-M) philosophy. This T-t-M approach advocates the importance of reducing the overall time taken to implement a project. Consider the potential benefits of

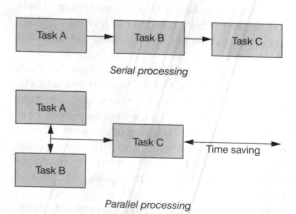

Figure 12.8   Serial vs. parallel processing

reducing implementation time. Firstly, a commercial return is produced sooner. Secondly, by being early into the market the opportunity exists to gain a price premium and/or market share. The T-t-M focus is achieved by parallel processing and, conversely, spending more time developing a robust planning specification.

Delegation

Effective managers realize that they cannot do everything themselves – they know that management is the art of delegation. The art is often to balance the degree of delegation with the appropriate span of control. The manager needs to understand the strengths, weaknesses and group dynamics of the team members.

Many managers have a problem with letting go, and need to remember that delegation extends the capacity to manage and frees the leader from the mundane. Additionally, if staff are encouraged to take decisions, overall decision making can be improved. The people 'on the spot' are more likely to have a fuller grasp of the situation and be able to make effective decisions.

Key principles of delegation include:

- Focus on the objective. Be crystal clear about what has to be achieved but flexible in how it is to be achieved.
- Delegate authority, not just responsibility. Empower people to make decisions and manage resources.
- Test people on smaller and less important tasks and gradually give the more able employee greater scope.
- Explain how tasks are monitored and define circumstances in which they should refer back to senior management.
- Refrain from undue interference but be watchful.

Team building

Clearly there is a need to use the skills and capacity of the team to the optimal level. It is important to have a core goal as this gives the team a focal point. Each team member must understand their contribution to this collective goal. As Wickens (1997) states, teamwork does not depend on people working together but upon working to obtain the same objective.

A winning team has the right combination of skills. These should blend and complement each other. The environment should be positive and supportive but not complacent or overly relaxed.

Basic team-building principles which can be applied to a marketing project are:

- Encourage a positive supportive environment. It is acceptable for mistakes to be made but lessons should be learnt from them.
- Show and encourage respect for each other. Encourage constructive criticism as opposed to personal attack.
- Link individual reward to group performance.
- Disagreement and discussion should not be suppressed and ideas should be listened to. However, this should not detract from effective decision making.

Crisis management

There will be times when things go dramatically wrong and a crisis point is reached. The basic premise of crisis management is to take urgent action in response to unexpected events. By definition, the process is reactive in nature and invariably is a turning point. However, it does not negate prior planning. Management can develop a series of scenarios and have appropriate responses available as a contingency. This scenario planning allows a crisis management approach to be developed in advance.

Additionally, we may be given prior warning of a pending problem. Often there is a gradual worsening of events until the point of crisis is attained. If these signals are picked up early enough decisive action can be taken before the problem becomes a crisis.

A key idea is to maintain confidence and for management to be clearly in control. Basic techniques include:

- Assess the situation coolly and establish the facts before taking any rash action.
- Draw up a plan of action and establish a management structure.
- Set up a communications system to receive and disseminate information.
- Separate the trivial from the important and prioritize tasks.
- Be decisive and take responsibility.

Summary

Do not downplay the importance of implementation. Organizations need not only to consider the development of strategy, but also to address issues that turn strategy into reality.

The key to successful implementation is the application of basic management principles – leadership, systems and resourcing are all important. Such factors must be taken within the context of the organizational culture and business environment that exists.

Prior to implementation, it is wise to consider how easy the task(s) is likely to be. This relates to the importance of the task and the level of associated change. The attitude and influence of interested parties will also have a significant impact on the ease, or otherwise, of implementation.

Internal marketing techniques and the deployment of standard project management principles, such as objective setting, planning and delegation, facilitate a workable framework for the implementation of strategy.

References

Adair, J., *Action Centred Leadership*, McGraw Hill, 1984

Berry, L. and Parasuraman, A., *Marketing Services: Competing Through Quality*, Free Press, 1991

Bonoma, T., 'Making Your Marketing Strategies Work', *Harvard Business Review*, Vol. 62, No. 2, pp. 68–76, 1984

Kakabadse, A., *The Politics of Management*, Gower, 1983

Piercy, N., *Market-Led Strategic Change*, 2nd edition, Butterworth-Heinemann, 1997

Wickens, P., *The Road to Nissan*, Macmillan, 1997

Further reading

Piercy, N., *Market-Led Strategic Change*, 2nd edition, Chapters 14, 15, Butterworth-Heinemann, 1997

CHAPTER 13

Control

About this chapter

Control mechanisms aim to translate strategic plans into specific actions. The purpose is to ensure that behaviour, systems and operations conform to corporate objectives/policy. Marketing managers need to be aware of a range of control variables: financial measures, budgets, performance appraisal and benchmarking.

Introduction

The term 'control' has received a bad press. The phrase smacks of coercive action, limiting freedom and keeping costs to an absolute minimum. The reality is somewhat different and managers should consider the control process as simply a mechanism to protect your strategic plans during implementation. Murphy's law states: 'if anything can go wrong, it will go wrong.' Hence a control system detecting and pre-empting the inevitable problems that accompany implementation is a valuable asset.

Control can be defined as attempting to guarantee that behaviour and systems conform to, and support, predetermined corporate objectives and policies. Such 'hard-edged' views illustrate the importance of linking behaviour to overall strategic direction. This is a fundamental reason for having control systems.

Control – the basic principles

The basis of control is the ability to measure. In essence it compares what should happen with what actually happened or is likely to happen. Given the importance of measurement, a tendency exists to measure what is easy to quantify rather than what is important. Project managers must guard against this and focus on the key areas. Good control systems often detect and rectify problems before they become significant and managers should remember that prevention is better than cure. Try to be proactive rather than reactive.

The process is broken down into a series of simple steps. Firstly, a target is set. Ideally, this is integrated into overall strategic planning. Secondly, a method of measurement has to be determined and implemented. Finally, measured results are compared with the predetermined target(s) and corrective action, if required, is undertaken.

There are two sides to the control equation – inputs and outputs. If only output is considered then the system is one of inspection as opposed to control. Correctly addressing both sides of the equation allows management to optimize the process and take a strategic view. Typical inputs include:

- *Finance*. Investment, working capital and cash.
- *Operations*. Capacity, usage, efficiency and application of machines, systems and other assets.
- *People*. Numbers, quality and skills of staff.

Output is measured in terms of overall system performance. Performance is derived from a combination of efficiency and effectiveness:

- *Efficiency*. How well utilized are the inputs? Do we make maximum use of finance, minimize cost and operate at optimal levels of capacity?
- *Effectiveness*. Are we doing the right things? This relates to actual performance and will include sales revenue, profit, market share and measures of customer satisfaction.

Remember, it is better to pursue effectiveness. For example, a company may be a very efficient producer (low cost, high volume, etc.) but relatively ineffective at finding buyers for its goods.

Control systems can operate as simple feedback loops. Figure 13.1 illustrates the concept. However more sophisticated systems of *feedforward control* are possible. Such systems try to pre-empt problems by anticipating

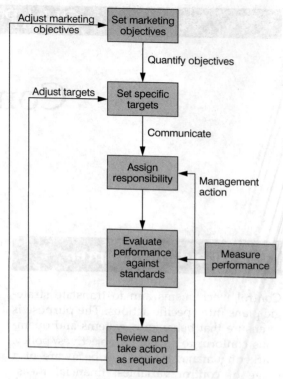

Figure 13.2   Marketing control systems

the effect of input(s) on overall performance. However, such systems are more complex and consequently more difficult to set up.

Figure 13.2 illustrates the application of a basic control loop to the marketing management process. Here marketing objectives, such as increasing market share, are translated into performance targets. These targets define a specific measurable basis against which managers will be judged. The objective of increasing market share would be quantified. For example, we may aim at a 7 per cent increase over twelve months. Responsibility for achieving the target is assigned and actual performance is evaluated against planned performance. The adjustment of the process is achieved by management action and/or altering the objectives or standards within the system. In this way, the system becomes flexible and can react to changes in performance and the business environment.

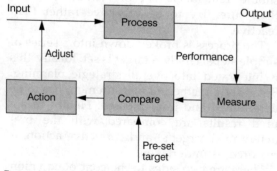

Figure 13.1   Feedback control

What makes an effective control system?

Control systems require careful design. Generic principles exist which are common to all effective control mechanisms. As with management processes, it is important to retain a degree of flexibility and common sense. The project manager can deploy the following principles to ensure effective control:

- *Involvement.* This is achieved by encouraging participation in the process. Management can achieve desired results via consultation. For example, staff could contribute towards setting targets. Their own staff development needs could be considered along with the required tasks. Correctly applied, the process enhances morale, promotes ownership and develops the skills base of employees.
- *Target setting.* There are two important factors. Firstly, the target criteria should be objective and measurable. How these are assessed needs to be communicated and agreed in advance. Secondly, they need to be achievable but challenging.
- *Focus.* Recognize the difference between the symptoms and the source of a problem. While it may be expedient to treat the symptoms, tackling the source of the problem should eliminate it once and for all.
- *Effectiveness.* The tendency exists to measure efficiency as opposed to effectiveness. Efficiency is the usage and productivity of assets. Effectiveness is about doing the right things. Ideally, we want measures of efficiency applied to areas of effectiveness. In reality we tend to apply efficiency measures to areas easiest to measure. Be careful to measure what is important, not what is easy to quantify. Additionally, measurement should be accurate, valid and consistent.
- *Management by exception.* Management attention is directed to areas of need. Identifying what constitutes an exception to

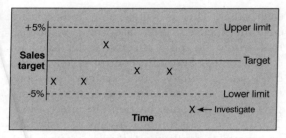

Figure 13.3   Tolerance control chart. X = actual sales

the norm is a useful exercise in its own right. The process involves setting tolerances and benchmarks for normal operation. Management action only becomes a priority when pre-set limits are breached. Figure 13.3 shows a simple tolerance control chart. This is based on planned sales revenue plus or minus a tolerance of 5 per cent. If the levels are exceeded, or in a proactive system appear as if they may be breached, management will begin to take an interest in the process.

- *Action.* Good control systems promote action. Such systems do not just detect problems, they solve problems. Basically, actions adjust the inputs to the process. For example, extra resources could be made available to deal with a backlog or a process or procedure could be redesigned to make it more effective.

Problems of control

A good control system is not easy to develop. The project manager requires an awareness of the general problems associated with control systems. No system is perfect and no control system offers a hundred per cent accuracy. Often, the concern is keeping operations and plans within acceptable limits.

Three problems are commonly associated with control systems. Firstly, such systems can be *costly*. Here the benefits of control and subsequent improvements are outweighed by the cost of the control mechanism. This often relates to large bureaucratic systems – layer upon layer of administration is built upon each other. This is self-serving rather than customer-focused, often absorbing resources that would be more effectively deployed in core activities. Secondly, control systems *stifle effort and creativity*. Such systems promote uniformity and conformance to pre-set targets. They become barriers to innovation. Thirdly, control promotes a view of *inspection as opposed to development*. Systems often deal with the symptom rather than the root of the problem. In such cases, there is a tendency to be constantly 'fire fighting' and looking for the quick fix as opposed to developing a better overall method of operation. The effect is to filter and/or suppress information from those with the power to radically overhaul a poor system.

Management control

Having reviewed the basic concept of control, we can now focus on the key aspect of management control. Management control takes place at a number of different levels within the organization (see Figure 13.4). Control criteria apply at strategic, operational and tactical levels. The control variables at one level become targets for the next level down. Effectively, this means that a 'cascade' system of control is in operation. Senior/strategic levels use fewer, more critical, control vari-

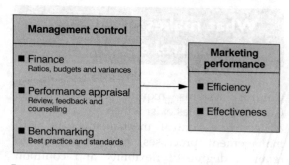

Figure 13.5 Management control related to marketing

ables. These are predominantly financial in nature and focus on divisional or strategic business unit (SBU) targets. The operational level relates to project or departmental activities and encompasses financial and non-financial information. The tactical level relates to group or individual performance and the focus is on productivity.

Good performance means that employees (at all levels) have a clear view of what the priorities are, what they should be doing currently, how their area of responsibility contributes to overall performance and what levels of achievement are acceptable.

Management control will focus on finance, performance appraisal and benchmarking. The relative importance of each may vary with level of management. Financial measures will give both short-term and long-term control data and are fundamental to decision making. Performance appraisal examines the personnel and human resource aspects of management. Finally, benchmarking is a means of comparison and identification of best practice. As Figure 13.5 illustrates, management control is applied to marketing in order to establish marketing performance. Remember, performance is a function of efficiency and effectiveness.

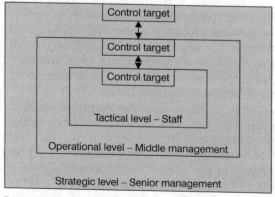

Figure 13.4 Cascade control

Financial control

Financial control techniques are vital to successful strategy. Such techniques apply to both the planning and operational phases of projects. We will focus on three main financial control activities: ratios, budgeting and variance analysis.

A basic understanding of financial terminology is required. Ultimately all business activities are measured in financial terms, and managers require a grasp of accounting terms. Key terms include:

- *Assets.* Items that have value to the business. Assets are subdivided into two categories. (i) *Fixed assets* – retained by the business, in the long term, for continual use. Typical examples include buildings, machinery, vehicles and long-term investments. (ii) *Current assets* – items that are readily convertible into cash or cash itself. Such assets are to be used in the short term. Typical examples include stock, cash and debtors (those owing the organization money).
- *Liabilities.* Financial obligations owed to others. *Current liabilities* are those debts which must be paid in the near future. Therefore cash will be required to meet current liabilities. Additionally, *capital* invested by the owner can be classified as a liability as it is technically owed to the owner.

Ratios

A simple and effective control technique is to express performance in terms of ratios. Ratios should not be used in isolation but should be considered in relation to trends and comparisons with planned or standards ratios. Remember, they are no more than indicators and rarely identify the source of a problem. However, managers can identify key ratios for their areas of responsibility, and these provide a quick and effective way to establish performance and highlight areas warranting more detailed analysis. Figure 13.6 outlines the uses of ratios.

Ratios represent a snapshot of the firm's financial/productivity position and fall into four general categories (see Figure 13.6): profitability, liquidity, debt and activity. Remember,

Ratio analysis	
Use	**Application**
■ Trend analysis	■ Profitability
■ Comparison	■ Liquidity
■ Highlight key areas	■ Debt
	■ Activity

Figure 13.6   Use and application of ratios

when calculating ratios it is important to be consistent with the terms used. For example, how is profit defined – before or after tax?

Profitability ratios

Here, effectiveness is measured by evaluating the organization's ability to produce profit. Profit margin is expressed in terms of a ratio of profit to sales. The profit margin is a key trading concern. Clearly, the profit margin can be enhanced by raising selling price and/or reducing costs.

Return on capital employed (ROCE) is expressed as net profit as a percentage of capital. It examines to what extent an investment is paying off. It can be applied to an entire business or to specific projects requiring capital investment. ROCE is used to indicate the extent to which an investment is justified or to compare investment opportunities.

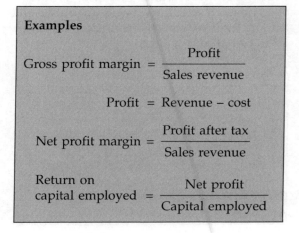

Examples

$$\text{Gross profit margin} = \frac{\text{Profit}}{\text{Sales revenue}}$$

$$\text{Profit} = \text{Revenue} - \text{cost}$$

$$\text{Net profit margin} = \frac{\text{Profit after tax}}{\text{Sales revenue}}$$

$$\text{Return on capital employed} = \frac{\text{Net profit}}{\text{Capital employed}}$$

Liquidity ratios

Ratios evaluate the ability to remain solvent and meet current liabilities. The firm needs to be able to convert assets into cash in order to meet payment demands. If the current ratio is more than 1, sufficient assets exist to meet current liabilities. The quick (or acid-test) ratio gives a stricter appraisal of solvency as it assumes stock is not automatically convertible into cash. Ideally, this ratio should be 1 to 1. However, many businesses operate with lower acceptable ratios. If the ratio is too high it may suggest that the organization does not make optimal use of its financial assets (e.g. holding too much cash).

> **Examples**
>
> $$\text{Current ratio} = \frac{\text{Current assets}}{\text{Current liabilities}}$$
>
> $$\text{Quick ratio} = \frac{\text{Current assets} - \text{inventory}}{\text{Current liabilities}}$$

Debt ratios

These ratios help determine the company's ability to handle debt and meet scheduled repayments. They examine the extent to which borrowed funds finance business operations. If creditors begin to outweigh debtors this may signify overtrading – inability to collect money owed.

> **Examples**
>
> $$\text{Debt to assets ratio} = \frac{\text{Total liabilities}}{\text{Total assets}}$$
>
> $$\text{Debt to credit ratio} = \frac{\text{Debtors}}{\text{Creditors}}$$

Activity ratios

These ratios determine how effective the organization is at generating activity, such as sales from assets. These activities often relate to business cycles or processes, such as the time taken to turnover stock or collect debts. For example, the greater the stock turnover the better for the organization. An additional example, common in retailing, is sales per unit of floor space. This gives a measure of retail effectiveness.

Essentially, such ratios measure the relationship between inputs and outputs.

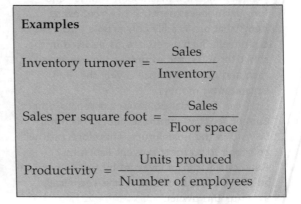

> **Examples**
>
> $$\text{Inventory turnover} = \frac{\text{Sales}}{\text{Inventory}}$$
>
> $$\text{Sales per square foot} = \frac{\text{Sales}}{\text{Floor space}}$$
>
> $$\text{Productivity} = \frac{\text{Units produced}}{\text{Number of employees}}$$

Budgeting

The processes of strategic development and budgeting are intrinsically linked. To be blunt: no budget equals no strategy! The budgeting process translates marketing strategy into financial terms which, whether we like it or not, are the way all plans are expressed, evaluated and controlled.

Budgeting is the single most common control mechanism. It serves not only to quantify plans but also to co-ordinate activities, highlight areas of critical importance and assign responsibility.

Many industry practitioners would agree with Piercy (1997). He talks about the 'hassle factor' – difficulty, time, negotiation, paperwork, etc. – associated with budgeting.

This serves to highlight two points. Firstly, budgeting is about resource allocation. Secondly, budgeting is a political process (negotiation, bargaining, etc.) necessary to obtain required resources.

Before managers can prepare a budget, there are certain fundamental requirements which must be met. These relate to:

- *Budget guidelines*. The organization's policy and procedure relating to budget formulation must be understood. These set out assumptions, methods and presentational requirements.
- *Cost behaviour*. Management must understand what drives costs within their area of responsibility. Additionally, it is important to be clear on how costs are allocated. For example, what is the basis of overhead cost allocation?
- *Timescale*. A specific time period needs to be set. This could be for a fixed budgetary period, such as a financial year, or alternatively a 'rolling budget' could be prepared. Here, the budget is split into manageable time periods, and outline forecasts are updated at regular intervals. New periods are added as the budget progresses.
- *Objectives*. Specifically, what are we aiming to achieve and how is it being assessed? Corporate or departmental goals should be translated into resource and subsequent budgetary requirements.

Approaches to budgeting

Many approaches exist to formulating a budget. Most organizations have developed a historic way of approaching the task. Recent times have seen a move towards greater objectivity and the need to justify assumptions and requirements. Common methods of budgeting are:

- *Historic*. Traditionally the main determinant of a future budget is previous expenditure. Organizations simply base the budget on previous financial data. Adjustments are made for factors like inflation and level of activity. The model is basically incremental in nature – last year, plus or minus some factor, with managers concentrating on justifying or challenging changes.
- *Zero-based*. Budgets are systematically re-evaluated and senior management establishes priority within the context of overall financial constraints. The process involves examining activities and deriving the cost and resulting benefit from these activities. Alternative methods of achieving objectives are simultaneously considered and there is often a trade-off between activities. The method relates to analysing objectives and tasks and is highly 'political' in nature.
- *Activity-related*. Here budgets are based on often crude measures of activity. Simple calculation rules such as percentage of sales, or average industry spend, are used as precursors to determining available funds.

Variance analysis

Finally, in this section on financial control, variance analysis is reviewed. Basically, this examines the variation between actual and planned results and is a concept applicable to a range of activities. It is commonly used along with budgetary control. The actual results are compared with budgeted forecasts and then the variance is examined in order to determine the reason for the difference. Variance analysis allows the organization to identify the main areas of concern and break problems down into component parts. For example, in marketing, variance analysis is often applied to sales price and sales volume. Standard formulae are useful in calculating the effect of these variables on overall revenue:

- Variance in sales revenue = Actual revenue – planned revenue
- Variance due to price = Actual volume × (planned price – actual price)
- Variance due to volume = Planned price × (actual volume – planned volume)

Consider the following example. We plan to sell 4200 units at £25 per unit. However, due to market conditions, we actually sell 3850 units at £16 per unit. Hence the variance in sales revenue is:

Variance in sales revenue
$$(3850 \times 16) - (4200 \times 25) = -43\ 400$$

Variance analysis can be used to determine whether the loss of sales revenue is predominantly due to the lower than expected volume or failure to maintain planned price:

Variance due to price
$$= 3850 \times (16 - 25) \quad = -34\ 650 \qquad 80\%$$

Variance due to volume
$$= 25 \times (3850 - 4200) = \underline{\ -8\ 750 \qquad 20\%}$$
$$ -43\ 400 \qquad 100\%$$

Therefore, we can see that 80 per cent of the failure to achieve planned revenue is due to the lower unit price. Management could then investigate why the planned unit price was not achieved.

Variance analysis is not limited to price and volume calculations. A wide range of factors can be analysed in this fashion (e.g. profit, cost and market size).

Performance appraisal

Performance appraisal concerns achieving better results from groups and individuals. A performance appraisal framework is based on planned objectives, levels of achievement and competence. The focus is on the control and development of staff, and is critical to project implementation. Effective performance appraisal requires managers to have good people skills and appraisal should be constructive in nature. It is about doing a better job. Three key skills are involved: reviewing performance, giving feedback and counselling.

- *Reviewing performance.* The performance of individuals or groups should be reviewed continuously as part of normal management activity. Additionally, there may be a formal review which summarizes activity. Objective criteria should be used as a basis of review. Such criteria should be communicated and agreed in advance. Work and personal development plans should be considered in tandem with set criteria.
- *Giving feedback.* Feedback relating to performance is based on actual results, or observed behaviour. It is important not to just focus on the negative – credit should be given where it is due. When giving feedback, managers should be specific and describe rather than judge results. By reference to specific actions and behaviours, managers can more readily focus on key aspects of improvement.
- *Counselling.* Performance appraisal should be positive in nature. In order to build on strengths and overcome weaknesses, management may well have to counsel staff. This is particularly relevant to areas of under-performance. Counselling needs to consider performance, not personality, and invite a degree of self-appraisal. The aim should be to identify and agree problems and then choose required actions.

Benchmarking

In order to be 'the-best-you-can-be', it pays for organizations to compare themselves with leading performers. Benchmarking provides a method of enabling such comparisons to take place.

Benchmarking is defined as:

A systematic and ongoing process of measuring and comparing an organization's business processes and achievements against acknowledged process leaders and/or key competitors, to facilitate improved performance.

However, benchmarking is more than just copying. The process is about continuous improvement and becoming a learning organization. The credo is one of adaptation rather than adoption. Ideas, practices and methods have to be screened and adapted to specific business situations. Benchmarking falls into three general areas:

- *Competitive analysis* – reviewing competitors' activities, strategy and operations so the organization can improve its performance.
- *Best practice* – determining the best way of undertaking an activity. This could involve examining activities in unrelated areas of business or industry. For example, a computer manufacturer could benchmark a mail-order retail company in order to improve its stock control system. Equally, best internal practice could be identified and spread to other units or departments within the organization.
- *Performance standards* – targets to be met or surpassed. For example, if the average industry conversion of enquiries into sales was 1 in 20 and the organization achieves 1 in 25, what does this say about its sales process?

The process of benchmarking

Benchmarking comprises a four-stage approach. This is illustrated using the 'Deming cycle' (Watson, 1993): plan, do, check and act (see Figure 13.7). The planning stage involves identifying what to study and who or what should act as the benchmark. Common areas to benchmark are customer service levels, logistic and distribution methods, product quality and 'time-to-market' cycles. Organizations will benchmark against competitors, acknowledged leaders or successful internal activities. Next, conduct research. This may involve co-operation and direct contact with the benchmark. Alternatively, secondary data may be used to establish standards and actions. The data is then analysed. This involves establishing the extent of performance gaps and identifying assignable

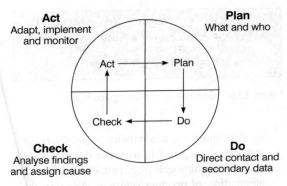

Figure 13.7 The Deming cycle applied to benchmarking (*Source*: Watson, 1993)

causes for such gaps. Finally, the lessons learned are adapted, as appropriate, and applied in order to generate improvement in performance.

Controlling marketing performance

In contrast to mechanical systems, marketing activities are inherently more volatile. This is due to a constantly changing business environment driven by the needs and wants of the market. Measuring marketing performance is a process of determining appropriate criteria by which to judge activity. Kotler (1997) identifies four main areas associated with the control of marketing activity (see Figure 13.8):

- *Annual planning.* This has the purpose of evaluating the extent to which marketing efforts, over the year, have been successful. Evaluation will focus on analysing sales, market share, expenses and customer perception. Commonly, sales performance is a major element of this analysis. All other factors provide explanation of any variance in sales performance.
- *Profitability.* All marketing managers are concerned with controlling their profit levels.

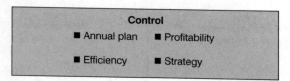

Figure 13.8   Control of marketing activities

By examining the profitability of products, or activities, it is possible to make decisions relating to the expansion, reduction or elimination of product offerings. Additionally, it is common to break distribution channels and segments down in terms of profitability. Remember, it is important to have a systematic basis for allocating costs and defining profit.

- *Efficiency control.* Efficiency is concerned with gaining optimum value from the marketing assets. Managers are looking to obtain value for money in relation to marketing activity. The promotional aspects of marketing (sales, advertising, direct marketing, etc.) are commonly subject to such controls (see Figure 13.9).
- *Strategic control.* There is a need to ensure that marketing activities are being directed towards strategic goals and that marketing is an integral part of the overall process of

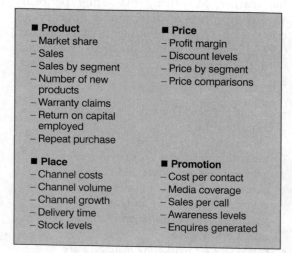

Figure 13.9   Control of marketing activity

delivering value. A strategic review will aim to assess that marketing strategy, and subsequent implementation, is appropriate to the marketplace. A review of this nature will take the form of a marketing audit – a comprehensive examination of all marketing activity to assess effectiveness and improve marketing performance.

These areas of marketing control are general in nature and specific measures of marketing performance are required. Performance measures and standards will vary by organization and market conditions. A representative sample of the type of data required to successfully control marketing activities is shown in Figure 13.9. The aim is to break the general areas (annual plan, profitability, efficiency and strategy) into measurable component parts to which responsibility can be assigned.

Remember, in the context of marketing a balanced view is required. No one variable should dominate the control process. For example, marketing strategists have been guilty of following a credo of 'market share at any cost'. While such a variable is important, it is not a panacea and consideration needs to be given to other factors such as profitability. Additionally, marketing control should only measure dimensions over which the organization has control. Rewards, sanctions and management actions only make sense where influence can be exerted. Control systems should be sensitive to local market conditions and levels of competition. For instance, developing markets and mature markets may require different control mechanisms.

Summary

The essence of control is the ability to measure and take action. Control systems are concerned with efficiency and effectiveness and often operate as simple feedback loops. In marketing terms, control ensures that what is supposed to happen actually happens and is a mechanism to protect strategic plans when they become operational.

Effective control systems have focus, involve people and promote action. Management control extends to cover finance, performance appraisal and establishing and maintaining performance benchmarks. Marketing managers are concerned with the following control mechanisms: annual plans, profitability, efficiency of marketing and strategic control.

References

Kotler, P., *Marketing Management*, 9th edition, Prentice Hall, 1997

Piercy, N., *Market-Led Strategic Change*, 2nd edition, Butterworth-Heinemann, 1997

Watson, G., *Strategic Benchmarking*, Wiley, 1993

Further reading

Piercy, N., *Market-Led Strategic Change*, 2nd edition, Chapter 12 , Butterworth-Heinemann, 1997

Index

Aaker, 3, 73, 87, 104, 118
ACORN, 34, 35
Acquisition and merger, 133
Adair, 151
Administrative VMS, 134
Age, 29
Aguilar, 13, 14, 15, 73
Air 2000, 19
Air France, 19
Alfa Romeo, 116
Alliances, 131
Allison's, 115
Alpert and Raiffa, 72
Amazon, 136
Annual plan, 168
Ansoff, 101
Assets, 163
Aston Martin, 18
Audi, 115
Auditing tools, 58
Avis, 116

Babycham, 116
Balanced score card, 6, 87
Behavioural variables, 29, 36
Benchmarking, 162, 166
Berry and Parasuraman, 155
Best practice, 167
BMW, 51, 114
Bonoma and Shapiro, 48
Bonoma, 42, 150
Booz et al., 123
Boston Consultancy Group (BCG):
    growth share matrix, 59, 60, 61
    strategic advantage matrix, 95
Bottom-up planning, 144

Brand:
    company and individual, 118
    equity, 117
    extension, 119
    strategy, 118
    stretching, 119
Britannia, 19
British Airways, 19
Buckley, 111
Budgeting, 164
    activity related, 165
    zero based, 165
Burnside, 55
Business definition, 2
Business ethics, 80
Business evaluation, 124
Buying process, 28
Bypass attack, 99

Cadbury, 30, 119
Campari, 116
Cartier, 39
Cash cows, 60
Caterpillar, 85
Change, 5
    cyclical, 5
    evolutionary, 5
    importance, 153
    level of, 153
Christopher et al., 134
Chrysler, 17
Clairol, 115
Coca-Cola, 52
Cognitive learning, 28
Cognitive styles, 58
Competitive advantage, 92, 94, 96

Competitor analysis, 18
Competitor focused, 7
Concept development, 124
Conditioning, 28
Consortia, 133
Constraints on innovation, 56
Consumer buyer behaviour, 25
Contraction defence, 101
Control chart, 161
Control system – marketing, 160
Control, 152, 159
    cascade, 162
    financial, 162
    loop, 160
    problems with, 161
Core competencies, 2
Corporate brand, 118
Corporate governance, 79
Corporate planning, 139
Corporate vision, 83
Corporate VMS, 134
Cosco, 80
Cost leadership, 92
    drivers, 92
Counter defence, 100
Crisis management, 157
Cultural fit, 133
Culture, 25, 151
Current ratio, 164
Customer focused, 7
Customer involvement, 125

Dalrymple, 67
Davidson, 57, 95, 96, 104, 110, 112
De Gaulle, 66
De Mooij and Keegan, 25
Debonair, 19
Debt to asset ratio, 164
Debt to credit ratio, 164
Decision-making pyramid, 65
Decision-making unit (DMU), 41, 154
Defensive strategies, 99
Delegation, 157
Delphi forecast, 69
Deming cycle, 167
Developmental activity, 129
Diffenbach, 13, 14, 65
Differentiated product, 122
Differentiation, 92, 93
Diversification, 102
Dogs, 60
Doyle, 23, 141

Drucker, 64, 85
Drummond and Ensor, 81
Dyson, 57

Easyjet, 19
Ecover, 115
Effectiveness, 160, 161
Efficiency, 160, 168
Employee markets, 134
End-user focus, 93
Ensor and Laing, 30
Esso, 115
Euro-Fighter, 133
Exit strategy, 105
Experience curves, 96
Exploratory research, 129
External analysis, 13

Family life cycle, 30
Family Policy Studies Centre, 30
Family, 26
Feedback, 152
Feedback control, 160
Feedforward control, 160
Ferrari, 18
Flank attack, 99
Flank defence, 100
Focus, 91
Ford, 119, 134
Forecasting, 65
Forecasting techniques, 65
Fragmented industries, 95
Freud's theory of motivation, 26
Frontal attack, 99
Fulmer and Goodwin, 91

Galer, 72
Gap analysis, 89, 128
Gender, 29
General electric multifactor portfolio matrix, 61,
    62
Generic strategy, 92, 94, 96
Geodemographics, 34
Globalization, 132
Go, 19
Gortex, 116
Green, 82
Groupthink, 67
Groupware, 126
Guerrilla attack, 99

Halifax Building Society, 133
Hard measure of innovation, 56
Harley Davidson, 115
Hartley, 64
Hedonistic factors, 28
Heinz, 118, 119
Henry and Walker, 128
Honda, 132
Hooley *et al.*, 51, 53, 54, 95
Hurst *et al.*, 58, 59
Hybrid systems, 144

Idea evaluation, 124
Idea generation, 124
Implementation, 9, 149
Implementation skills, 150
Incrementalize, 154
Individual forecasting, 66
Industry analysis, 16
Ingroups, 67
Innovation, 126
    dilemma, 128
    exchange of information, 127
    teamwork, 127
Innovation audit, 55
Integration, 141
Internal analysis, 50
Internal audit, 53
Internal marketing, 134, 155
Inventory turnover, 164
Irn-bru, 52
IVD Ltd, 116

Jain, 122
Janis, 67, 68
Janis and Mann, 67
Jicnar's classification of social class, 32
Jobber, 112, 115
Johnson and Scholes, 4, 54, 79, 80, 82, 83, 133
JVC, 132

Kakabadse, 154
Kaplan and Norton, 6, 87, 88
Kellogg's, 115, 119
Key players matrix, 154
Kim and Mauborgne, 57, 58
Kit Kat, 115
KLM, 19
Knowledge management, 125
Komatsu, 85, 87
Kotler, 167
Kotler *et al.*, 20, 54, 99, 100, 115, 122, 135

Lamborghini, 18
Lawson, 30, 32
Leadership, 150
Learning, 154
    attitudes and beliefs, 27
Leeds Building Society, 133
Lehman and Weiner, 20
Lever Bros, 118
Levitt, 82
Liabilities, 163
Long-range planning, 3
Lotus Notes, 126
Lotus, 18
Lucozade, 115

Makridakis and Wheelwright, 69, 72
Management by exception, 161
Management control, 162
Managers, 37
Managing innovation, 126
Market analysis, 21
Market challengers, 98
Market conditions, 104
Market development, 101, 129
Market followers, 98
Market leaders, 98
Market nichers, 99
Market orientation, 7
Market penetration, 101, 129
Market research, 124
Market scope, 82
Market sensing, 72
Marketing functions audit, 55
Marketing mix, 155
Marketing plan, 140
Marketing plans:
    strategic, 140, 143
    tactical, 140
Marketing strategy, 7
Marketing strategy audit, 54
Marketing structures audit, 55
Marketing systems audit, 55
Marketing uncertainty map, 129
Marks & Spencer, 119
Maslow's theory of motivation, 27
McDonald, 61
McDonald's, 52
McKinsey & Co., 153
Mentzer and Cox, 67
Mercedes, 51
Metaphors, 56
Miaoulis and Kalfus, 37

Mission statement, 80
Mitchell, 39
Mobile defence, 101
Modelling, 66
Monitor framework, 39
Montanari and Bracker, 61
Morgan, 56
Morris, 42
Motivation, 26
Multi-brand, 118
Multi-dimensional planning model, 142
Multi-functional teams, 125
Murphy and Staples, 31

Networks, 133
New product development (NPD), 123, 125
New product lines, 123
New to world products, 123
Newport News Shipbuilding, 80

O'Connor and Galvin, 126
Objective setting, 156
Objectives:
    corporate, 85
    functional, 86
    hierarchy of, 85
    operational, 86
    SMART, 84, 156
    Strategic Business Unit, 86
    strategic, 84
Offensive strategies, 99
OPEC, 71
Operations, 160
Orange PLC, 122
Organizational assets, 51, 55
Organizational buyer behaviour, 41
Organizational capabilities, 50, 110
Organizational climate, 55
Organizational competencies, 51, 53, 55
Overhaul, 153
Overkill, 153

Pantene, 115
Parallel processing, 125, 156
Pareto affect, 37, 38
Pearce and Robinson, 85
Pearson, 128
Pepsi, 115
Perceived risk, 28
Perception, 27
Perceptual mapping, 115
Performance appraisal, 162, 166

Personal influences, 26
PEST, 5, 15, 18
Peugeot/Citröen, 17
Piercy, 65, 72 142, 154, 164
PIMS, 102
Planning, barriers to, 141
Plummer, 38
Porter, 4, 92, 94, 95, 97, 105
    'five forces' model, 16, 17, 18
Portfolio analysis, 59
Positioning, 8. 107, 114
Positioning alternative, 116
Positioning defence, 100
Power and politics, 142
Pre-emptive defence, 100
Primary activities, 97
Procter & Gamble, 118
Product:
    actual, 122
    augmented, 122
    core, 122
    fail
Product augmentation, 93
Product development, 101, 121, 124
Product development strategy, 122
Product imitation, 123
Product improvement, 122
Product innovation, 123
Product launch, 124
Product life cycle (PLC), 103
    industry, 103
Product/market matrix, 101
    expanded, 102
Product modification, 122
Product orientation, 6
Product perception, 93
Product scope, 81
Productivity, 164
Productivity audit, 55
Profile variables, 28, 29
Profit, 163
Profitability, 167
Psychographic variables, 29, 38
Psychological influences, 26
Purchase occasion, 38

Question marks, 60
Quick ratio, 164

Range brand, 119
Ratio analysis, 163

Ratios:
  activity, 164
  liquidity, 164
  profitability, 163
Reference groups, 26
Reichheld and Sasser, 135
Relationship drivers, 135
Relationship marketing, 134
Relationship strategy, 135
Reposition, 123
Resource allocation, 141
Resources, 151
Retain customers, 136
Return on capital employed (ROCE), 163
Revuelta, 86
Richer Sounds, 81
Ries and Trout, 116, 117
Risk, 132
Rolex, 39
Roll-out strategy, 124
Rose and O'Reilly, 32, 33
Rover, 132
Ryanair, 19

Sales orientation, 6
Sarah Lee, 119
Sathe, 74
Scanning, 13
Scenario planning, 70
Scottish Power, 81
Scottish Tourist Board, 132
Secondary activities, 97
Secondary data, 124
Segmentation, 8, 23
  benefit, 36
  criteria, 28
  demographic, 2
  geographic, 34
  industrial, 40
  organizational, 40
  organizational macro, 47
  organizational market, 46
  organizational micro, 47
  process, 24
  socio-economic, 31
  usage, 37
Segments:
  Euro-consumer, 35
  evaluating market, 107
Selective attention, 27
Selective distortion, 27
Selective retention, 27

Self-image, 28
Seven S's, 153
Sharp, 132
Shell, 71, 72
Shell directional policy matrix, 62, 112, 113
Sheth, 44, 45
Skills:
  HRM, 152
  implementation, 150
  project management, 152
  technical/marketing, 152
SmithKline Beecham, 82
Social factors, 28
Social influences, 25
Social learning, 28
Sony, 57
SPAR, 115, 134
Specialized industries, 95
Stakeholders, 79
Stalemate industries, 95
Stars, 60
Steers *et al.*, 27
STEP, 15
Strategic alignment of assets and competencies, 111
Strategic analysis, 4
Strategic choice, 4
Strategic drift, 5
Strategic fit, 133
Strategic goals, 84
Strategic groups, 18, 19
Strategic implementation, 4
Strategic intent, 79
Strategic management, 3
Strategic marketing management, 8
Strategic planning, 3
Strategic wear-out, 104
Strategy, 2
  inconsistent, 94
Sun Zsu: *The Art of War*, 97
Supplier markets, 134
Support of innovation, 58
SWOT analysis, 63
Synergy, 2, 153

Tactical marketing, 140
Targeting, 8, 107, 111
Taylor Nelson, 40
Team building, 157
Tesco, 119
Tesco clubcard, 136
Time-to-market, 156

Tinson, 26
Tolerance, 161
Top-down planning, 143
Toshiba, 132
Toyota, 18
Trend extrapolation, 66
Tucker, 119
TVR, 18

Uncertainty map, 128
Under-investment, 126

VALs framework, 38
Value chain, 59, 97, 111
Van Der Heijden, 71

Vandermerwe and L'Huillier, 36
Variance analysis, 165
Vertical marketing system (VMS), 131, 134
Virgin, 118, 119
Vision, 139
Volatility, 5, 104
Volume industries, 95
Volvo, 115, 119

Wack, 72
Watson, 167
Webster and Wind, 44
Webster–Wind framework, 43
Wheelen and Hunger, 84
Wickens, 157